GARY MacEOIN

Northern Ireland: Captive of History

NORTHERN IRELAND:

CAPTIVE OF HISTORY

"If you think you're not confused, you just don't understand what's going on," goes a Belfast saying. To thousands of Americans, the conflict in Northern Ireland seems to have reached a muddled and hopeless impasse. As the daily bombings and mounting death toll have become staple news items, the personal tragedies and individual suffering of this divided people have receded into the background. Seemingly endless, senseless, and irreconcilable, the struggle has lost the clear-cut moral lines it once had. Yet the very confusion of the moment makes this a particularly opportune time for a tough-minded, comprehensive, and lucid analysis of the causes and issues, the parties, leaders, and events that constitute the core of the conflict. *Northern Ireland: Captive of History* is such an analysis.

Writing with sympathy and wisdom and drawing on personal experience as well as careful research, Gary MacEoin unravels the complex skein that is Northern Ireland today. For the Irish, he asserts, the past is more real than the present, and what they do, think, and say is intelligible only through their history—a history distorted by myths held by both sides. MacEoin places

(Continued on back flap)

Other books by Gary MacEoin

Revolution Next Door: Latin America in the 1970s
Colombia, Venezuela and the Guianas
Latin America: The Eleventh Hour
Agent for Change
Cervantes, an Interpretative Biography
What Happened at Rome?

NORTHERN IRELAND:

CAPTIVE OF HISTORY

Gary MacEoin

HOLT, RINEHART AND WINSTON
New York   Chicago   San Francisco

Library of Congress Cataloging in Publication Data

MacEoin, Gary, Date
    Northern Ireland: captive of history.

    Includes bibliographical references.
    1. Northern Ireland—History.   I. Title.
DA990.U46M135   641.609   73-15161
ISBN 0-03-012491-3

First Edition

To my wife, Jo, who shared many of the tribulations
and some of the dangers involved in assembling the
data for this book; to our children, Dottie and Donald;
and to their children, Mary Kathryn, Nancy Clare,
and Gary

Acknowledgments

Joseph O'Malley, editor of *This Week* (now *Profile*), never tired of my innumerable queries. His knowledge of the contemporary Irish scene is exceeded only by his readiness to share his information.

Padraig O'Curry, commuting between London and Paris, was equally diligent in keeping me informed on what the press of those two capitals reported and commented from Northern Ireland.

Others whose contributions I record with gratitude include:

In Northern Ireland: Alfie Hannaway, Bishop Richard P. C. Hanson, Frances Murray (Association for Legal Justice), Reverend Desmond Wilson, Edwina Stewart (Northern Ireland Civil Rights Association), Reverend Ian Paisley, Monica Patterson (Women Together), Henry Kelly, Reverend Patrick Egan, Reverend Martin Smyth, Mary Gordon (SDLP), Thomas Kane, Billy Kelly, Reverend A. J. McAvoy, Jim and Ruby McDonald, Hugh Stockman, Reverend Charles Daly, Reverend Anthony Mulvey, Reverend Christopher McCarthy, Phyllis Meehan, Joy McKeever.

In the Republic of Ireland: Sean O Suilleabhain, Margaret MacCurtain, Reverend Donal Flanagan, Reverend Enda McDonagh, Reverend Tomas O Fiaich, Erskine Hamilton Childers, Desmond Fisher, Sean MacReamoinn, Ruairi O Bradaigh, Louis McRedmond, Reverend Terence Patrick McCaughey, Cathal Loughney, Reverend Charles Gray-Stack, Brian Loughney.

In Great Britain: Terry Sheehy, William Dykes, Sigmund Eisner, Reverend Herbert McCabe.

In the United States: James J. Lamb, Jim Best, Padraic N. MacKernan, Finbar O'Kane, Michael Cunneen, Rona Field, Eoin McKiernan.

Contents

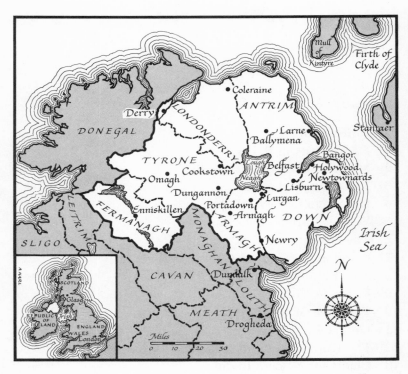

NORTHERN IRELAND: Division by counties and location of principal places mentioned in text, also including adjoining areas of the Republic of Ireland and Scotland.
Inset: Ireland and Great Britain.

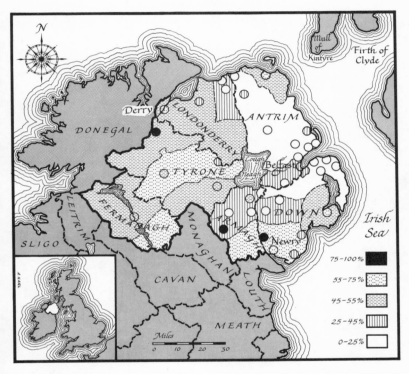

NORTHERN IRELAND: Proportion of Roman Catholics in each local government jurisdiction according to the 1961 census.

*As to Ireland, [the English] know little more than
they do of Mexico, further than that it is a country
subject to the King of England, full of Boggs,
inhabited by wild Irish Papists; who are kept in
Awe by mercenary troops sent from thence [i.e.,
from England]; And their general opinion is that
it were better for England if this whole Island
were sunk into the Sea; For they have a Tradition,
that every Forty Years there must be a Rebellion
in Ireland.*

—JONATHAN SWIFT,
letter to Lord Chancellor Middleton, 1724

*They say it is the fatal destiny of Ireland that no purposes
whatever which are meant for her good will prosper or take
effect; which, whether it proceeds from the very genius of the
soil, or influence of the stars, or that Almighty God has
not yet appointed the time for her reformation, or that he
reserves her in this unquiet state still for some secret
scourge which shall by her come to England, it is hard to
know but much to be feared.*

—EDMUND SPENSER,
in sixteenth century

Introduction

Northern Ireland is neither a nation nor a state. Legally, it is a subordinate part of the United Kingdom. Historically, it is an insubordinate part.

—RICHARD ROSE [1]

Americans have for several years become accustomed to having their appetite for dinner disturbed by television news pictures of savagery in Northern Ireland, of carnage in hotels, supermarkets, and neighborhood saloons, of men picked apparently at random to be tortured and murdered in cold blood.

To the average American, whether he is one of the more than 16 million [2] of Irish descent or simply a neighbor, business associate, or lodge brother of some of that 16 million, it makes little sense. Rather it doesn't measure up to what he knows.

The Irish immigrants who built the canals, the railroads, and the subways of America adjusted to pluralist living within a democratic framework more easily than almost any other group. Their children have won a reputation for being charming, easygoing, good-living. The Scots-Irish of an earlier immigration are more reserved, true to their Scottish origins. But they are even more committed than other Irishmen

1

to sophisticated notions of law and order, as befits the group from which emerged Andrew Jackson, Richard Nixon, and nine other American presidents. In the United States, these two groups of Irishmen, even when they differ in religion, live comfortably with each other and with everyone else.

The conflict between these two groups in Ireland has fortunately not significantly affected their relations here, not yet at any rate. There are, nevertheless, evidences of back-washes of different kinds. While most of the millions of Irish birth or descent are only vaguely concerned, growing numbers feel the need to do something about the scandalous situation in their ancestral home. Some, like the "Fort Worth Five"—New Yorkers jailed for nearly two years in Texas for refusing to tell a grand jury what they knew about arms smuggling—have carried their commitments in directions that have brought them into conflict with United States law-enforcement agencies.

Later it will be necessary to evaluate the religious content in this conflict which pits Catholic against Protestant in Northern Ireland.[3] For the moment I will distinguish the protagonists by terms relatively free of overtones: the Unionist majority, which seeks to retain the existing constitutional union with the United Kingdom, and the Nationalist minority, which sees a united Ireland free of political ties to Britain as the ultimate goal. Each of these has its adherents in the United States, and some of the responses here to developments in Ireland are such as to raise issues of general concern.

Most obvious is the growth of organizations which identify with the Nationalists—the Irish Northern Aid Committee, the American Committee for Ulster Justice, the National Association for Irish Freedom, and the Irish Republican clubs. These organizations send several hundred thousand dollars a year to support Nationalist causes in Ireland, some of which ends up as the arms and explosives which maintain the terror campaign of the Irish Republican Army (IRA), an organization which is illegal in both parts of Ireland. Paradoxically, those who are religiously and socially most conservative here tend to back the most militant elements of the IRA in Ireland.

The activities of the Scots-Irish are so far more muted on this side of the Atlantic, but they maintain a substantial network of Orange lodges both in Canada and in the United States. Ian Paisley and other ultra-Unionists have brought them an outspokenly anti-Catholic message, stirring up bad feelings in the American South in particular.

Both sides have been active in Washington, the Unionists being the more successful so far in that they have blocked the attempts of the others to get an open declaration of Administration or Congressional sympathy for the Nationalist cause. Numbers, however, are on the other side, and numbers count in elections. Mr. Nixon's roots are in the Unionist camp, but it does not follow that Washington will stay neutral forever.

It did not do so on former occasions. More generally, the anti-British sentiments of the vast majority of Irish Americans have for a century been a potent negative factor in Anglo-American relations. Other irritants, especially financial and economic, have been intensified in the recent past. A recrudescence of Irish-American sentiment, if the British adopt the hard line in Northern Ireland (which informed observers today do not completely rule out), could have a disturbing and potentially damaging impact on our basic foreign policy.

Elsewhere around the world, most notably in Canada and Australia, the descendants of Irish emigrants are many and often powerful. They too must be affected in their attitudes, judgments, and reactions by events in Northern Ireland. But no emigrant community is so immediately involved as the million Irish-born and several million of Irish descent in Great Britain. Their situation becomes ever more ambiguous as young English soldiers continue to die in Belfast. Some extremists already propose for them the solution President Idi Amin of Uganda recently applied to the Indians in his country. Expulsion of the Irish en masse from England is today unthinkable. But so are many of the things that are happening in Northern Ireland. Already a deep gulf has been opened in England, forcing the Irish into an emotional ghetto and reversing the trends of half a century. Job discrimination has become significant, especially for newcomers. The strains are spreading to new areas, affecting such things as trade between the two countries and British investment in the Republic of Ireland. Both countries stand to lose.

Northern Ireland is, of course, far from unique in having within its boundaries two communities which have formed images and expectations of each other that prevent them from reaching a stable and peaceful equilibrium. Similar situations exist on both smaller and vastly broader scales, and the scale seems to have little relationship to the intensity and intractability of the problem. The American will think immediately of the conflict between blacks and whites in the United States, a conflict that has gone through scores of convolutions since it was supposedly settled by the Civil War, and which is today in many ways more widespread and complicated than ever. It is a situation which every American recognizes he will have to live with for the foreseeable future, and which most Americans believe—rightly or wrongly—is objectively insoluble with our present level of intellectual and cultural evolution. The same is true of Northern Ireland if the solution is left to the interplay of its internal political forces, as has been the situation for the past 50 years. But, as I hope to clarify later, I do not think it is true when the conflict in Northern Ireland is inserted into the broader framework in which it belongs.

One important difference, important at least for the expectations of those involved, exists between the experience of blacks in America and that of Northern Ireland's minority. Since their importation as slaves into America, blacks always constituted a depressed and underprivileged group. Northern Ireland's Catholics are descendants of the original owners and rulers of the land, from which they see themselves as wrongfully dispossessed. In this respect they are closer to the American Indian, but that comparison is also limited. Notwithstanding various recent token protests, such as the occupations of Alcatraz, the Bureau of Indian Affairs in Washington, and Wounded Knee, the Indian is no threat to the federal government. His potential is marginal. Northern Ireland, however, has a doubtful balance of power, the majority in constant fear of being overtaken, stripped of privilege, and annihilated. Even if the danger of annihilation is objectively imaginary, it is real to those affected.

Israel and Cyprus offer closer comparisons. Israel, whose conflicts with Arabs within and outside its borders have kept the Middle East in turmoil for the entire period of Northern Ireland's existence and continually threaten to draw the great powers into world war, is smaller than the historic province of Ulster and has just about twice the population of Northern Ireland. The Arabs see themselves as wrongfully dispossessed, just like the minority in Northern Ireland. Yet if the Israelis take back the refugees and give them full citizen rights, they fear they will be swamped, as the majority in Northern Ireland does.

Cyprus is an even smaller problem in numbers and geographic extension, a mere 600,000 people in an area two-thirds the size of Northern Ireland. The Turkish minority is less than a fifth of the population, but it is divided from the Greek majority by animosities which have historic roots hundreds of years older than those of the two communities in Northern Ireland. The constitution adopted after Cyprus became independent in 1960 gave the Turks 30 percent of the legislative seats and the vice-presidency. Similar concepts are proposed for Northern Ireland in London's 1973 White Paper (which will be discussed later). But the arrangement has not worked in Cyprus. The Turks have boycotted the government since 1964; and while both sides oppose formal partition, the communities have since been effectively partitioned, with 4000 United Nations troops keeping the peace.

An important factor, nevertheless, distinguishes Northern Ireland from both Israel and Cyprus. The causative factors of the conflict in Ireland have effectively ceased to exist. What remains is principally the emotional carry-over, together with the personal readjustments called for by a new power equilibrium more consonant with the underlying realities. Not so in the other two cases. That of Israel is particularly obvious. The Catholic community of Northern Ireland, even if it had dictatorial powers, would seek neither transfer of property nor reparations for past loss; and the same would be true if the north were integrated into the Republic of Ireland. Israel is faced with the unresolved plight of a million and a quarter refugees. At a higher level, the presence of Israel in the Middle East, with its superior technology and its lines of communication to the United States and the other Western powers, is seen by its neighbors as a threat to their existence. All the great world powers have economic or strategic reasons for supporting one side or the other. Any solution will be opposed by some as benefiting their rivals.

Economic and strategic pressures are less acute in Cyprus. But Greece and Turkey have by no means abandoned their millennial struggle for influence in the eastern Mediterranean, and Cyprus remains a focal point for their conflicting ambitions, a point that brought them to the brink of open war in 1964. In addition, the cultural gulf deriving from the religious beliefs and practices of the Orthodox Greeks and Moslem Turks is vastly greater than that between the two Christian communities in Northern Ireland. While they themselves conceive of their differences largely in religious terms, the objective fact is that Roman Catholicism and Protestantism have long since found an equilibrium in Northern Ireland, as elsewhere, even if special circumstances make an awareness of that objective fact still rare.

Another hopeful factor in the Northern Ireland situation is that the reasons why Britain created this political entity 50 years ago have lost their validity. Britain, thanks to the nuclear era and the European Economic Community, no longer has strategic or economic motives for maintaining a political and military presence in Ireland, and in consequence it has abandoned its centuries-old effort to dominate the neighboring island militarily and absorb it culturally. Its involvement in the affairs of Northern Ireland has become an economic liability and a diplomatic embarrassment. It is forced to maintain laws which are in conflict with the European Convention on Human Rights. So many troops are deployed in Northern Ireland that it cannot fulfill its NATO commitments. Its citizens run the risk of being blown up even on the streets of London. Even the Prime Minister's residence at Ten Downing Street, one of the symbols of authority and stability for Englishmen, has had to be encased in steel as a protection against Irish terrorists. For all these reasons, in addition to the steady loss of young British soldiers, Britain would dearly love to write the last chapter. All it now wants is to honor commitments made to those who were earlier its supporters, the descendants of its colonists.

The violence in Northern Ireland, therefore, is not an isolated event without significance in the broader context of world affairs. To find a solution satisfactory to all the interested parties would signify a giant step toward the resolution of one of the most bitter and long-lived conflicts between neighbors. Ireland might serve as a lesson and preview of what will be faced around the world when nations more recently carved up—Germany, Korea, Vietnam—struggle later for their reunification.

But there is no likelihood of an automatic solution simply by letting things take their course. On the contrary, the story of the past five years is one of steadily mounting tension, growing bitterness, and escalating violence. Given present world rivalries, one cannot exclude the possibility that outsiders will use the conflict for their own purposes. Ireland has always fascinated Marxist theoreticians, ever since Marx wrote Engels in 1867: "I used to think the separation of Ireland from England impossible. I now think it inevitable." This thought has been echoed in *Tricontinental*, a revolutionary magazine published in Havana, Cuba. "A blow delivered against British imperialist bourgeois rule by a rebellion in Ireland has a hundred times greater significance than a blow . . . in Asia or in Africa. . . . Ireland, unique today in Europe, remains in the struggle for its national liberation."

Though few in numbers, Communists of Russian, Cuban, and Chinese ideology are all represented in Ireland, and their views influence not only the thinking of Irish Republican Army (Officials) but a much broader spectrum of opinion. Historian Liam de Paor, a moderate and respected commentator on contemporary affairs, recently wrote in an Irish newspaper: "It is not only in the North that the historic relationship conditions the present situation, since the Republic may be regarded as being in many respects a neocolony of Great Britain." Indications are also present of a growing coordination between extremist groups in Ireland and in other trouble areas around the world. *The New York Times* reported in August 1972 that the CIA and other Western intelligence services claimed to have traced numerous connections between the Japanese terrorist "Red Army," a Palestinian guerrilla organization, the Uruguayan Tupamaros, an Italian "Red Brigade," and the IRA. These organizations were said to have set up a central coordinating office in Zurich late in 1971. In March 1973, the Irish navy intercepted off the Irish coast a German-owned coaster carrying five tons of arms, ammunition, and explosives, with a top IRA leader on board. The armaments, believed to have been taken aboard in Libya, had originated in Russia, East Europe, Belgium, Britain, and the United States. A high Libyan official told a news conference some days later that his government was in fact financing the IRA. Given all these circumstances, the continuing conflict in Northern Ireland must remain a concern not only of the Irish, but of everyone.[4]

The quotation from Richard Rose given at the beginning of this chapter identifies Northern Ireland as being legally a subordinate part of the United Kingdom. This status goes back to the 1920s when five-sixths of Ireland—the Free State—became a self-governing dominion with the same autonomy as Canada, South Africa, and Australia in what was then the British Empire. The remaining sixth, an area of 5200 square miles in the northeast corner comprising 6 of the country's 32 counties, continued its previous close association with the former kingdoms of England and Scotland and the principality of Wales in what was henceforth known as the United Kingdom of Great Britain and Northern Ireland.

The Government of Ireland Act of 1920, by which the United Kingdom Parliament at Westminster created Northern Ireland, gave to the subordinate government, set up at Stormont near Belfast, a House of Commons, a Senate, and a Governor-General. The House had 52 members elected by universal suffrage, each from a separate constituency. Originally, members were elected from multimember constituencies by the system of proportional representation then and still used in the neighboring Free State (now the Republic of Ireland); a system designed to ensure significant representation of minorities.[5] This system was, however, quickly dropped by Stormont without protest from Westminster. The Senate, elected by the House, provided some checks to its power; like the British House of Lords, it could delay the enactment of legislation.

Stormont's authority extended to labor, agriculture, commerce, education, town and country planning, the levying of some local taxes, the administration of justice, and the maintenance of internal law and order. The United Kingdom government retained and exercised all functions relating to foreign affairs, armed forces, navigation, postal services, and income tax. A complicated system of allocating revenue between Northern Ireland and the United Kingdom government enabled each administration to reimburse itself from the total revenue of the area for the services it provided.

In the 1920s Northern Ireland was highly prosperous and more than paid its way. Subsequently it declined relative to the general economy of the United Kingdom, and for many years it has been subsidized in common with such other depressed areas as Scotland and Wales. The level of subsidization is disputed. A White Paper attached to the financial statement for the Northern Ireland budget for 1972–1973 put the subsidy for social services, agriculture, and unemployment benefits at $330 million (£133 million). Professor Norman Gibson of the New University of Ulster has calculated the total at more than $500 million (£200 million). That would make it some 40 percent of Northern Ireland's total expenditures of $1220 million.[6] In recognition of the fact that major economic and other decisions affecting Northern Ireland are made by the Westminster Parliament, the region elects 12 of that body's 600 members.

Belfast, capital of Northern Ireland, contains nearly a third of the state's one and a half million people. Its big expansion from its seventeenth-century beginnings as a small market town at the head of a wide, deep, sheltered fjord at the mouth of the Lagan river was begun during the nineteenth century when the herons and gulls were chased from the mudflats and piles were sunk 30 to 40 feet to carry the buildings that now form the city center. The fine basaltic scarp of Cave Hill rises to a height of 1100 feet over the northern suburbs, a geologically recent formation of lava rock which makes the adjoining valleys rich and fertile. The rise of Belfast corresponded with the economic decline of the rest of Ireland that followed the Act of Union of 1800 which put an end to Ireland's separate Parliament located in Dublin. Belfast, which then had 20,000 inhabitants, expanded rapidly to become Ireland's only center of heavy industry, specializing in shipbuilding and engineering, as well as in the manufacture of linen. Today it also manufactures food, drink, and tobacco, and aircraft production has become important, while the weaving of linen has yielded to synthetic fabrics. More than half of the manufacturing workers of Northern Ireland are in Belfast, and three-quarters of the state's external trade—most of it with Britain—passes through its port. The concentration of industry during the nineteenth century here rather than elsewhere in Ireland was politically motivated for the benefit of the Unionists who then as now were heavily concentrated in and around Belfast, though one should not overlook the greater readiness of its inhabitants to adjust to industrial processes, the so-called Protestant ethic. And for the same reason, the policy of the government of Northern Ireland since 1920 has continued to favor the expansion of Belfast by locating new industry in Unionist areas. Again, however, we must note other influences. In Ireland, both north and south, the meshing of all economic life with that of neighboring Britain for the past several centuries has steadily drawn the population toward the east coast from the less-developed western half of the island. The River Shannon forms the dividing line in the south, the River Bann in the north.

Roman Catholics constitute the largest religious denomination in Northern Ireland, and their proportion of the population has remained practically unchanged since the beginning of the century. They formed 34.4 percent of the total in 1911, 33.5 percent in 1926, 33.5 percent in 1937, 34.4 percent in 1951, and 34.9 percent in 1961. Presbyterians come next with 29 percent, followed by Church of Ireland with 24 percent, and Methodists with 5 percent. Other small groups of Protestants account for the other 7 percent. Jews number a statistically insignificant handful. The fertility rates for Roman Catholics are considerably higher than for all others. Live births by 1000 married women in 1960–1962 were 288 for the former group and 163 for the latter, and the average family size was 4.69 and 2.88, respectively. The fertility differential between the two groups became significant only after 1937, and its effect can be seen in the growth of the number of Catholic children in primary schools. They were 34.8 percent of the total in 1924, 36.5 percent in 1934, 39.4 percent in 1945, 42.8 percent in 1951, 45.5 percent in 1957, and 51 percent in 1968.[7]

Public profession of atheism is practically unknown. Social integration is possible only within the network of tribal allegiances which mark one as either a Roman Catholic or a Protestant. The person who does not go to any church is still

identified as a Catholic unbeliever or a Protestant unbeliever. The Church of Ireland is part of the Anglican Communion, but its members generally identify with the "low
church" or nonconformist side of Anglicanism. They are
called and call themselves Protestants.

In the United States, Episcopalians (Anglican Communion) tend in general to hold liberal views on doctrinal
issues, while Presbyterians are moderates, and Roman Catholics are conservatives. No similar correlation exists in
Northern Ireland. A survey made of people in Northern Ireland and Great Britain in 1968 by an opinion research center
found little difference in the level of doctrinal conservatism
between Presbyterians and Church of Ireland communicants,
or between them and Roman Catholics. An average of 80 percent of the respondents in Northern Ireland expressed clear
agreement with five conservative theological statements of
position, while in Britain only 49 percent were in agreement.
The cultural self-identification of each group in Northern Ireland by opposition to the other group probably functions as a
support of fundamentalist beliefs and as an obstacle to theological evolution.[8]

The extent of the influence of religious allegiance on
the conflict in Northern Ireland, which will be treated later,
forces the author to define his own position. I was born and
spent my early years in an overwhelmingly Roman Catholic
rural community in the west of Ireland. According to family
tradition, the first of my father's paternal ancestors to reach
Ireland was a Cromwellian soldier, and his family had been
Protestant until his grandfather married a Catholic and raised
the children as Catholics. My mother's paternal line goes
back to the twelfth-century Anglo-Normans. Both my grand-
mothers were of old Gaelic stock. The combination makes us
a very typical Irish family indeed.

Today in Northern Ireland, polarization of the communities has forced apart Catholics and Protestants regardless of
personal respect and affection. The bitterness of the Black
and Tan War (1919–1921), during which I grew up, caused no

such response in my village. The few Protestant children came to the one school, shared the same games and escapades. Our only resentment was their daily half hour of liberty while we swotted catechism. One of my most vivid childhood recollections is my parents' practice of inviting each year, between Christmas and the New Year, a neighboring family with whom they were on terms of friendship usually reserved in that society for close relatives. We enjoyed an excellent meal, followed by games, good conversation, and songs. The only indication that the two families belonged to different religious traditions came at departure time when my mother would sing the *Adeste Fideles,* then replay the same music on the piano as Mrs. Hutchinson closed the evening with *Oh, Come All Ye Faithful.*

Work as a newsman in Ireland from 1934 to 1944 took me to all parts of Ireland, north and south, and gave me an unusual opportunity to make friends across the conventional barriers. My first experience of the collective frenzy with which the Orangemen each July 12 commemorate the Battle of the Boyne (1690) was in 1936. That was a quiet year, in contrast with 1935 when the marches had led to three weeks of burning and wrecking, with the loss of 12 lives, in one of Belfast's worst outbreaks of sectarian rioting. The bowler-hatted marchers wore elaborate sashes and collarettes over their dark suits. Were it not for their stern, set faces, they might pass for a Shriner convention. The banners recalled past glories, William of Orange crossing the Boyne, the breaking of the boom as the siege of Derry was raised. From time to time, a banner saluted the virtue of temperance, about the only salute it would receive that day. Union Jacks streamed from windows and were waved by onlookers. "To hell with the Pope" was scratched with unimaginative monotony on every wall and billboard, the current four-letter disposition of His Holiness not having then come into its own. Bands playing partisan tunes whipped marchers and onlookers into a frenzy of exaltation. The key instrument was the Lambeg drum, struck with short sticks in such a way as to cause the drummer's knuckles to bleed profusely, the mark of a true professional. In such a context a spark is all that is needed to start a pogrom.

Thirty years subsequently spent in many parts of the world gave me new perspectives on the heavy load of history which weighs on Ireland. In a residential men's club in Trinidad I learned a profound lesson from my next-door neighbor. The moral, social, and cultural values of an Irish Catholic and a Northern Ireland Protestant are indistinguishable. "I have been in every one of the thirty-two countries," says journalist Douglas Gageby, a Protestant who was born in Belfast and works in Dublin, "and in all my travels I have never been conscious of two Irelands. . . . People talk, drink, walk, eat, and worship God in much the same way (in the North) as they do in other parts of Ireland. . . . They sin and die in very much the same way." [9] Their tastes, likes, and dislikes differ in only one respect. The northern Protestant has an aversion for the English which his Catholic counterpart usually does not bear. Having once discovered this important truth, I had no difficulty in verifying it time and again, and most recently by my dealings with many Protestants in Northern Ireland while researching this book. That such an identity of values objectively exists, even though those people viewing each other through their myopic prejudices cannot yet see it, is a major reason why I foresee a solution without the need to annihilate or even displace either community.

Exposure to the updating of the Roman Catholic church which was begun at Vatican Council II [10] gave me, I believe, a further clue to what the northern Protestant regards as an invincible obstacle to his acceptance of citizenship in a united Ireland in which he would constitute a minority, the nature of the church to which his fellow Irishmen give allegiance. As will appear in the course of this book, there were good reasons why it developed the way it did. Unfortunately the vision of this Irish Catholicism is distorted by the obscurantism and arrogance of nineteenth-century Rome,

with illusions of Tridentine certainty and Constantinian gran-
deur. Self-righteous, authoritarian, contemptuous of Protestants; it is a church little touched by the spirit of Pope John
and of the Vatican Council, still committed to imposing its
views of right and wrong even on those who do not accept its
pretensions. The northern Protestant wants no part of it. I
agree with him.

I am not suggesting that all this makes me neutral. It has
never been my ambition to be neutral where the rights of innocent people are involved, and I believe that the innocent
suffer on both sides in Northern Ireland. I hope rather to
have acquired a perspective not common among those who
write about these issues. I shall be content if I can share it.

1

No Neutrals in Belfast

Steady on your aim with the petrol bomb—
Don't throw it, son, till the Peelers come.
                    —A contemporary "Fenian" ballad

And when we got to Weirsbridge, sure 'twas a glorious sight
To see so many Orangemen all ready for a fight,
To march around the old remains, our music sweet to play;
And the tune we played was "The Protestant Boys"
Right on to Dolly's Brae.
                    —An Orange ballad

Northern Ireland is a battleground. Terror grabs at every throat. Bombs explode in stolen cars abandoned on city streets, in hotels, in supermarkets. Drivers watch constantly for road obstructions designed to prevent hit-and-runs from speeding automobiles. To drive over one of these axle-high humps at more than five miles an hour will smash up one's car, and very likely bring a volley of machine-gun fire from the nearby military post. At night the British army patrols, young faces blackened, prowl like alley cats through the poorly lit darkness. They press flat against grimy walls, then dash from one doorway to the next, semiautomatic FN rifles or Sterling submachine guns at the ready. Sad-faced women peer from darkened windows. One thinks of her missing husband, hunted by the police, out there somewhere with only a pistol in a shoulder holster to protect him. Another shudders and crosses herself as she recalls that her teen-age son picked up the empty milk bottle when he left a while ago. Is he now on some corner, waiting for the patrol, a petrol bomb at the ready? Yet another sends her blessing after the soldiers and prays they will catch the "murdering terrorists" they are looking for. But none of them has much confidence in the efficacy of prayer. They accept as inevitable each new upsurge of the centuries-old war.

What are they fighting about? The concrete, existential issue can be most clearly seen in the ghetto communities of Belfast, the Catholic Falls and the Protestant Shankill, separated since the riots of August 1969 by a 15-foot-high barbed-wire fence incongruously known as the Peace Line. Here the struggle is quite clearly for territory, to maintain one's living space against encroachments from the other side, to penetrate a step here and a step there when the enemy is distracted.

Hardest to understand is that the territory each guards literally with his life consists of squalid slums, wretched houses 70 to 80 years old, little better than hovels, packed together in endless rows. A typical house has a frontage of 13 feet and is 20 feet in depth from front to back. The door opens directly onto the narrow street without yard or lawn. The area at the back for coalbin and toilet is no more than ten feet in depth, with a high wall to cut it off from a similar layout beyond.

A siege mentality dominates. People switch homes, even though they do not own them, only if driven out in communal riots, or if they make the decisive jump to another country. Short of such an irreversible step, which is also traumatic since it involves a kind of desertion, there is almost no local movement. One's immediate neighbors are also protectors.

They can be counted upon in sickness, unemployment, or forcible ejection. Outside is a hostile world, equally absorbed in its own concerns, equally frightened of a stranger in its midst.

Alfie Hannaway is one of these people.[1] His credentials in the predominantly Roman Catholic Falls Road district, where he has lived since his birth in 1922, are impeccable: internment as a young man, two brothers openly identified with defense of the neighborhood during and since the 1969 burnings and shootings by Orange mobs. Of medium height and clean-shaven, he dresses quietly and speaks with a schoolmasterish deliberateness that contrasts with the rapid-fire, poorly enunciated speech of working-class Belfast. Since 1945, Alfie has occupied the same house on Oranmore Street, tenant of a private landlord. In the distant past, private enterprise in Belfast could make a profit out of providing rental homes for the workers employed in factories, an activity it has handed over almost entirely to the public authorities since the creation of the Northern Ireland state in 1922. Alfie's home belongs to that earlier period, as do most of those around him. These houses follow a standard pattern. From the street one enters almost directly into a living room measuring 11 feet by 8, behind which is a dining-kitchen area. Upstairs are two bedrooms, each the same size as the living room. That is all. Although there is running water, there is no bathroom. The toilet (still sometimes a dry closet) is outside in the backyard, alongside the coalbin. Here Alfie and his wife have raised five children, three boys and two girls, a family slightly below the average for the Catholic ghetto. Having worked uninterruptedly for many years, Alfie can afford a refrigerator and a washing machine. But he still has no telephone. There is only one telephone in the entire street.

As a child and youth, Alfie followed the ghetto patterns. He went to Catholic schools and learned that all things Irish are identified with truth, beauty, and the spirit of Catholicism, that his loyalties belonged to an Irish nation whose flag he was forbidden to display, and that the Protestants who lived a few blocks away and went to the public school were his enemies because they cursed the pope and flew the British Union Jack. He learned Irish ballads, Irish dances, and Irish music. He participated fervently in the Irish-style football and hurley at nearby Casement Park, a playground named to commemorate a Belfastman who sought German help for Ireland during World War I and was hanged by the British for his pains.

With hundreds of others whose life style caused the police to question their loyalty to the Northern Ireland regime, Alfie was, at the age of 17, interned without trial during World War II. Like many of his companions, he spent his time studying Irish, the form of the Gaelic language that was once the vernacular of all of Ireland and much of Scotland and England, now commonly spoken only by small communities in remote parts of Ireland. (Today it also is an official language of the Republic of Ireland and obligatory in the schools there.) Irish had a practical function for the internees because it enabled them to communicate without their captors' being able to understand them. But for Alfie, as for others before and since, it did something more basic. He discovered that Irish was not just a group of dialects forming the subject of a quaint revival in part of Ireland, but that it was the most important Celtic language in the Indo-European family, related not only to Latin and Greek but to Phrygian, Hittite, and Tokharian, with a literary tradition older than any European language except Greek and Latin.

That discovery gave him a self-identification no longer cast in emotionally unacceptable molds and simultaneously opened up a world of culture. Today Alfie's bedroom—the only island of solitude in his tiny home—is dominated by bookshelves which, on close examination, are seen to hold mostly dictionaries, grammars, and other teaching aids and literary texts. These volumes are not only a source of personal joy but are utilized in the neighborhood Irish classes to which he devotes his spare time, without pay of course. The Republic of Ireland has for 50 years been using oceans of

rhetoric and material inducements to encourage its citizens
to learn and speak Irish, but the results are minimal. What is
apparently lacking is the mystique provided by British and
Northern Ireland jails and internment camps.

Alfie had an unusual stroke of luck when he got out. Although lacking any specific skills or training, he got a job
which made all the difference to his subsequent life. Two
Jewish refugees from Nazi Europe had started the business
of textile screen printing in the Lower Falls in the late 1930s.
When Alfie was released from internment in 1945, they gave
him a job as a cleaner and handyman. He was there only a
short time when a high officer of the Royal Ulster Constabulary (RUC) called on the owners to notify them they had
employed an undesirable. Fortunately for Alfie, the Jewish
immigrants didn't understand the language of Belfast. If they
had, they would immediately have fired him, and the police
would have hounded him out of one job after another until
he gave up the hopeless effort and drifted in frustration into
active service with the illegal Irish Republican Army (IRA).
The prospects there might not be great, but at least a man's
self-respect survived. Instead, Alfie stayed on and in due
course worked his way up from sweeping floors to the post of
production manager.

Once a suspect in Belfast, nevertheless, always a suspect. Even if a man did nothing more treasonable than teach
Irish in his spare time, his name remained on police dossiers.
In August 1971 the Stormont government secured the approval of its London overlords to reinstate internment without charge or trial as a counter to a wave of bombings being
conducted by the IRA. A few days later, as Alfie was walking
to work one morning, three men in civilian dress jumped him
on the street and began to force him into a car. Fearing that
his assailants might be a murder gang of Orange extremists,
he tried to struggle free. One of them quickly produced a
gun, and Alfie decided to go quietly. As it turned out, they
were police, and they took him directly to the interrogation
center. Under the internment law, the police can hold a sus-

pect for 48 hours of interrogation, without allowing him to call a lawyer, and without having to notify anyone that they even hold the individual as a suspect. At the end of 48 hours, they must either release or intern him. Even then, they do not have to specify any charge, but they must permit him to notify his family.

But Alfie was again lucky. A young girl on her way to class had witnessed the kidnapping and spread the news at school. By midafternoon it had drifted back to Alfie's wife who checked at the plant and learned that her husband had failed to show up for work. The plant manager telephoned police and military authorities all around Belfast, everywhere getting the stock reply that there was no record of any such person in their hands. In this the law was on their side. They didn't have to admit anything for 48 hours. The plant manager finally contacted his London office, and it in turn pulled political strings in Whitehall. When Whitehall put the squeeze on Stormont, Alfie was let go after only 20 hours of questioning. "You must be a very important man where you work," the interrogator commented sourly, as he dismissed him.

Alfie regards himself as one of the more fortunate. All around are people who are under far greater stresses. Phyllis Meehan, for example, has been a "wire widow" since her 25-year-old husband Colm was "lifted" by the police in August 1971 and interned behind barbed-wire fences in the "cages" of Long Kesh camp four miles outside Belfast. Mrs. Meehan is outgoing, her smile of welcome transforming her entire face.[2] But when she sits clutching her youngest in the living room and stares moodily into the fire, the lines of tiredness show. She could use some makeup, and a visit to the hairdresser would work wonders for the jet-black hair that hangs long around her shoulders. But these are luxuries quite remote from her day-to-day reality. With four children under the age of five, she lives in a house similar to Alfie's but slightly bigger, with outside toilet and without bath, refrigerator, or washer. Catholics who identify openly with the culture represented by the flag of the neighboring Irish Republic and patronize Irish dances and games cannot get employment in businesses dominated by the Orange Order. That means that they are refused employment not only with the state or local authorities but also most big business and industry. The best they can hope is to gain some service job for and in their own ghetto, delivery of bread or milk, storehand, home repairs, and the like.

Colm had steady work as a truck driver in such a service firm owned by a relative, but his salary ended with internment and Phyllis had to turn to welfare. Fortunately for her, a Labor government in Britain after World War II had forced the reluctant government in Stormont to bring social and health as well as educational services up to the level of those in Britain itself. (The Stormont reluctance was not motivated by the cost, because London was going to pay, but by its recognition that Catholics as the depressed segment of the population would be the principal beneficiaries and would be better placed than previously to withstand job discrimination.) As mother of four preschool children who require her full-time attention at home, Phyllis was able to get $25 a week in welfare payments, and a further $7.50 a week from a Quaker-supported fund called rather quaintly the Innocent Victims Fund. She could get by on this income but for two factors. The quality of the food supplied at the internment camp is so bad the internees refuse to eat any of it. She must, consequently, send Colm a food packet each day. In addition, he was always a heavy smoker and camp life has increased his craving.

The life of the "wire widows" is a very special one. Phyllis is visited for hours each day by Joy McKeever, whose husband Frank is also interned at Long Kesh. Joy is in a particularly anomalous position in Belfast, a Protestant married to a Catholic. During the relatively long period of peace since the previous communal riots in 1935 up to the outbreak of the present disturbances in 1969, considerable intermingling of Catholic and Protestant families occurred in the

small side streets connecting the Catholic ghetto of the Falls
with the Protestant ghetto of the Shankill. In such a street the
McKeevers lived next door to Joy's Protestant parents. But
the Peace Line erected in August 1969 left the McKeevers in
Cooper Street on the Protestant side. They were not alarmed
at first, being reasonably safe in their obscurity. They
paraded neither Frank's religion nor the symbols of his cultural identification. Many who knew Joy's parents assumed
that her husband was also a Protestant.

The McKeever anonymity ended when he was "lifted"
in November 1971, just two weeks before their first child was
born. Each evening since, she watches a soldier lock the gate
in the Peace Line, cutting off her escape route, and she turns
out the lights early whenever she hears hoodlums shouting
obscene threats on the street. It is now her ambition to find a
place in the Catholic ghetto, as most of the Catholics in these
cross streets have already done. But "safe" housing is at a
premium. Meanwhile, during the day Joy spends every free
moment with her baby at the Meehan home. There Phyllis
and she discuss unceasingly the prospects for the release of
their husbands, the news they learned at the most recent of
their weekly visits to Long Kesh, the indignities they suffer
at the hands of guards and searchers each time they go there,
the constant barking and snarling of the guard dogs.

Under questioning, they will formulate the political objectives for which their husbands are suffering. They want to
see Ireland free and united as the fulfillment of a centuries-
old dream. They want, more immediately, a regime which
will guarantee an end to discrimination in voting, housing,
and jobs, so that their children will have a fair chance in life.
But these are not their felt concerns. What they think and talk
about incessantly is the day-to-day struggle against the temp-
tation to run away from the threats, the fire bombs, and the
sniper fire which has enveloped them for more than three
years. They regard it as a duty not to yield. They see themselves as defending their homes and neighborhoods from the
unrelenting pressure of the enemy who is only a stone's

throw away. If at the moment there is no hope of expanding the area controlled by their side, at least they must prevent the seizure of any redoubt by the enemy.

The issue that most agitates Joy and Phyllis and others in their situation is the morale of their interned husbands. "Up in the zoo in a cage with the monkeys" was one child's recollection of his father after his first visit to Long Kesh. He expressed precisely what was on the mind of his mother and the other wives, who see their husbands forced to live indefinitely almost like animals.[3] The indefinite duration of internment particularly disturbs them. When London suspended the Stormont regime in March 1972 and named William Whitelaw as Minister of State for Northern Ireland with dictatorial powers, their hopes rose. Whitelaw, an archetypal figure of the British "establishment," independently wealthy, enormously energetic, and with a reputation for getting on with people, set out to persuade the Catholic community it could trust him. Accordingly, a few internees were released each week, and tension grew among the relatives of those still held. All they would talk about was the mood of expectancy in the camp, the men each morning washing, shaving, packing their things, then gathering in threes and fours to watch for the arrival of the superintendent with his "Long Kesh roulette" list.

Gradually, however, people came to believe that Whitelaw was using the men as pawns in his political game, and the mood changed. Bitterness was intensified further in November with the unfolding of what was proclaimed to be the British solution to the issue of internment. Simon Hoggart,[4] one of the most prestigious of English newsmen covering Northern Ireland, described the "special commissions" then created as "a Kafka-like perversion of justice . . . mock courts where the only evidence comes from hidden spies, informers and special branch policemen [British English for detectives]. . . . Not only is the evidence hearsay . . . but the police are not even obliged to say where and how they heard it." By mid-January 1973, the commissions had seen

206 of the internees and released 77 of them. Meanwhile, another 93 men and 1 woman had been detained, increasing by 16 the total number held. And as people like Joy and Phyllis angrily add, not a single member of the Ulster Defence Association (UDA) or other extremist Orange armed groups had been held under the Special Powers Act from the reintroduction of internment in August 1971 up to January 1973.[5]

Joy and Phyllis are equally bitter about what they describe as the partisanship of the British army. The soldiers had been welcomed when sent in to keep order in August 1969, after the Stormont police and paramilitary forces had sided openly with the Orangemen. But the honeymoon was brief. As people like Phyllis and Joy see it, the soldiers soon decided openly to sympathize with the Ulster Defence Association, a force of Orange vigilantes claiming 43,000 members and heavily armed.[6]

When the UDA start firing in, our lads have to reply quickly, because the army never shows up for half an hour, even when their post is only a block away. And when they come, they don't turn on the aggressors but on the boys defending us. They sneer at us if we protest. "Why should we interfere with the UDA," they ask. "You sons of bitches are the only ones who fire on us." Some of the soldiers are not so bad, but you can never trust a Scots Guard. Every one of them is a bigot. They hate us just because we are Catholics. When they were leaving at the end of their tour of duty, they came through the street in jeeps, swilling whiskey, singing Protestant songs, and threatening to kill every "papish bastard" in the country.

But most of the conversation is about the children. "They never get a night's sleep with the shooting. We lie on the floor, and that's not safe either, because the high-velocity bullets ricochet when they come through a window. The kids are terrified. And even during the day it's dangerous to let them out because of the patrols and the snipers." There have in fact been many studies of the impact of the climate of violence on Belfast children, some of which received considerable exposure on United States television. Tests of children evacuated from Belfast schools which previously had an excellent academic record showed grade-school pupils now two years behind their age groups. Emotional abnormalities are very common, especially when a father or mother has been killed or interned, or is "on the run" (in hiding); or when the mother has cracked under the pressures and is in a psychiatric ward or being treated.[7]

The boys are uncontrollably aggressive. Every uniform holds an enemy. When evacuated to peaceful surroundings, they need retraining to respond normally to a police officer or bus driver. The girls have nightmares. Their vivid memories are of doors burst open in the middle of the night, soldiers with blackened faces shining lights on them and tossing them from their bed in order to bayonet the mattress and rip up the floorboards in search of arms. Even small children as well as the grown-ups talk about the "Tartans" and other street gangs loosely integrated into the UDA. They had slashed a teen-age girl from up the street on the face with a razor. They had carved UDA on the hands of a child. They had blown out the brains of Malcolm and Peter Orr, two Protestant youths who were too friendly with Catholics. They had raped the Widow McGlenaghan and killed her 15-year-old imbecile son. "Are you a Fenian?" they challenged passersby on the street.

The word "Fenian" is itself a significant example of the persistence of tradition in Northern Ireland. The Fenians were a revolutionary organization founded in New York and Dublin in 1858 to work for the creation of an independent Irish republic. It was quickly condemned by the Roman Catholic authorities in Ireland who saw it as the equivalent of the Italian revolutionary movements which were then threatening the pope's extensive kingdom in central Italy. A formal papal ban was added in 1870, and this caused the Fenian Society as such to die out and prevented the Irish Republican Brotherhood which grew out of it from ever gaining popular support among clerically dominated Irish Catho-

lics either at home or in the United States. Yet even today to
the Protestant in the north of Ireland every Catholic is still a
Fenian, part of a worldwide conspiracy dedicated and committed to his annihilation.[8]

How real this fear is of an international Catholic conspiracy actively engaged in plotting the destruction of the loyal
Protestants of Northern Ireland can be seen by the visitor to
the Shankill. If he is coming from the Falls, he does not
move uninterrupted through the side streets that connect
these two neighboring districts. First, there is the official
barrier of the Peace Line, which can be passed during the
day through gates in the barbed-wire fence. Also there are
usually unofficial barricades, perhaps supported by antitank
emplacements, manned by IRA men with stockings over
their faces, on the Catholic side, and the UDA boys with
goggles, mask, and bush jackets on the Protestant side.

Jim McDonald is as representative of Belfast's Protestants as Alfie Hannaway is of its Catholics. Rev. Martin
Smyth, Grand Master of Belfast's Orange Order, a top leader
of the group of extremist Protestant organizations known as
the Ulster Vanguard, and a Presbyterian minister, vouches
for him as a faithful member of the Orange Order. Jim's home
is little different from Alfie's. It is one of a long row of
reddish-brown brick houses, built right on the street. Outside, the only difference is that Jim may and does exhibit the
flags portraying his loyalties, the Union Jack and the Ulster
flag consisting of the cross of St. George centered with a red
hand and a crown.[9] Within, it is furnished somewhat better,
but it also lacks a bath and indoor toilet. As a Protestant, Jim
has always had a steady job. When he left school at 15, he
was apprenticed in a factory for five years and qualified as a
latheman. He now has year-round work as a maintenance engineer in a factory, earning $100 a week with overtime. He
can consequently afford a washer, refrigerator, and other
comforts denied the typical Catholic slum resident who earns
$50 a week in less-skilled work or collects $25 unemployment benefits for a family of five. As the family consists of

only two children, a girl of eight and a boy of seven, Jim's wife, Ruby, can also pick up extra income at a nursery school in the morning and as a barmaid at an Orange club at night.

Jim, aged 33, is clean-cut and clean-shaven. A serious man with a ruddy complexion, he has the preciseness one expects of an engineer and exudes a sense of competence. He smiles easily and is not self-important. For both Jim and Ruby, the central fact of their lives is the terror in which they and their children live. Jim tends to be almost resigned to it as a fact of life. She is more bitter in her expression and more insistent on corrective action. They claim that they used to have Catholic friends but admit that they no longer have any. Raised in their separate schools and separate cultures, the McDonalds are even more dependent on their myths for their knowledge of their Catholic neighbors than are those neighbors for their knowledge of them. The difference is that the Catholic ghetto is less self-sufficient, forcing its residents sometimes to venture forth. The McDonalds never have either desire or need to move beyond their own sectarian circle.

Many distorted facts are consequently inserted into the myth and become an element of misunderstanding. The family size is particularly significant. "These Catholics are tricky people," Jim McDonald says. "They are trained to use every device to get money without working. Their priests tell them to have large families so that they will outnumber us at the polling booths and swamp the welfare rolls. So they breed like rabbits." The Catholics, for their part, see the two-child family of the typical Protestant couple as proof of the moral degradation which takes possession of people who are dominated by selfishness and break the natural law. Neither side pays any attention to sociologists who match up family size and economic levels. They ignore the fact that poor Hindus or Buddhists have as many children as poor Roman Catholics. They simply refuse to believe that difference in the birth rates for Catholics and Protestants of the same income groups in the United States are today statistically insignificant, a major change from an earlier period when Catholics as a group were poorer than Protestants and had bigger families.

The issue is, nevertheless, one of the most basic in the conflict. The proportion of Catholic children to all children in Northern Ireland has risen substantially since 1937, and—as already noted—Catholic primary school children constituted more than half of all schoolchildren in 1968. Yet the proportion of Catholics in the general population rose less than one and a half percentage points from 33.5 in 1937 to 34.9 at the 1961 census, the last to record religious affiliation. To maintain the two-to-one proportion, which they believe essential to prevent their physical liquidation—and certainly is essential to maintain their control of the levers of power—the Protestants were forced to discriminate in jobs and housing. In housing, it was relatively easy. Private houses in Northern Ireland are a luxury within the reach only of the wealthy. Public housing was provided by local authorities controlled by their Protestant majorities. They could make a newly married Catholic couple wait up to 12 years for a place of their own. Similarly, employment in local and central government, as well as in industry and commerce, was guaranteed for all Protestants but not for young Catholics. Those unwilling to accept the double limitation of having to raise a family in the already crowded home of parents of one of the couple and live on welfare or in marginal activities emigrated in sufficient numbers to maintain the desired population mix. Between 1937 and 1961, the latest years for which there are figures, 21 percent of the Catholic population emigrated but only 8 percent of the Protestants.[10] Even with this heavy emigration, more than 30 percent of the men in the Catholic ghettos were unemployed.

Jim McDonald does not deny these facts, but he defends the discrimination exercised ever since the state was founded as a necessary weapon of Protestant self-defense. "There is discrimination everywhere in the world," he says, "including the United States, and here it was not excessive." [11] The

Catholics recognized this, he insists, and they would continue to accept discrimination were it not for "outside agitators" who had a safe haven in the neighboring Republic of Ireland, from where they carried out the instructions of their Roman Catholic leaders. It was all a plot hatched by the Vatican. Frightened by the steady advance of the Communists in Italy, the pope needs a secure base from which to launch his long-planned offensive for world domination. If only he could get rid of the million Protestants, Ireland would be ideal.

Seen in this perspective, the stand of the Orangemen becomes logical. They see themselves not as the aggressors with a two-to-one edge, but as the tiny David facing the 500 million minions of the Vatican Goliath. Their fear is as real as that of the Catholics over in the Falls, a fear confirmed by every sniper bullet that whizzes into their streets from nearby Ardoyne and by every car-bombed bank and supermarket in the city center. And there can be no solution while half a million Catholics continue to constitute a papal Trojan Horse in their midst. No rabble-rouser, Jim McDonald has nevertheless become a hard-liner. He does not trust any Catholic, and he believes that force is the only language his opponents understand. That is why the place of honor in his living room is given to the two documents which express for him his identity, his memberships in the Orange Order and in the UDA.

But can intelligent and even moderately educated people really believe such nonsense? They can and do, because they trust their leaders in the Orange Order, and that is what those leaders tell them. Typical of the Orange leadership is Rev. Martin Smyth, 44-year-old son of a Belfast plumber. At the age of six he decided to become a preacher as a result of "a decided personal experience with Christ," and since 1953 he has proclaimed the Christian message as an ordained minister of the Presbyterian church. He has also, since 1969, been an organizer and leader of Ulster Vanguard and other extremist organizations which maintain illegal armies and under whose protective umbrella savage sectarian rioting and large-scale murder of civilians have flourished.

As Grand Master of the Belfast Orange Lodge, the biggest and most influential of the 10 or 12 lodges into which the Orange Order is divided, Mr. Smyth is one of the most powerful men in Northern Ireland. Orangeism reveals very little about itself. Mr. Smyth, while refusing to state its strength, says it is "basically religious and only coincidentally political, a fellowship of all who embrace the Reformed faith, founded to safeguard the interests of the Protestant people against the aggressions of the church of Rome which historically claims to have power over princes." [12] Others estimate its strength at about 100,000. When the flourishing satellite organizations for women and young people are added, it emerges as Northern Ireland's only all-embracing fraternal grouping, actively involving more than 90 percent of the Protestant community in places.

Many interpret its role very differently from Mr. Smyth. Rev. Terence McCaughey, also a Presbyterian minister from Belfast, deplores "the divisive and sectarian nature of the Orange Order . . . used consistently—even by ministers of the gospel—as an instrument to foment hatred and fear of their Roman Catholic neighbors . . . the means of deceiving honest people into believing that they have everything in common with the Archdales, the Brookes, the Chichesters and the Cunninghams [prominent establishment families of Northern Ireland], and nothing with their Catholic neighbors." [13]

The negative role of the leadership of Northern Ireland has been consistent throughout the lifetime of the state. Terence O'Neill, Prime Minister from 1963 to 1969, records in his autobiography the problems he had when he tried to establish a code of conduct for cabinet ministers. He describes his predecessor, Basil Brooke (Lord Brookeborough) as "a man of limited intelligence . . . in the hands of his dominating wife . . . difficult to shake from some of his more idiotic ideas." Yet Brooke ruled Northern Ireland for 20 years. He had the power and influence to make profound changes, if he had so wished. "The tragedy of his premiership," according to O'Neill, "was that he did not use his tremendous charm and his deep Orange roots to try and persuade his devoted followers to accept some reforms. In twenty years as Prime Minister, he never crossed the Border, never visited a Catholic school, and never received or sought a civic reception from a Catholic town. His latter days were taken up with two pet aversions. First, he was determined never to recognize the trade unions; and second, he condemned planning, which he regarded as a socialist menace." [14]

The role of the Orange Order in Northern Ireland since the founding of the state has been very similar to the role of the Communist party in the Soviet Union. Although not officially a part of the system of government, it dominated the executive, the legislative, and the judicial branches. Only its members could hope to gain office, and they showed their appreciation openly by carrying out the policies it formulated. A major part of the activity of the leadership of the Orange Order is keeping the rank and file convinced that the real enemy is the Roman Catholic church. [15] "We have to fight the pretensions of the church of Rome," Mr. Smyth says. "I am convinced that it has never stopped its efforts to obscure the gospel, and I believe we must contend for the way of salvation through Christ." The same message comes from Thomas Orr, Grand Master of Scotland. In a speech at an Orange ceremony in July 1972, he charged that the English government was withdrawing from its commitments to Northern Ireland because it was preoccupied with the negotiations for entry into what he called "the Roman Catholic European Council." The reference was to the European Economic Community with which London was in fact negotiating. Orr also said he had heard that the pope was involved in the trouble in Northern Ireland, that Cardinal Heenan of Westminster had warned Wilson and Heath, leaders of the two major parties in the British Parliament, that entry into the European Common Market would be difficult unless they did more for the Catholics in Northern Ireland. The other Presbyterian minister with whom Mr. Smyth shares the intellectual and spiritual leadership of the Orange masses, Rev. Ian Paisley, is even more outspoken. He refers to the pope in his public speeches as "old Red Sox" and denounces his church as "the scarlet whore of Rome." For the doubter, he has in his high-ceilinged library a sheaf of antipapal literature, alongside his twisted blackthorn stick and his musket.

To the outsider it is hard to understand how the Orange Order manages to provide for its members not only a sense of involvement but an absolute conviction that they can depend upon it for all the truth they need to ensure success and salvation in this world and in the next. Douglas Gageby, a Protestant native of Northern Ireland who has made a successful career as a journalist elsewhere, nevertheless gives us some measure of insight in his description of an Orange celebration on July 12, the day sacred to the memory of William of Orange who saved us from "brass money, wooden shoes and popery." The main speaker, among a group of important politicians, was the Reverend Samuel Millar. "He reads the Word of God for us," Gageby reported,

nothing less joyful than the raising of Lazarus. He reads with what elocution classes call "feeling," head thrown up to the sky, teeth clenched, and when he comes to the bit "He groaned in His spirit and was troubled," the Reverend Samuel Millar groans with the Lord. . . . Men and women. We aren't for long; soon we are a generation of vipers. "Christ is good, He is good," he shouts. God loves us; He wants to take the hatred from our hearts. But we have spurned the message of the Gospel; it is not enough for us to follow the Reformed Church, not enough to be Orange, not enough for us to be just hearers.[16]

Gageby adds perspicaciously: "Those who had read their Joyce might take the speech of the Reverend Samuel Millar and compare it with the sermon in *A Portrait of the Artist*. There is not so much difference between the northern Presbyterian and the southern Jansenist."

One detail differs, nevertheless, between north and

south. The power of the Roman Catholic church over politicians in the south is substantial; that of the Orange Order over politicians in the north is total. Gageby brings it out again in a description of the one prime minister of Northern Ireland who tried to bring the two communities together. Even while he was making the effort, he had to identify unambiguously as an Orangeman. Here is how Gageby records Captain Terence O'Neill's participation in a July 12 procession in his constituency.

Half the parade has gone past us when on the other side of the road, not far ahead of the banner which depicts Moses viewing the Promised Land, among the Ahoghill Loyal Orange Lodge 414, there is a familiar face. A smile, bows here and there, nods of the head. Clasping a small plastic mackintosh in his left hand, a gavel tied with ribbons in his right, wearing one of his good suits but hardly his best, bowler-hatted of course, his neck hung with the Orange collarette—a smaller version of the sash—comes Captain Terence Marne O'Neill at the same pad and shuffle as his fellow-brethren. He walks and smiles; his greeting is folksy, with that jerk of the neck which to a northern man is sufficient to show recognition without introducing any note of *plámás* or flattery, as much as to say that he is just one of the boys who sit on the bridge of a summer evening, spitting into the river Main. He does not look like one of the boys, but he acts on this occasion like one of them and, in common with the rest, as he passes the Orange Lodge, raises his bowler.

How the Orange Order acquired that influence and power would require relating a long history, part of the history which Ireland can neither live with nor without. It is also part of the two mythical versions of history and of life which sustain the division of Northern Ireland into a loyal majority and a disloyal minority. Before coming to the history, it is necessary to explore further the content of these conflicting myths.

2

Myths to Live — and Die — By

Northern Ireland has too many Roman Catholics and twice as many Protestants, but very few Christians.

—Anonymous

People like Alfie Hannaway and Jim McDonald, the ordinary men in the street in Northern Ireland, identify friend and foe by religious affiliation. But without realizing it, they give the words a sociological, not a theological, content. There was a theological justification—though, I suspect, more rationale than justification—when English kings and parliaments ordered all Catholics to be regarded as rebels, since the pope had told them they owed no allegiance to a schismatic ruler. But all that was several hundred years ago. Neither side today seeks to convert the other, nor fears religious absorption by the other. Indeed, there is less change in religious allegiance here than almost anywhere else in the world, with the possible exception of solidly Moslem countries. Nor is there any way to stay neutral. To live in Northern Ireland involves joining one community or the other. "Even an atheist," says Richard Rose, "must be a Protestant or a Catholic atheist in order to have a status in the society." [1]

What then does it mean to be a Catholic or a Protestant? It means, first of all, to divide the world into "us" and "them." A Catholic refers to them as "Prods"; a Protestant as "papishes," "Taigs," or "Fenians." [2] But there is never any reference whatever to either us or them unless the speaker is certain that all the people he is addressing are "us." A person introducing one of them to a group of us is expected to send up a danger signal, since otherwise some of the party might assume the newcomer was one of us and speak indiscreetly. A mention of the school he attended or the street on which he lives normally suffices.

Being a Catholic or a Protestant means to belong to a community, a community always at war with the other, openly or potentially. It means to have a different set of loyalties, a different attitude to the state and its laws, but much more deeply, a different set of assumptions and values. Each has its own starting point, a conflicting set of claims to the same elements. Each lives by a myth which makes his position reasonable for him, that of the other absurd and obscene. And each has his separate schools and other social institutions to perpetuate the respective myths and protect individual and community from exposure to and contamination by the other's myths.

Myths are expressed in words, and often a single word has a special meaning for one or both. Hannaway and McDonald would, for example, both call themselves Irishmen.[3] For Hannaway that conjures up an identification with all those living in Ireland and the millions of Irish birth or descent in the United States and elsewhere who stand for a nation free and undivided, holding as its birthright the entire island of Ireland. It is a nation with a proud and glorious past. It developed a high civilization when the rest of western Europe—including England—was sunk in ignorance and paganism after the barbarian invasions had destroyed the Roman Empire and all but wiped out Christianity. Irish monks then brought both the faith and learning back to

Europe, monks who had saved Latin and Greek for posterity
in their tiny cells on remote islands off Ireland's west coast.
Nobody could have gone to Catholic schools without remembering some of their names: Saint Columba from Derry who
evangelized Scotland from his foundation at Iona; Saint Co-
lumbanus who had gone all the way to Bobbio in Italy, right
to the pope's doorstep; St. Gall in Switzerland; and the
curiously named Alcuin, leading luminary of the court of
Charlemagne.[4]

There might be some vagueness about when these
events occurred, but two dates are fixed in every mind to
mark the beginning and the end of the glory that was Ireland
while she was mistress of her own fate: the coming of Saint
Patrick in 432, and the Anglo-Norman invasion in 1179. In
between came the monasteries dotting the countryside and
the great centers of learning like Clonmacnois to which the
nobles of England and France sent their sons to be turned
into scholars and gentlemen. And somewhere toward the end
of the period came marauding Norse pirates who sacked the
monasteries and scattered the students, draining the wealth of
the country and leaving it too weak to defend itself when the
Anglo-Normans decided to add it to their other conquests.

The Anglo-Norman invasion is the basis for an important
element of the Hannaway myth. He lives chronologically in
the twentieth century, and as he looks all the way back to the
twelfth, one stubborn fact faces him. The Irish never accepted defeat, never gave in, but were always defeated. They
had their moments of glory. They won battles. They even
won campaigns. But they lost every war. To live with that
fact is not easy. It calls for some kind of sublimation. And the
myth incorporates the needed sublimation. It offers, in a semi-
formulated way, the view of conflict between cultures which
the English historian of civilizations, Arnold Toynbee, has
developed in his elegant style. When there is a clash of two
cultures or civilizations, usually one is both militarily and
spiritually superior, and it quickly conquers the other and

imposes its way of life and attitudes. But on rare occasions, while one is materially and militarily more powerful, the other excels at the level of the spirit, and you can have a long stalemate, as you have had in Ireland for almost eight centuries. But ultimately—and here is the faith that keeps the weak from giving up—the spirit must triumph over matter. The defeated Irishman absorbs and incorporates his English conqueror, who immediately turns around and becomes his comrade and leader in another round of unending struggle.

This concept of absorption is an important element of the myth. It was formulated within a few years of the arrival of the Anglo-Normans by a Welshman known to history as Giraldus Cambrensis (Gerald from Wales) who made the earliest surviving news report on the progress of the conquest after a quick survey of the occupied areas. To his horror, the newcomers from England were already adjusted to Irish ways of living, dressing, and eating, even speaking the Irish language and marrying Irish wives. An inspired headline writer, Gerald coined a phrase which every child raised in every Catholic school in Ireland has had drilled into him, generation after generation. They were *more Irish than the Irish themselves*.[5]

There are positive and negative aspects to this element of the myth. Positively, it opens up the concept of recognizing as Irish anyone who is willing to identify with this particular vision. Hannaway has no problem about accepting as Irish those leaders who were Protestants: Wolfe Tone in 1798, Robert Emmet in 1803, poet Thomas Davis, and social reformer John Mitchel, the mystic Unitarian from Ulster, in the middle of the nineteenth century, Charles Stewart Parnell, and more recently folklorist Douglas Hyde, poet William Butler Yeats, Gaelic enthusiast Ernest Blythe, and politician Erskine Childers, elected President of the Republic of Ireland in 1973. Hyde, a clergyman's son, could attend Protestant worship as Ireland's first president, just as Robert Briscoe, mayor of Dublin a few years ago, could go to the synagogue. The only conversion required of them was an emotional identification with an Irish people understood in the terms just described. For Hannaway, in consequence, the identification is not exactly coterminous with religious affiliation. It includes all Roman Catholics (the exceptions are minimal and insignificant) and those Protestants assimilated to the way of thinking of the Catholics who constitute the determining element. And so in today's Northern Ireland, where the last several years of violence have intensified polarization along religious lines, the political party which supports the aims of the nonviolent civil rights movement, the Social Democratic Labor Party (SDLP), includes a Protestant among its top policy makers. He is Ivan Lee Cooper, chosen by Derry's Catholics in 1968 as chairman of the Citizens Action Committee, and elected by them the following year as one of the six members of Stormont representing Catholic-dominated constituencies which subsequently joined forces as SDLP.

The negative aspect is that, in spite of the acceptance of pluralism in religion, the Hannaway myth imposes as a measure of an individual's Irishness the ability to identify totally with one type of "Catholic culture." This starts with a set of moral values fixed in the rigidities of the Counter-Reformation Church and embracing the reactionary stand of the papacy against the Enlightenment, the French Revolution, and the social transformation of Europe in the nineteenth century. It stresses the rights of property and favors a rigidly hierarchical system in which the Church—as a "perfect society"—sets the rules for the state and the state imposes them on the citizen. Its esthetic values start with those of the Irish peasant, the element in society most protected from "foreign influences." His dances, his folk music, his poetry all tend to be taken as models. This aspect of Irishness has always been a problem for Protestants, almost all of them—for reasons to be explored later—coming from a background of comparative wealth and esthetic development. Yeats found it a real complication, referring to the process by which he consciously identified himself with the Irish literary revival and the development of national consciousness at the turn of the century as his "baptism of the gutter." [6]

For McDonald, most of this past in which Hannaway glories simply does not exist. His history begins with the Plantation of Ulster in the first decade of the seventeenth century. Before that, and from time immemorial, Ireland had been sunk in the superstitions of popery, the perverted form of Christianity described in the Book of Revelations, its leader the incarnation of the "scarlet woman of Babylon" on his throne in the Vatican. Then, as now, the papists were trained in every form of deceit and treachery, committed to the overthrow of their lawful sovereign, the king of both England and Ireland, for which purpose they constantly conspired with the king's enemies, domestic and foreign.

McDonald is in his own mind as Irish as any other inhabitant of the island. The fact that his ancestors came from the other side of the Irish Sea at an identifiable moment in the past does not alter that fact. Unlike those of his community who subsequently moved to America, he seldom feels the need to call himself Scots-Irish.[7] His people came here with a double mission, to implant the true Reformed religion and to hold this territory for the king. This is their home, the only home they have or want. Being Irish has for him no connotation of disloyalty to the Crown. He is simultaneously Irish and British, in the same way as most Welsh and Scots can be British while maintaining their regional identity. Rebellion and treason are for him characteristics not of the Irishman, but of the "Fenian," his favorite term for all who identify with the Ireland of Hannaway's myth.[8] But while he is pro-British, he tends to dislike the English with a far greater intensity than do those other Irish who are anti-British. He is conscious that the English regard him as a "colonial," and therefore a step down in their class structure. He is further conscious of his dependence on London, a dependence today spelt out with great clarity in the heavy subsidization of the economy of Northern Ireland.

Religion is more central to the conflict for McDonald

than it is for Hannaway.[9] His leaders, people like Ian Paisley
and Martin Smyth, both Presbyterian ministers, are deeply
steeped in the polemical anti-Catholic literature of a century
ago. They keep reminding him that popes insisted openly for
centuries that a Catholic owes no allegiance to a heretical
prince, and that what one pope teaches cannot be reversed
by a successor. They paint a picture of the million Protestants
in Northern Ireland as the object of a continuing international conspiracy, a beleaguered minority whose salvation
depends on eternal vigilance and unceasing resistance to any
and every attempt of the enemy within to improve his condition or increase his power. By his logic, he cannot accept
Catholic supporters in the same way in which Protestants can
join the other side. In order to join him, the Catholic must
openly repudiate his religion, after which he will be brought
to tour the Orange lodges and regale their members with his
exposés of clerical villainy. Similarly, the Protestant who frat-
ernizes with Catholics is automatically suspect. Marriage of a
Protestant and a Catholic forces the two into the Catholic
community, a process rendered even more inevitable by the
insistence of the Catholic religious authorities on a commitment from the Protestant partner to raise all children of the
marriage as Catholics. Understandably, this rule is further
proof for the average Protestant of the lengths to which Rome
will go to destroy all he stands for.

What Paisley and Smyth tell their followers merely con-
firms for them the history they learned at school. When their
ancestors had occupied the best lands of Ulster, in accordance with the king's directives, they had allowed the former
owners to remain in the hills and marshes, a kindness for
which they were ill-requited. In 1641, just a generation after
the original settlement, the dispossessed Irish rose in Ulster,
claiming that they were supporting King Charles I against his
rebellious Parliament. They drove many of the colonists from
their homes and murdered not a few of them. It took eight
years and the personal intervention of Cromwell to restore
the balance and introduce more settlers to replace those

slaughtered. And once again before the end of that century, the threat was renewed when the ever-rebellious natives supported King James II after Parliament had deposed him and given the crown to William of Orange. A repetition of the earlier slaughter was only averted by the heroic stand of the Apprentice Boys of Londonderry. They withstood hunger and the superior arms of their opponents in a three-month siege, giving William time to marshal his forces, raise the siege, and push forward to the Boyne where a great victory on July 12 confirmed for all time the "Protestant liberties" of loyal Ulstermen.[10]

After these two major challenges, the settlers determined there would be no third round. The first part of the eighteenth century in Ireland was devoted to stripping the Catholics—disaffected by definition—of property, power, and education. The colonists saw the operation as both necessary and defensive in its nature, as later colonists would see similar despoliation and pacification of natives in South Africa, Rhodesia, and Kenya.

Such was the success of these measures that by the second half of the eighteenth century, the Protestants in Ireland were able to indulge in a double political and social venture. They were so sure of their control at home that they sought to ease the controls exercised over them by England, a process encouraged by the parallel movements toward autonomy in the American colonies. Simultaneously, the class differences between members of the upper-class Established Church of Ireland (Anglican) and the lower-middle-class Presbyterians, previously muted in the face of the overriding threat of "the common enemy," rose to the surface. The conflict within the Protestant community has never been fully assimilated into the mythical histories of either side in Northern Ireland. It is, nevertheless, of basic importance to an understanding of continuing tensions and possible lines of community evolution.[11]

The laws by which the Catholics were dispossessed applied not only to them but to all dissenters or recusants, that is to say, to all who refused to subscribe to the beliefs of the

Established Church. London's policy in the settlement of loyal subjects of the Crown on escheated Irish lands in the sixteenth and seventeenth century was to limit grants in freehold to Englishmen who could be counted upon to be faithful to the Established Church. But each freeholder was obligated to introduce a number of tenants according to the size of his grant, and few farmers were willing to migrate from England to work a family-sized farm on which he would have to pay rent. Scotland, however, where land was of poorer quality than in England, could provide as many applicants as might be needed, and even though they were Presbyterians, it was decided they should be accepted. The result was a class division between Presbyterians and members of the Established Church in Ulster. As the Catholic threat receded, the differences between these two groups grew, causing many Presbyterians to move from Ulster to America, where they played a significant part in the War of Independence, siding with the colonies against England. Those who remained followed the fortunes of the emigrants, projecting for themselves an emancipation from religious discrimination such as the Constitution of the United States guaranteed. The French Revolution further encouraged this mood, leading to the formation of such organizations as the United Irishmen, into which Presbyterian leaders welcomed Catholic supporters, and culminating in a series of uprisings in 1798, one mainly Catholic in the southeast and another mainly Presbyterian in the north.

This Catholic-Presbyterian alliance was always ambiguous. All the members of each faith had in common was the desire to end the hegemony of the Established Church and cut for themselves a part of the action. The Catholics shared none of the Presbyterian dreams of inalienable human rights, as Americans had; still less of French liberty, equality, and fraternity. As yet, most Irish in America were Ulster Presbyterians. The emotional identification of Irish Catholics with "the land of the free" would not start for another 50 years, and they shared the pope's horror of the French Revolution with its rejection of the divine and the distortion of human values. The Presbyterians, for their part, did not share, indeed scarcely suspected, the Catholic dream of equal access to and influence in the new political institutions they would build together. They assumed a Protestant Parliament in which they would be the spokesmen and decision-makers for the Catholics as well as themselves.

Other factors were simultaneously at work, factors calculated to smash the fragile understanding between Presbyterians and Catholics. Many big landowners cleared prosperous Presbyterian tenants from their land, giving it to Catholics willing to live at a lower level and hand over a higher proportion of the produce to the landlord. Such Presbyterian tenants formed secret societies, which were to coalesce in the Orange Order, and developed terrorist methods to stop Catholics from undercutting them at auctions for tenancies. Then in the early nineteenth century, the Catholics began to organize politically and press for an end to discriminatory laws. The Presbyterians, as a group, decided, after prolonged internal polemics,[12] to form a united Protestant front in the Orange Order against the pretensions of Rome, a front that has held firmly ever since. Even today the main sectarian dynamism of the Orange Order is provided by working-class Presbyterians under such charismatic leaders as Paisley and Smyth, although the top levels of Orangeism are still heavy with upper-class politicians, business magnates, and landed gentry, identified with the Church of Ireland. Meanwhile, the older tradition of religious tolerance and political liberalism has survived in certain Presbyterian families, often families in which son follows father in the Church.

Although polarization tends to identify them as part of the Catholic community in the Hannaway sense, they have important distinguishing characteristics. Their cultural values stretch back to John Knox, and they would never dream of changing them for those of the Irish-peasant, priest-led way of life. Their republicanism derives from the secularist concept of the French Revolution, and leans today toward socialism. Several of these values were brought together in the civil rights movement of the 1960s,[13] especially among the student organizations of Queen's University, Belfast. The Official wing of the Irish Republican Army [14] has accepted the same values, but by traveling a very different road. So has Bernadette Devlin, and that may be the main reason why her appeal for an Irish nationalism free from religious overtones has failed to appeal to a wider public. Irish society is desperately conservative, the conservatism of the Catholic church confirming the universal immobility of the peasant. Nevertheless, these strands of liberalism, of socialism, of anarchism, and of identification with the oppressed are all around, and they will not be stamped out.

The maintenance of these two contradictory myths requires the physical as well as the emotional isolation of each community from the other. The physical isolation began with the seventeenth-century settlements. Bernadette Devlin describes in the opening paragraphs of her autobiography the layout of the town in which she was born. "The structure of Cookstown hasn't changed in the three hundred years of its existence. At one end is the Old Town, the original settlement, which is Protestant to this day. At the other, where the rebels once camped, now stands the Catholic area." [15] Since the Orangemen began their periodic pogroms in the middle of the nineteenth century, every pogrom has forced the members of each community to shrink more tightly into the protection of its own ghetto. The violence since 1969 has carried this process farther than ever before, making it progressively more difficult for one side to know the other. In the intervals of distension between outbreaks of violence, friendships are formed across barriers. But with the next round come social pressures no individual can resist.

It starts even before school. Infants prattle different nursery rhymes. As soon as they walk, they learn different games. At their respective street corners they learn different curses. In school they are segregated from each other. When the state was founded in 1920, it provided for subsidization

of all denominational schools. Gradually, however, the Protestants of various denominations gave up most of their
schools in favor of the public schools, which are in effect
nondenominational Protestant in much the same way as were
the public schools of the United States in the nineteenth century. The Catholic schools exist not only to give religious instruction but to perpetuate the myth. Bernadette Delvin says
of her high school that it was "a militantly Republican
school," with everything "Irish-oriented." She suggests that
not all Catholic schools were as extreme as hers, but many
are. And today, extracurricularly, the students learn while
still in grade school how to conduct hit-and-run attacks on
the British soldiers. While they pour stolen gasoline into stolen milk bottles to make Molotov cocktails they sing an old
sea chantey with new words:

> Burn, burn, burn the soldiers,
> Burn, burn, burn the soldiers,
> Burn, burn, burn the soldiers,
> Early in the morning.

To which equally youthful and bloodthirsty voices from
the other side of the Peace Line are not slow to respond:

> Now, down on the Falls
> where the papishes dwell,
> to hell with their chapels
> their priests as well.

Curiously enough, the Stormont regime seemed perfectly happy with a system that ensured the perpetuation of
communal divisions. It is significant that Catholic schools in
Northern Ireland got more from the public purse than those
in the neighboring Republic of Ireland with its 95 percent
Catholic population.[16]

Attitudes toward the Irish language form another element in the conflict. English is the normal language of com-

munication and of instruction in both communities. After
seven centuries of resisting the extreme, and often hysterical,
efforts of the English to stop the use of their language, the
Irish finally yielded in the late nineteenth century to the
pressure, thanks in large part to the decision of the Catholic
church to accept English. But by then, it had become a badge
of resistance. The growth of the Sinn Fein (meaning *ourselves* [17]) separatist movement in the first two decades of
this century included as a basic tenet the commitment to
restore Irish as the everyday language of the Irish people, a
commitment that for some meant bilingualism, for many the
elimination of English as a vernacular, and the consequent
protection of the masses from exposure to the "irreligious
and pagan" influences which reached them in that language.
Since the creation of the Irish Free State in 1922 (which became the Republic of Ireland in 1949), all parties there have
been committed in principle to implementing this Sinn Fein
policy, giving a high priority in education to speaking and
writing Irish, and requiring a high level of proficiency for
entry to the civil service and for many other posts. Many citizens today have a limited ability to understand Irish and to
express themselves in it, but its restoration as a vernacular
has not occurred, and the will to make this change seems almost to have died along with many other dynamic elements
of the Sinn Fein ideal.[18] In Northern Ireland, on the contrary,
where English is the only official language, Irish retains its
role to identify the minority. As noted in the previous chapter, Hannaway speaks it fluently and spends his spare time
teaching it to others.

A vital part of the two myths is their contrasting interpretations of the creation and purpose of the state of Northern
Ireland. For Hannaway, the division of Ireland into two
states by the British in 1920 was a culminating demonstration
of Albion's perfidy. It had never been in doubt, according to
his version of history, that the island of Ireland was a political, social, and cultural reality distinct from that of the neighboring island. The only claim the English could assert to any

part of it was one based on force, brute and unjustified. The Irish in every generation had rejected that aggression and expressed their rejection in arms. By the twentieth century their sovereign will was clear beyond question. In election after election, held under English rules and supervised by English guns, four out of every five Irishmen had declared for independence. What more democratic will could exist?

Not at all, says the contrary myth. Without going back further in the chain of justifications, the decision of the Irish Parliament in 1800 to join the kingdoms of Ireland and Great Britain in the United Kingdom established once and for all the exclusive jurisdiction of the Westminster Parliament over Ireland. The Bill of Rights enacted by Parliament when it gave the crown to William of Orange guaranteed the protection of the Reformed religion and its adherents, making it the duty of Parliament to ensure that Protestants would never come under the power of the government of renegades and cutthroats which the pope was preparing to seize Ireland. What it should have done was to stamp out that conspiracy, as it had been forced to do so often in the past. But failing this will, it was obligated to save from the disaster as much of Ireland as it could reasonably expect to hold; and that was precisely what was done in drawing the border to encompass the greatest area which would still have a safe Protestant majority.

On the one side we have a minority which sees itself as cheated by force out of its birthright, isolated from the rest of the Irish people, and always drawn by the most natural instincts to correct that injustice. On the other, there is a community that constitutes a majority of the area it actually controls politically, but always unsure of that control because it depends to such a great extent on the support of Britain, always further insecure because its domestic "disloyal" minority has the backing not only of the 3 million inhabitants of the neighboring Republic but behind them of many millions of Irish birth and descent in the United States, Australia, and Britain. Behind these again are 500 million minions of the pope to be found in all parts of the world. A community that feels so threatened necessarily sees all change as frightening. The steady secularization of life in England is in their eyes a betrayal of the principles of the Act of Settlement which guaranteed the dominance of Protestantism, and thus a weakening of the English will to protect them. They similarly regret the end of an Empire whose builders and defenders had been their strongest friends. The election of John Kennedy as President of the United States brought a new threat. An Irish Catholic in the White House boded only evil for them through new pressures on a Britain ever more dependent on the United States. The ecumenical thrust of Pope John XXIII and the Second Vatican Council only further disoriented them. Their self-identification had long been in terms of denial of all the settled things Roman Catholicism had dogmatically proclaimed. The new Catholicism deprived them of their shadow. Even if their church attendance is higher than that of Protestants in Britain or the United States, for many it is more a rejection of Rome than affirmation of personal convictions. The only way to read Rome's change is as a new venture in hypocrisy, one accepted at face value around the world and consequently increasing Rome's power and their own isolation.

One malevolent aspect shared by both myths is a glorification of physical force, which is more total, however, on the Protestant side. The Catholics recall victories in battles long past, while downplaying the wars lost in spite of those battles. They glory in the Anglo-Irish War of 1919–1921 which culminated in the creation of the Free State. This they attribute to the valor in battle of the IRA, though history is far less categorical in distributing credits for the result. As to the contemporary IRA, their view is more equivocal. They share the goal of a united Ireland free of all British control, and most of them believe that the use of force is ethically and morally justifiable in the pursuit of that goal. But in the present circumstances they judge it to be self-defeating. They have been gravely disillusioned over 50 years by the high-sounding words of successive Dublin governments without any corresponding deeds on their behalf. Particularly since World War II, they have reconciled themselves to a long "captivity," and they want domestic peace to achieve the gains possible within their minority status. For that reason, they rejected the IRA tactics in the 1950s,[19] and few of them sympathize fully with the IRA today. Nevertheless, they are convinced that only the IRA has saved them from annihilation in pogroms of the past, as well as in the recent and continuing assaults on their ghettos by Orange extremists. London recognizes their dilemma, and—as will be seen—has in recent years made major attempts to persuade them that they no longer need IRA protection. But so far, without avail.

The Orange myth stresses the two threats of annihilation their forefathers overcame in the seventeenth century. The folk memory recalls the many Scots-Irish who played a leading part in expanding the American frontier in the Indian Wars, a role interpreted as essentially a defense of religion against superstitious savages, their own role at home. Today they identify with the whites in South Africa and Rhodesia, and even with the Portuguese attempts to cling to the remnants of empire in Africa.

The Orange Order began as a secret society committed to imposing its will by physical force. It was by far the most numerous and aggressive of the contending forces during the nineteenth century, suppressed for a time but emerging with new strength thanks to friends and members in government and the army. It was "the Orange card" (in the form of sectarian riots in Belfast) played by Randolph Churchill in 1885 that defeated Gladstone's Home Rule bill, or so at least the myth has it. Once again in 1912 the Orangemen appealed to physical force to prevent the political change which the great majority of Irishmen then wanted. Sir Edward Carson told the cheering crowds: "They may tell us, if they like, that this is treason. . . . We are prepared to take the consequences." Soon he had 100,000 trained and armed men under his command, pledged to use "all means which may be found necessary to defeat the present conspiracy to set up a Home Rule parliament in Ireland." [20] The Orange myth gives these men exclusive credit for staving off the threat at that time and for the creation of the separate state of Northern Ireland eight years later. What is certain is that Carson's initiative convinced Irish nationalists that their commitment for half a century to democratic and constitutional methods would never gain their objectives. The result was the formation of the Irish Volunteers, an organization which would in due course become the IRA and has plagued the Orange state ever since. The Orange mythmakers quickly recognized the importance of the IRA. As far back as 1918 they forged a document which purports to be the oath by which the IRA binds its members. As an insight into the mentality of the people who made it up and to those who constantly reprint it in widely distributed hate sheets, it merits extensive quotation.

I swear by Almighty God . . . by the Blessed Virgin Mary . . . by her tears and wailings . . . by the Blessed Rosary and Holy Beads . . . to fight until we die, wading in the fields of Red Gore of the Saxon Tyrants and Murderers of the Glorious Cause of Nationality, and if spared, to fight until there is not a single vestige and a space for a footpath left to tell that the Holy Soil of Ireland was trodden on by the Saxon Tyrants and the murderers, and moreover, when the English Protestant Robbers and Beasts in Ireland shall be driven into the sea like the swine that Jesus Christ caused to be drowned, we shall embark for, and take, England, root out every vestige of the accursed Blood of the Heretics, Adulterers and Murderers of Henry VIII and possess ourselves of the treasures of the Beasts that have so long kept our Beloved Isle of Saints . . . in bondage . . . and we shall not give up the conquest until we have our Holy Father complete ruler of the British Isles. . . . So help me God.[21]

Like the French colonists in yesterday's Algeria and their English counterparts in today's Rhodesia, the Orangeman is an "ultra." He is ready to break the law to support his definition of the regime, convinced that the continual use of both legal and extralegal force is essential to containing this enemy. While recent successes by the IRA have been few and marginal, it continues to be his justification for every denial of civil rights to the minority, all of whom he presumes to be disloyal. The majority believes that, because of the IRA, it must keep the minority down. The minority believes it cannot reject the IRA while the majority is committed to holding it down. Such is the dilemma on the horns of which Northern Ireland is uncomfortably impaled.

3

The Orange State

Partition petrified Northern Ireland as a historical fossil.
—PATRICK O'FARRELL [1]

I am an Orangeman first and a politician and a member of
this parliament afterwards. . . . All I boast is that we are a
Protestant parliament and a Protestant state.
—LORD CRAIGAVON, while Prime Minister in 1934 [2]

The Orangemen had never wanted their own separate
state. From the early nineteenth century their goal was to
maintain the union established in 1800, a system which ruled
Ireland from London through a local administration which
they themselves dominated and which ensured a "Protestant
ascendancy" over the disloyal natives. When, in the second
decade of the twentieth century, they saw that England was
no longer willing to hold the disaffected Irish, they moved to
ensure that the historic province of Ulster be retained under
direct British rule. In this northern part of Ireland, the population was in equal parts Protestant and Catholic, and they
figured that British diplomacy and force would keep them

dominant there while allowing the rest of the island to go its shameful way. But London was determined to achieve what it regarded as a definitive resolution of the Irish problem. The Orangemen would have to accept their separate state. That forced them to scale their demands down to an area in which they were confident they could hold a permanent majority, two-thirds of Ulster, inaccurately named Northern Ireland.

The new regime was installed in 1921 to the accompaniment of the worst sectarian riots that Belfast had experienced up to that time. The collapse of the British administration in the rest of Ireland under the combined impact of a massive campaign of noncooperation and the guerrilla warfare being conducted by the IRA created in the north a climate of tension and fear. The claim of the Sinn Fein Parliament to jurisdiction over the entire island was accompanied by IRA attacks on police and military installations in the north as well as in the rest of Ireland. The Orange leadership saw the need to demonstrate continuously the determination of its followers not to be absorbed as a minority into a self-governing Ireland. An inflammatory speech by Sir Edward Carson during the July 12 celebrations in Belfast in 1920 provoked riots in Derry and Belfast a few days later. Tension rose further the following month when IRA gunmen killed a police inspector just a few miles from Belfast. He had been sentenced to death in absentia by an IRA court as the person principally responsible for the assassination, by a posse of Black-and-Tans, of Cork's Lord Mayor, and the court had sent an execution party which tracked him from Cork to his new assignment in the north.

This invasion from the south produced a sense of fear and outrage, starting a wholesale expulsion of Catholics from jobs and homes. About 200 Catholics and 100 Protestants were killed in the course of these pogroms between 1920 and 1922, a proportion reflecting the greater strength of the Protestants in men and arms, as well as the fact that the police forces adopted a partisan stand, treating the Protestants

as loyal supporters of the government and the Catholics as
enemies pledged to its overthrow. Belfast, which was 75 percent Protestant and 25 percent Catholic, was the scene of
most of the violence, the victims usually being slain in cold
blood, not in the heat of battle. In a six-month period in 1922,
160 murders were recorded in Northern Ireland, 115 of them
in Belfast—72 Catholics and 43 Protestants.[3]

The Anglo-Irish Treaty of 1921, which gave dominion
status to the rest of Ireland, contained provisions that increased the misgivings of the Orangemen. A clause designed
to make the treaty more palatable to majority Irish opinion
stipulated that the entire island would come under the overriding jurisdiction of the Parliament in Dublin which the
treaty envisaged, unless the Parliament already functioning
in Northern Ireland voted its area of jurisdiction out within
six months. The Stormont Parliament quickly passed the
required resolution, thus ensuring the continuance of Northern Ireland in the form established by the 1920 Government
of Ireland Act.

A further threat, nevertheless, still hung over it. The
treaty had additionally stipulated that, if Stormont voted for a
separate Northern Ireland, a joint commission would be set
up by the Westminster, Stormont, and Dublin governments
to redraw the partition line "in accordance with the wishes of
the inhabitants, so far as may be compatible with economic
and geographic conditions." Since the city of Derry, the
counties of Tyrone and Fermanagh, and the southern parts of
Armagh and Down—all of them situated along the existing
border—had Catholic majorities, this clause constituted a
threat that the area of Northern Ireland might be shrunk to
half its size, left only with the city of Belfast and its immediate hinterland. It was not until 1925 that this threat was
lifted, in circumstances to be described later. For more than
three years it hung over the new state, raising the fears for
survival of the majority to the same extent that it raised the
hopes of escape for the minority. By the time this threat of
early death was lifted, the character which the regime would

retain for 50 years had been established. Only Protestants could be automatically regarded as loyal citizens. Every Catholic must be assumed to seek the destruction of the state and the absorption of its territory into the neighboring Free State. From that day to this each side insists that the other was responsible for launching Northern Ireland on a course which required the government to treat a third of the citizens as permanently disloyal. In view of the emotional atmosphere of those first years, it is difficult to see how any other outcome was possible. If there is blame, it must fall on the politicians in Britain who drew the border to ensure the exclusion of as much of Ireland as possible from an Irish state, the creation of which they no longer had the power to prevent. It was they who built in the intransigent minority. The rest followed of its own weight.

The classification of being disaffected was not the only disability with which Catholics had to contend in the new state of Northern Ireland. They were also as a group economically underprivileged, with the corresponding cultural and educational disadvantages. This condition, while variously interpreted in the respective myths of the two communities, was solidly rooted in history. Up until the Catholic emancipation in 1829, Protestants had a monopoly of all but menial jobs in the public service in the whole of Ireland and Great Britain. They had a similar monopoly of ownership and control of industry, banking, and commerce. This situation was little changed in what is now Northern Ireland, not only during the foundation of that state in 1920, but subsequently. In the rest of Ireland, where Catholics were in the majority, the pressures to open up a share of the jobs for Catholics grew rapidly as the nineteenth century progressed. Nevertheless, the higher civil service, as well as the upper levels of police and the judiciary, continued to be staffed predominantly by Protestants, many of them brought over from England, until the Free State was established in 1922, and the same imbalance continued in industry, banking, and commerce.[4] Subsequently, the proportion of Catholics in high government positions rose rapidly in the Free State. It also has risen, though less rapidly, in the private sphere. Even today, the proportion of Protestants in key posts in commerce and finance tends to be significantly higher than their proportion of the general population.

For its initial appointments in 1922, the government of the Free State named five Protestants to its nine-man High Court. It also chose a high proportion of Protestants for the Senate. The chief civil servants, in large part Protestant, were continued in office. Northern Ireland, on the contrary, did not name a single Catholic to the Senate or the judiciary, nor to any major administrative position.[5] The 1920 Act of the Westminster Parliament provided that elections in Northern Ireland should be under a system of proportional representation to ensure a fair representation for minorities. The same system was established by the Free State, and a clause in its constitution gave it further security, a protection continued in the constitution of the Republic of Ireland. Only once—in 1959—did a government in power in the Republic attempt to jettison this provision, and the electorate rejected the proposed constitutional amendment when it was submitted to plebiscite.[6]

One of the anomalies of elections in Northern Ireland follows from the ghettoization of the two communities. In many constituencies either the Unionist government or an opposition party has had a majority so overwhelming as to exclude a contest, and the candidate of that majority was returned unopposed, thereby effectively excluding a considerable proportion of the electorate from ever exercising the franchise. Only the lower house of Stormont was directly elected by the people, this house in turn electing the senators; and for the 20 years up to 1965, 23 of the 52 members of the lower house were returned unopposed. The Unionist party always held a large majority of the Stormont seats, the deputies who would support the government on the critical issue of survival of the regime fluctuating between 40 and 42 of the total of 52. It abolished proportional representation in

1929, though not because of any immediate threat from the antipartitionists. The problem created by the previous elections in 1925 was different. They had reduced the official Unionist party seats to 33 from the 40 secured in the first election in 1921, while making no change in the number of seats—12—held by antipartition candidates. The other seven had gone to Independent Unionists, Unionist Labor, and Independents.[7]

What the government feared was a growth of this trend to a point where it might possibly give some participation in the system to the antipartitionists as a balance of power, in the same way as the Irish Parliamentary party had earlier used its wedge in Westminster to promote its purposes, allying in turn with Conservatives and Liberals. The abolition of proportional representation brought the Unionist party back up to 37, a level from which it has fluctuated only minimally ever since. The main loss has been to the parliamentary system itself, since it left the voter with no options other than the extreme one of rejecting the basic assumptions on which the state as such rested.

Abolition of proportional representation, however, could not by itself achieve all the benefits sought by the regime. Control of the allocation of housing required a majority in every local government area, and this was difficult for Protestants to gain in areas where Catholics had substantial majorities. With its absolute control of the Stormont Parliament, however, the regime was able to work miracles by gerrymander. Here the classical case was Derry. Thanks to the policy of ghettoization, the Catholic population was concentrated mainly in one sector of the city. It was consequently possible to divide the city into three wards, one of which contained half the city's voters and elected eight council members, the others having about 25 percent each of the voters, one electing eight members and the other four. The first ward had a 90 percent Catholic majority, while the other two had each a Protestant majority of about 60 percent. The end result was that 20,000 Catholic voters elected 8 councillors, while

10,000 Protestant voters elected 12. Under the law only householders and their wives had votes. If all adults over 21 had a vote, the Catholic majority would be even bigger but still would not affect the outcome.[8]

The city council not only allocated public housing preferentially to Protestants but cut back progressively on the number of new houses in order to prevent growth of the Catholic community. Only 136 houses were built by the Derry city council since 1958, and not a single one after 1966.[9] In 1969, when the control of housing was transferred to another body, in circumstances to be explained later, over a thousand houses in the city were occupied by more than one family, and in several cases dwellings originally built to house one family were occupied by seven or eight families. The waiting list for housing contained the applications of more than 1500 families, nearly all of them Catholics. The average waiting time for a newly married Catholic couple to get a place of their own had grown to ten or more years.

The same pattern of gerrymander was established wherever there was a manageable Catholic majority. In Omagh, the 39 percent of the voters who were Protestant elected 12 town councillors, while the 61 percent who were Catholic elected 9. In Armagh, which was 54 percent Catholic, the Catholics elected 8 councillors also, to the 12 elected by the Protestant minority. In Dungannon, the Catholic majority had 7, and the Protestant minority 14. In County Fermanagh, the Catholic majority had 6 of 26 seats on the county council, 7 of 21 on the Enniskillen town council, and 30 of 84 on other town councils. Fermanagh was chosen in 1967 to test a pilot scheme for a restructuring of local government, the entire county being placed under a single authority. But the restructuring did nothing to lessen the gerrymander. Of the 53 members of the new body, 36 were Protestants. The English Duke of Westminster, who has a residence in Fermanagh, commented shortly afterwards that the Unionist party in the county is run by "a dictatorship . . . of less than half a dozen people." [10]

The other great instrument of Protestant supremacy was the control of law and order. The Royal Ulster Constabulary (RUC) was set up in 1922, and as a result of representations by the authorities of the Free State to the London government, the Stormont regime officially undertook to maintain a balance of one Catholic to every two Protestants on the 3000-man force. That provision was never observed. In the late 1960s, Catholics comprised less than 10 percent of the force. The 1920 Act reserved to the British Parliament and the London administration all armed forces; it delegated to the Stormont regime control only of the police. In fact, the RUC was equipped as a military force with armored cars and automatic weapons, and it has always functioned as such. A militia was created to support it, the Ulster Special Constabulary usually known as the B-Specials. It was from the outset almost 100 percent Protestant. "It is also from the ranks of the Loyal Orange Institution that our splendid Specials have come," wrote the Unionist Belfast Newsletter on July 12, 1922, when the force was already 50,000 strong.[11] The atmosphere and outlook of the B-Specials is described by one of their historians, Wallace Clark. He quotes an early commander in a charge to his recruits: "I want men, and the younger and wilder the better." [12] The B-Special was given a uniform and a rifle or automatic weapon on induction, and he took these home with him. His training consisted, in addition to some drill, of 48 hours of weapons practice in his first year. He got none of the grounding of a regular policeman in criminal law or even in riot control. "The most outrageous thing they have ever done in Ireland," was the editorial comment of the London *Daily Mail*. "These are the very people who have been looting Catholic shops and driving thousands of Catholic women and children from their homes." [13]

No police force in the world, not even that of South Africa, has a wider discretion than that enjoyed by the RUC and the B-Specials under the Special Powers Act introduced as a temporary measure in 1922, renewed annually until 1933, and then made permanent. It is a measure which embarrasses the British government. When it signed the European Convention for the Protection of Human Rights and Fundamental Freedoms, it had to insert a reservation for the area of Northern Ireland for which it accepts international responsibility because of the many clauses in the Special Powers Act which conflict with the Convention. The act gives powers of search, arrest, and imprisonment, without warrant, charge, or trial, to any police officer. The authorities may suspend at will any and all of a citizen's basic rights, from habeas corpus to freedom of the press. He can be interned indefinitely without appeal or a right to know the reasons for his detention. The police do not even have to reveal the fact that they hold him for 48 hours, and during that time he can be interrogated without the right to a lawyer. He has in fact no legal safeguards when facing interrogation, if he has been arrested "on suspicion of acting, having acted, or being about to act" contrary to the peace. Specifically, "a person examined under this regulation shall not be excused from answering any question on the ground that the answer thereto may criminate or tend to criminate himself."

The National Council for Civil Liberties, a British organization composed of leading members of all that country's political parties, set up a commission in 1935 to inquire into the operation of the Special Powers Act. "The Northern Ireland government," the commission reported,

have used Special Powers towards securing the domination of one particular political faction and at the same time towards curtailing the lawful activities of its opponents. The driving of legitimate movements underground into illegality, the intimidating or branding as law-breakers of their adherents, however innocent of crime, has tended to encourage violence and bigotry on the part of the government's supporters, as well as to beget in its opponents an intolerance of the "law and order" thus maintained. The government's policy is thus driving its opponents into the way of extremists. . . . The close relations maintained by the government's leading members with the Orange Order, coupled with the little use made of Special Powers against activities notoriously productive of disorder, provides some show of reason for the view that the government permits the perpetuation of, rather than seeks to quell, sectarian troubles. The widespread allegations of "placing" in government offices, the fact that important judicial and official positions are withheld from practising Catholics, the personal ties between the Executive and the Orange Order, and the frankly sectarian speeches made even by Ministers, are all disquieting features of the political life of the Six Counties.[14]

Sectarian speeches by cabinet ministers had been a feature of the regime from its inception, and the report of the Council for Civil Liberties did nothing to alter this or any of the other features it condemned. Sir James Craig, when he was Parliamentary Secretary to the British Admiralty, set the tone for such speeches in 1920. Craig was to become first Prime Minister of Northern Ireland the following year and to be raised to the British peerage as Lord Craigavon in 1927. Addressing shipyard workers in Belfast in October 1920, just after their threats and violence had forced 5000 Catholic fellow workers to quit their jobs, he said: "Do I approve of the action you boys have taken in the past? I say yes." [15] Two years later, while Prime Minister, he boasted that "it is also from the ranks of the Loyal Orange Institution that our splendid B-Specials have come." [16]

Unlike the Unionists, whose Orange Order embraced in its membership a third a Northern Ireland's Protestant men and through them maintained a monolithic control over Protestant opinion, the opposition groups never established anything approaching a common voice until August 1970 when a coalition was created of the major opposition groups committed to nonviolent policies under the name of the Social Democratic and Labor party. The original opposition party, when the state was founded, was called the Nationalist party, the descendant of the Irish Parliamentary party which from 1885 to 1918 elected the majority of Irish representatives in the British Parliament and sat in that Parliament on a policy of winning by constitutional means the repeal of the 1800 Act of Union and the restoration of one parliament for all of Ireland.

At the first general election held in Northern Ireland in 1921, the Nationalist party won 6 seats and Sinn Fein also won 6, the remaining 40 going to the Unionists. Both the Nationalists and Sinn Fein refused to recognize the legitimacy of the regime or to take their seats. At the second general election in 1925, nine Nationalists were elected but no one from Sinn Fein. Two Nationalists took their seats immediately and the others joined them at different times over the next two years. They refused, however, to become an official opposition until the conciliatory gestures of Terence O'Neill as Prime Minister caused them to change their minds in the mid-1960s. During the entire intervening period they had never formulated an alternative program for government, limiting themselves to the single issue of ending the partition of Ireland. They frequently walked out of Stormont in protest against a particular decision of the Unionist government, sometimes staying away for as long as a year.

Paralleling the function of the Orange Order in relation to the Unionist party is the Ancient Order of Hibernians, a carry-over from the Catholic defense organizations of the eighteenth century, in relation to the Nationalist party. The equivalency is, however, more nominal than real. The membership of the Hibernians is small, about 2.6 percent of the Catholic population, and the organization is primarily a social grouping of the middle class, with none of the working-class involvement which characterizes the Orange Order. The conservatism of the Nationalist party is illustrated by its refusal in June 1968, just when the civil rights movement was boiling up, to approve of a policy of civil disobedience. Party leader Eddie McAteer, in opposing the proposal, said he suspected that "there is no real desire for this much sought holy grail of good community relations" among Catholics in Northern Ireland.[17] Only nine months later he lost his seat in Parliament to a civil rights leader, John Hume.

Because of the impossibility of wresting control of the machinery of government from the Unionist party, there was never any practical inducement on the part of those opposed to it to join in a coalition or a single party based on minimum agreement. In consequence, tiny splinter parties have always existed. In 1965, ten parties named candidates, and candidates from six of them were elected, as well as one Independent. They included, in addition to the Nationalists, the Northern Ireland Labor party and Republican Labor. In spite of the high level of trade-union membership, Labor has never been able to win more than a few seats, the polarization for and against the political regime overriding the conflict of interests that exists between labor and capital which dominates politics in Britain. The Labor party, while deploring sectarian divisions and generally sympathetic to the claims of Catholics for equal treatment, represents principally the Protestant workers; and in times of open sectarian conflict, as in 1935 and again in the past few years, it is forced by the rank and file to identify with the Unionists. Republican Labor, on the other hand, is a minuscule group, supported mainly by those few Catholics who see the solution in a revolution which would bring into existence a socialist republic in all of Ireland.

Thanks to the Special Powers Act, the Orange Order, and the police, a peace of exhaustion had come to Northern Ireland by the end of 1923, although it was not until a year later that a four-and-a-half-year curfew in Belfast was lifted. The shipbuilding and engineering industries had been prosperous before and during the First World War, and the area of Northern Ireland was among the most economically developed parts of the United Kingdom when it began its career as a separate state. In 1921, however, the bitter political conflict contributed to the slump that then affected Britain. The Irish still had a market for their agricultural produce across the Channel, but the border cut off trade with the rest of Ireland. Derry in particular suffered the loss of its natural hinterland to the west.

Ulster industries had been designed to serve an empire and were not suited to a small territory. The decline in overseas markets in the late 1920s and the 1930s hit them severely. In 1923, 18 percent of workers entitled to unemployment benefits under compulsory insurance schemes were unemployed, a figure that rose to 25 within a few years, declined to 15 briefly, then rose again to an average of over 25 throughout the 1930s. These are all gross figures. The various devices used to give job preference to Protestants meant that the net unemployment level for the Catholic community was much higher. Derry suffered more acutely and more continuously than any other area. Its principal activity is shirtmaking, an activity that employs women almost exclusively, and it has become a tradition there for the women to go out to work while their husbands and grown sons are idle.

The years of relative peace after 1924 lowered the tension between Protestant and Catholic to such an extent that labor leaders decided to try to bring them together and enable the workers to speak with a single voice as the depression threatened to engulf them all in a common catastrophe. They cooperated in October 1932 in a massive demonstration in Belfast for an increase in unemployment benefits. Street battles with the police occurred in the Shankill and along the Falls Road. Police gunfire killed a Protestant on one street and a Catholic on another. The worker movement held together, however, and the government felt it wise to meet some of the demands.

It was obvious to the government that a continuing alliance of Catholic and Protestant workers would destroy the foundations on which the state had been built. Sir Basil Brooke set the tone for a campaign designed to reawaken sectarian bitterness at an Orange rally on July 12, 1933. Brooke, then Minister of Agriculture, was subsequently Prime Minister from 1943 to 1963 and raised to the British peerage as Viscount Brookeborough. Referring to Protestants who employed Roman Catholics, he said he could speak freely on the subject because he had not a Roman Catholic about his own place. "I appeal to Loyalists, wherever possible, to employ good Protestant lads and lassies." A little later, he spelled out his message even more explicitly.

Thinking out the whole question carefully . . . I recommended
those people who are Loyalists not to employ Roman Catholics, 99
percent of whom are disloyal. . . . I want you to remember one
point in regard to the employment of people who are disloyal.
There are often difficulties in the way, but usually there are plenty
of good men and women available, and the employers don't bother
to employ them. You are disenfranchising yourselves in that way.
You people who are employers have the ball at your feet. If you
don't act properly now, before we know where we are, we shall find
ourselves in the minority instead of the majority.[18]

The message was echoed in August 1933 by Sir Joseph
Davison, Grand Master of the Belfast Orange Lodge. Davison
was named to the Stormont Senate in 1935 by the Unionist
majority in the House and subsequently became deputy
leader of the Senate. "When will the Protestant employers of
Northern Ireland recognize their duty to their Protestant
brothers and sisters and employ them to the exclusion of
Roman Catholics?" he asked in 1933. "It is time Protestant
employers of Northern Ireland realize that whenever a
Roman Catholic is brought into their employment it means
one Protestant vote less. It is our duty to pass the word along
from this great demonstration, and I suggest the slogan
should be: 'Protestants, employ Protestants!' " [19]

The sectarian appeals of the Orange leaders were successful in distracting the Protestant workers from their challenge to a social and economic system that was exploiting
them. Sporadic outbreaks of violence directed against the
Catholic ghettos built up to such a level of tension that the
government decided in July 1935 to ban the traditional
Orange parades on July 12. At the last moment, however, it
yielded to Orange protests and pressures and allowed the
parades which inaugurated three weeks of burning, wrecking, and killing in the most violent pogroms since 1922. More
than 500 Catholic families were driven from their homes.
Twelve people died from gunshot wounds, which in the
opinion of the Belfast coroner who presided at the inquests,
resulted from the inflammatory and provocative speeches of

"those so-called leaders of public opinion who stirred up big-otry among their followers." [20]

The official efforts to ensure priority of employment for Protestants have been supremely successful during the entire 50 years of the history of Northern Ireland. An analysis of the situation in government in 1961, for example, revealed that Catholics numbered 13 of the 209 officers in the professional and technical grades, and 23 of 319 in the administrative grades of the civil service. The technical and professional grades consist of engineers, lawyers, doctors, accountants, and similar specialists. In the Ministry of Home Affairs, re-sponsible for the police and the maintenance of law and order, only 1 of 20 administrators was Catholic, and in the sensitive Ministry of Health and Social Service, only 1 of 78. The top administrative grade, comprising assistant secre-taries and higher civil service posts, had only 1 Catholic of 53. Appointments are made by two bodies, the Placing Au-thority and the Establishment Authority, the membership of which is secret.[21] Twenty-two public boards, whose members are named by the government to run such services as those providing electricity, housing, tourism, and hospi-tals, have 49 Catholics in a total membership of 332.

The imbalance in membership of these boards is re-flected in their decisions and appointments. The hospitals board, which administers Northern Ireland's 97 hospitals, has only 31 Roman Catholics among the 387 specialist doctors who work in the hospitals, although the number of Catholic doctors in general practice is a third of the total number of doctors in the state, reflecting the Catholic proportion of the total population. The chief medical officer and his deputy are Protestants, as are the chief medical and dental officers and public health inspectors of all counties and boroughs. In the Courts of Justice, there was in 1968 one Catholic of seven high court judges, one of four county court judges, and three of nine resident magistrates. None of the three members of the land tribunal, the three members of the Commission for National Insurance, the six clerks of Crown and Peace, the six undersheriffs or the eight Crown Solicitors, was a Catholic, and only 1 of 26 clerks of Petty Sessions.*

Discrimination in local government is at the same level. The town of Omagh, 61 percent Catholic, employs 2 Catholics in a staff of 100 in the county hall, 2 of 70 in the education offices, and 2 of 35 in the rural council. Of 22 senior staff of the Tyrone county council, 1 is a Catholic. Tyrone's population is 55 percent Catholic. Dungannon, where the civil rights movement began, is over 50 percent Catholic. In 1963 it had more than 300 families on the waiting list for houses; some of them had been waiting for over 12 years. Council houses had meanwhile been allotted to several Protestants in comfortable circumstances, including a pharmaceutical chemist and an engineer employed by the council itself. Young Protestants—but not young Catholics—were given houses immediately after marriage.

Fifteen town employees, from town clerk to bricklayer, are Protestants. County Fermanagh, 53 percent Catholic, has 10 Catholics among 166 employees of the county council, and 10 Catholics among 179 employees of the education committee.[22] Discrimination in private employment has been equally blatant. The Catholic bishop of Belfast protested in 1966 that an engineering firm in the city had only 3 or 4 Catholics in a work force estimated at three thousand.[23] In response to the bishop's protest, the management of the firm said that Catholics did "not feel at home in a Protestant atmosphere." The more common defense is that the big factories happen to be in areas which are predominantly Protestant, and that it is natural for a firm to draw its workers—whenever possible—from its own neighborhood. But this explanation does not fit the facts. Mackey's, a big engineering firm, has one of its two Belfast plants located deep

* David Donnison, Director of the Centre for Environmental Studies, London, gives an indication of the limited extent of subsequent reform in *New Society* (July 5, 1973). He cites a suppressed official report as showing that 95 percent of the 477 civil servants in the top grades were still Protestants in 1973.

in the wholly Catholic Falls district, yet employs very few Catholics. It refuses to give any breakdown, but informed estimates put the number of Catholics in Mackey's work force at 100 of 8000. As for the shipyards, Lord Brockway said in the British House of Lords in June 1972 that only 500 of 8000 workers were Catholics.[24] A year later employment in the shipyards was up to 10,000 but the number of Catholics down to an estimated 150. At the same time, it is obvious that the concentration of Catholics in narrowly defined ghettos facilitates job discrimination. And in fact the location of new industries—subsidized by the government—in the Belfast area has been such as to keep them well away from the major Catholic ghettos.

Even more easily documented is the policy of building up the economy of the eastern part of the state, in which Protestants are concentrated, at the expense of the western part which is mainly Catholic. The government in 1965 accepted the Wilson Plan for economic development. It proposed four centers, all within a 30-mile radius of Belfast, for quick industrial development, while offering almost nothing to the western half of the state. In the same year, it accepted the Lockwood Report which rejected Derry as the site for a new university, in spite of the fact that Derry had a hundred-year-old two-year college which was available as a nucleus. Instead, the new university was located at Coleraine and the existing college in Derry was allowed to wither away for lack of official support. Geoffrey Copcutt, an English town planner brought over by the Northern Ireland government to design a new town it had determined to build close to Belfast, quit after one year, "disenchanted with the Stormont scene," as he said. Having studied the situation, he had urged the government to drop its plans for a new city and instead to give the state a reasonable balance by developing Derry. "It is the obvious choice," he said, "to expand as the center for higher education outside Belfast. It could prove the most promising way of unifying the present populations and integrating future immigrant communities." [25] But unification of the present population was the last thing the regime desired.

World War II brought to Northern Ireland the only period of significant prosperity it has enjoyed. As early as 1937 it had a foretaste of what would follow when a factory for the manufacture of military aircraft was opened with the encouragement of the British Ministry of Aviation. After the outbreak of hostilities, employment rose rapidly in the textile industry, shipbuilding, engineering, aircraft manufacture, and construction of airfields and other facilities required for the training of the rapidly expanding British armed services. A further increase in prosperity was given when the United States began to use the naval base at Derry and several airfields spread throughout Northern Ireland. Simultaneously, incentives to expand and modernize agriculture were introduced, as more distant sources of food for Britain were cut off by the German submarine blockade. Unemployment dropped for the first and only time to about 5 percent, and work permits were granted freely to migrants from the neighboring Republic of Ireland, though on the clear understanding that they would have to leave at the end of the war, a condition that was rigorously enforced when the time came. Hundreds of Catholics were interned without trial on suspicion of being disloyal, but on the whole relations between the two communities were excellent during this period. The economic situation eliminated the need for job discrimination, and the issue of discrimination in housing had become academic because construction of buildings for civilian use had been suspended in favor of the war effort.

With war's end the situation again deteriorated, though never to anything like the conditions of the 1930s. Two officially sponsored studies in the postwar period brought out very clearly the distorted and dependent nature of the economy of Northern Ireland. There had been major industrial development in the nineteenth century, at a time when the rest of Ireland was devoted almost exclusively to agriculture. The main industries then created were shipbuilding and linen, both of them heavily dependent on world markets for raw materials and for sales, and consequently subject to factors not controllable within the state. The sale of linen has been steadily declining since 1914, and shipbuilding—always subject to cyclical ups and downs—has in recent years experienced stiff competition from Japan and other countries. No new important industry was started in Northern Ireland from 1900 until an aircraft factory was started in 1937. And its location was determined, not by economic attractions, but by the need to put it as far away as possible from enemy attack during the war then anticipated and actually to start that same year. And once more, this was an industry even more dependent on outside sources of supply and demand for the end product than the earlier ones.

After 1945 a serious effort was made to diversify industry by offering cash grants, tax concessions, and other inducements for businessmen to start new businesses or expand existing industries. Total manufacturing investment since that time is estimated at $2 billion, about a quarter of it coming from 34 United States companies which provide some 20,000 jobs. Among the results has been a big growth in industrial production, the index standing at 176 in 1973 as compared with a base of 100 ten years earlier. Gross domestic product followed the same pattern. In 1963 it amounted to $1230 million, and by 1973 it was estimated to have increased by 75 percent over that figure.

Built-in problems nevertheless remained. The Isles and Cuthbert Report stresses the area's isolation from its "mainland," that is, the British market to which its economy is geared. Transport must be added to manufacturing costs, and transport is kept "unreasonably high" by well-organized monopolies. The fact that about half the total output of goods and services is exported makes this limitation very serious indeed, and it also makes the economy enormously dependent on variations in demand not subject to its control. In addition, because of the lack of minerals and other basic raw materials, the economy has a high propensity to import. Since the state was founded in 1920, it has had an unfavorable trade balance every year except during the war years of 1939 to 1945 when its agricultural products received preferential treatment in the British market.

Political pressure to provide employment in areas in which Protestants were concentrated combined with the economic benefit of being close to the state's major port. These considerations ensured the location of most new industries in the Belfast area. Some 9 percent of all manufacturing companies have suffered physical damage during the violence of the past several years. The president of the Confederation of British Industry has noted "a distinct break in the flow of outside investment" to Northern Ireland. "Many companies have lost business," said an October 1972 circular from his office, "because some of their customers were no longer prepared to rely on them as sole suppliers. Ancillary industries have been particularly hard hit, especially advertising and tourism. There has been a strong decline in the number of buyers visiting the Province, and some companies there have had difficulty in getting service engineers for the maintenance of plant and equipment." Among the problems businessmen had to contend with were several thousand explosions which caused property damage for which $30 million had been paid in reparations by mid-1972, with claims for a further $75 million outstanding at that time. Armed robberies, mostly of "political" inspiration, netted $750,000 in 1971 alone.

These various factors contributed to the failure of a 5-year plan announced by the government in 1965 which was to add 75,000 jobs by 1970 to the 180,000 then available in industry. Official figures recorded the creation of six thousand to seven thousand jobs each year, but job attrition by rationalization and closing of factories was at a higher rate. By June of 1973, industrial employment stood at 176,000, lower than it had been in 1965. Employment in agriculture declined because of mechanization, a trend calculated to speed up under the arrangements of the European Economic Community. The combined effect was an acceleration of the brain drain through emigration, and a high level of unemployment. The proportion of unemployed is normally some points higher than in Britain and fluctuates with the demand for Northern Ireland labor there. It rose above 9 percent of the work force in 1972, then dropped to 6 percent in mid-1973 as British exports rose with the decline of the pound in relation to most other European currencies.

Canada and Australia are the two preferred destinations of permanent emigrants. Canada in 1967 introduced more stringent conditions for immigration, with the result that the applications from Great Britain dropped 30 to 40 percent. But those from Northern Ireland have remained as high as ever, and so many of them are highly qualified, many are doctors, nurses, engineers, and professional people, that the number accepted rose from 1491 in 1969 to 2078 in 1972. "People now applying are highly qualified," a Canadian immigration official in Belfast said in late 1972. "These are the kind of people Northern Ireland cannot afford to lose. Not only the quality but the number of applicants continues to increase." [26] Australia does not have figures on the number of immigrants from Northern Ireland separate from those for Britain. Its Belfast office, however, reported 8452 applicants for assisted passages in 1971, treble the number in 1967, with 1700 of them in the two months immediately following the introduction of internment without trial. These are family applications, the average family containing six or seven members. Catholic emigrants tend to favor Australia and New Zealand, while Protestants go to Canada.

The general level of unemployment had risen by 1972 above 9 percent, twice the figure for Britain, and unemployment among men was over 11 percent. The differential between east and west remained significant, with a 7 percent rate in Belfast and 14 percent in Derry. Among men in Derry, the unemployment rate was unofficially estimated as exceeding 30 percent. As unemployment grew, the traditional factors came again into play, causing its main incidence to be felt by the Catholic workers. A survey in the Catholic ghetto of Ballymurphy in Belfast revealed an unemployment rate of 47 percent for men aged 16 years and older.[27] But new factors also had been inserted into the equation, facing the Unionist regime with a challenge that had never before confronted it.

4

Campaign for Civil Rights

*The most dangerous war is that which has its origin in just
claims denied or in a clash of opposing rights—and not merely
opposing interests—when each side can see no reason in justice
why it should yield its claim to the other.*

—EAMON DE VALERA [1]

The radical social changes introduced in Great Britain
immediately after World War II by the Labor governments
which held office from 1945 to 1951 were far from pleasing to
the rulers of Northern Ireland. It was impossible to challenge
the principle of closing the gap between classes, providing
free education at all levels with intake at the upper levels
based on merit, and establishing health and welfare programs
that would ensure minimum living standards for all citizens.
Yet the administrators in Northern Ireland feared—and as
the event demonstrated, with reason—that such programs
within their area of jurisdiction would upset the delicate balance of community interests based on discrimination by religious affiliation.

Labor governments in England have never been friendly
to Stormont. From the early days of the Northern Ireland

state, Labor spokesmen criticized the Unionist monolith as dominated by big business and consequently unsympathetic to the workingman. In addition, the votes of Catholics of Irish birth or descent are vital to Labor candidates in London, Liverpool, Glasgow, and other areas in which the Irish are concentrated in Great Britain.[2] And politically even more decisive, the Northern Ireland Unionist party is organically united to the British Conservatives. A minimum of 10 of the 12 members elected to Westminster from Northern Ireland have always belonged to it. This handful of votes went automatically to the Conservatives under the strict "whip" of Westminster conventions, a constant threat to Labor in the tight race of the two parties for control of Great Britain.

In these circumstances, Labor, when in power in London, was understandably unsympathetic to the Stormont arguments against extending to Northern Ireland the new health, education, and welfare benefits. To eliminate all discussion, it agreed to subsidize the operation to whatever extent might prove necessary, thereby eliminating Stormont's final expressed reason. But the real reason, the unspoken one, remained valid. As Stormont had feared, the Catholics soon discovered that they could now survive on welfare when they were unable to get a job. The pressure on young people to leave the country when they finished school consequently diminished. Instead, they could go on to the university. There they met Protestants of their own age, from whom they had been totally isolated during their entire former existence, and Catholic and Protestant students alike were absorbed into the new youth culture which was sweeping the world. The beliefs and prejudices of their parents ceased to be their exclusive motivations. They were learning to judge for themselves, to choose their own values and their own alliances. Simultaneously, and at least in part as a result of the changing outlook of youth, Catholics in Northern Ireland began to question the basic assumption that their survival and prosperity were dependent on absorption of Northern Ireland into the Republic of Ireland. Concretely, they saw that the Republic did not and could not afford to provide the education, health, and welfare benefits they were now enjoying as British citizens of Northern Ireland. In more general and philosophic terms, they questioned the kind and extent of freedom enjoyed by the ordinary citizens of the Republic. More and more of them came to believe that the leaders of the south, clerical and lay, had no real desire to see the country reunified, even if they continued to give lip service to that ideal. They seemed congealed in a socioeconomic system very similar to that of Britain half a century earlier, a system in which a few enjoyed prosperity and status while the ordinary people had to be content with meager living standards at home. And, unlike Britain in that earlier period, Ireland was able to maintain those standards only by the continuing export of a substantial proportion of the nation's young men and women. The practical conclusion they came to was that Catholics should shelve their long-term dreams and concentrate on securing for themselves equal rights and opportunity as citizens of the United Kingdom.

The first significant expression of the new thinking was a controversy in the early 1960s over the admission of Catholics to the Unionist party. All indications then were that this party would retain for the foreseeable future the monopoly of power enjoyed since 1921. It was, accordingly, perfectly logical that a Catholic who sought to share power should start by joining it. The response of the Unionist leaders revealed some of the system's absurdities. Sir George Clark, who was shortly to become chairman of the party's central control machinery, was first to comment:

I would draw your attention to the words "civil and religious liberty." The liberty we know is the liberty of the Protestant religion. . . . It is difficult to see how a Roman Catholic, with the vast difference in our religious outlook, could be either acceptable within the Unionist party as a member, or bring himself to support its ideals. Furthermore to this, an Orangeman is pledged to resist by all lawful means the ascendancy of the church of Rome.[3]

Clark was here unusually open in his total identification of the Unionist party with the Orange Order.

The party constitution does not bar Catholics by name, but the affiliation of Orange lodges to the party at the level both of the constituencies and of the central controlling groups creates obvious problems for Catholics seeking to join. The Orange Order nominates 122 representatives on the 718-member Ulster Unionist Council, and most of the other council members are Orangemen. Until the "thaw" in the late 1960s during Terence O'Neill's premiership, when four non-Orangemen were elected, all Unionist members of Parliament (except the few women, who are ineligible) belonged to the Orange Order. But an Orange member of Parliament who then resigned from the Order was repudiated by his constituency and resigned his seat. The party has never nominated or elected a Catholic to Stormont.

Clark's call to Orangemen to keep Catholics out of the Unionist party was quickly endorsed by the Prime Minister, Lord Brookeborough. Those who propose the admission of Catholics to the Unionist party, he said, "are charging against windmills and beating their heads against a wall on an issue that did not arise and probably will not arise." [4] His statement is the more striking when matched with his earlier assertion that "there is only room for one political party in Ulster." [5]

The civil rights movement in Northern Ireland began very modestly in 1963 in Dungannon, County Tyrone, a town which—as already noted—had at that time more than 300 families on the waiting list for houses, some for 12 years or longer.[6] The Protestant-dominated town council decided to demolish 50 prefabricated bungalows less than 20 years old, after moving the occupants to better quarters. The news angered Patricia McCluskey, a doctor's wife, and she organized a Homeless Citizens League to agitate for the transfer to these bungalows of Catholic families living in far more dilapidated and overcrowded accommodations. Almost immediately, 30 Catholic families who had been crowded into single rooms for which they paid up to half their income in rent moved in as squatters. When the league made inquiries at Stormont, it discovered that the council's claim to have filed plans with the housing ministry to develop the area in which the bungalows were standing was false. Instead, the council's purpose was to deny this housing to needy Catholic families. Other facts established by the league were that the wife of the council chairman owned slum property that should have been but was *not condemned,* and that a Unionist supporter owned a tenement housing 8 families consisting of 29 persons who shared one kitchen, one bathroom, and two toilets. Faced with so much publicity, the council finally yielded and granted the appropriate tenancies.[7]

Encouraged by this success, Mrs. McCluskey and her husband founded the Campaign for Social Justice in Northern Ireland in January 1964. Its aim was to publicize instances of discrimination, using the duplicating machine and the mails as its principal weapons. By bringing pressure on the authorities to redress specific grievances, it was hoped to uncover gradually the sectarian nature of Northern Ireland society. The associates of the McCluskeys were for the most part professional people without political ambitions and free from economic pressures. The Campaign affiliated with the British-based National Conference of Civil Liberties in 1965, and with the help of NCCL it formed the Northern Ireland Civil Rights Association (NICRA). By that time it had established contacts with important people in the Labor party in Britain, which were particularly useful because Labor had again returned to power, led by Harold Wilson, in 1964.

During these same years a change was taking place within the Unionist party which seemed to augur well for the civil rights movement. In 1963, Terence O'Neill succeeded Lord Brookeborough as Prime Minister. O'Neill was an Ulster aristocrat, claiming descent from the O'Neills who had ruled Ulster in a distant Gaelic past as well as from early upper-class settlers from England. Education in England and subsequent service in the British army had given him a back-

ground very different from the typical Unionist politician
whose horizons were bound by his experiences of sectarian
strife and partisan bitterness in Ulster. O'Neill soon made it
clear that he envisaged major change. The future of Northern
Ireland, he said, required cordial relations with the Republic
of Ireland, as well as internal readjustments to give Catholics
the benefits of their citizenship and lead them gradually to
accept the regime as their lawful government. To his fellow
Protestants he said that the only way to get Catholics to limit
their families was to improve their economic situation. "If a
Roman Catholic is jobless and lives in the most ghastly
hovel, he will rear eighteen children on national assistance
[welfare]." In 1965 he welcomed Sean Lemass, Prime Minister of the Republic of Ireland, at Stormont. This action,
taken without consulting his cabinet, was as startling to the
Irish as was President Nixon's 1972 visit to Communist
China for Americans.

The reaction to these and other gestures that O'Neill
made, however, was less reassuring for the civil rights leaders. The Rev. Ian Paisley, a rabble-rousing Presbyterian minister, was quickly catapulted to center stage. Paisley is head
of the Free Presbyterian church which he himself founded as
a protest against what he claimed was a "Romeward" trend of
the Presbyterian church in Northern Ireland. The son of a
Baptist minister from Ballymena, County Antrim, his background is hazy.[8] There is no record of his ordination, and it is
widely believed that he put his hands on his head and ordained himself. Before he became nationally known in the
mid-1960s for his opposition to the various efforts to reduce
denominational tension and secure equal rights for all, he already had a local reputation for Catholic-baiting. He made
some headlines in Belfast in 1956 when he claimed to have
saved a 15-year-old Catholic girl from being incarcerated in a
nunnery against her will. He was again in the headlines in
1959 when he threw a Bible at the head of a visiting ecumenical Methodist at a horse fair in his hometown of Ballymena.
His sermons are impressive because of his vibrant voice and

mountainous physique, as well as his complete command of scriptural reference. Roman Catholicism is for him "the scarlet whore of Rome," and when Archbishop Ramsey of Canterbury went to visit the pope in 1966, Paisley followed him to Rome to protest publicly that Ramsey had betrayed the Reformation. He later described a group which got in his way as "blaspheming, cursing, spitting, Roman scum."

Paisley set the tone for the Orange response to the efforts of O'Neill and others to build a bridge between the Protestant and Catholic communities. O'Neill betrayed Unionism, he said, when he entertained "a Fenian Papist murderer" at Stormont. The reference was to Sean Lemass, the Prime Minister of the Republic of Ireland, who had indeed fought in the Anglo-Irish War from 1919 to 1921, but whose subsequent career as a cabinet minister from 1932 onward had been characterized by moderation and a commitment to industrial development.

Paisley's concern went far beyond the O'Neill-Lemass meeting, however. The 1960s were a period of major progress in ecumenical understanding between Catholics and Protestants around the world. The election of Angelo Roncalli as Pope under the title of John XXIII in 1958 quickly produced a profound change of attitude within the Roman Catholic church, a change that was quickly recognized and welcomed by the World Council of Churches and other bodies representing the principal streams of the Reformation. In addition to challenging the Anglicans by protesting Ramsey's visit to Rome in 1966, Paisley turned on the Presbyterian church in Northern Ireland and accused it of a similar softness toward Roman Catholicism. During the annual meeting of the Presbyterian General Assembly, in Belfast in June 1966, he resorted to a tactic calculated to touch the deepest roots of sectarianism. He announced a parade of "loyalists" in Belfast, the route to "take in" Cromac Square, a completely Roman Catholic slum area.[9]

Parades in Belfast are a deep-rooted part of the culture, and so long as they stay within the living space of the community they represent, whether Protestant or Catholic, they seldom cause trouble. But Cromac Square is peculiarly sensitive, a small community just west of the Lagan river and isolated from the major Catholic ghettos. Ever since the last major pogroms in 1935, it had been off limits to any Orange procession. According to the folk understanding of Northern Ireland, the Paisley march through Cromac Square would be a symbolic reassertion of the Protestant ascendency, of the right of Protestants as victors in distant wars to remind the losers that they survive by privilege and not by right. In spite of Catholic protests, the O'Neill government decided to avoid a showdown with Paisley, whose popular backing was becoming daily more evident. A riot did in fact develop as the parade passed through Cromac Square, but nobody was killed. Two weeks later O'Neill assured Parliament there was "no evidence that the militant Protestant organizations are contemplating the use of violence." Within four days his assurance was shattered. An 18-year-old Catholic was shot dead leaving his work and his two companions were wounded. Within a short time, two others were killed in Belfast in incidents intended to intimidate Catholics.

Three men were charged with one of the murders, and one of them testified at the trial that the organization behind them was the Ulster Volunteer Force, a violent and extremist Protestant group. According to the London *Sunday Times*, the English newspaper which has given the most thorough and objective coverage of recent violence in Northern Ireland, the UVF functioned in "a nightmare world of casual violence, organized by trigger-happy hoodlums." The three suspects, all members of the Orange Order, were found guilty and sentenced to life imprisonment. O'Neill banned the UVF, describing it as "a sordid conspiracy of criminals against an unprotected people." [10] The Orange Order quickly expressed its disagreement with the verdict of the courts and the Prime Minister's confirmation of that verdict. The annual parade the following July 12 halted in front of Crumlin Road jail to pay its respects to the three murderers housed inside.

It was by now apparent that powerful forces within the Protestant community had substantial popular support for their efforts to negate the attempts to reconcile the two communities. O'Neill himself was long aware of this. After Labor gained control in Britain in 1964, he told Harold Wilson, the new Prime Minister, at their first meeting in May 1965, that his chief of detectives had told him that he (O'Neill) could walk through the Catholic Falls area without protection, but that a full bodyguard would not guarantee his safety in the extreme Protestant areas. His recognition of this situation caused him to move with the utmost discretion, and he did not encourage the appointment of Catholics to prominent public positions. Although their membership in statutory committees and boards improved somewhat during his term of office, a 1966 survey revealed that even then there were only 9 Catholics among 102 members of such bodies.[11] What he did was simply to insist that Catholics could not be automatically judged disloyal by the fact of being Catholics. His objective was a bridge between the two communities. But that was more than the extremists would tolerate. "A traitor and a bridge are very much alike," Paisley told his followers. "They both go over to the other side." [12]

While welcoming the O'Neill initiatives, Catholics were impatient for concrete results. Thanks to instant communications, the young people had been stirred by the student movement in the United States, starting with the 1964 unrest at the Berkeley campus of the University of California, a movement that had produced demonstrations at more than a hundred campuses by the first half of 1968. They had similarly followed the Black Power movement in the United States, from the Harlem riots in 1964, through Newark and Detroit in 1967, and the assassination of Martin Luther King in April 1968. This last event impressed them immensely. Many had accepted Martin Luther King's program of nonviolence and reconciliation as a model for their own conduct. His death increased their militancy, as did the outbreak of student unrest on French campuses, which led to a general strike and the paralysis of that nation less than a month later. The stage was set for confrontation when the Campaign for Social Justice took a stand on a new test case in Dungannon in June 1968.

Undeterred by the defeat suffered at the hands of Mrs. McCluskey and the Homeless Citizens League in 1963, the Dungannon town council attempted a particularly brazen move in June 1968. It evicted a Catholic family which had squatted in a council house and awarded the tenancy to a 19-year-old unmarried Protestant girl, secretary to a Unionist politician. The first to protest was Austin Currie, a young Nationalist member of the Stormont Parliament. But when he raised the issue at Stormont, he got nowhere. Housing, he was told, was the exclusive responsibility of the local authority. He then secured some additional publicity by organizing a "squat in" at the house on June 20, after which he persuaded the Civil Rights Association to stage a march—again imitating Martin Luther King—from Coalisland to Dungannon, a distance of four miles. Coalisland is a predominantly Catholic town, and the marchers assembled there without incident. It was to be a nonsectarian, nonpolitical march, and while the participants were predominantly Catholic, other elements in the community were prominent, including the Young Liberals and the Young Socialists, as well as veteran Communist Betty Sinclair, president at that time of the Civil Rights Association. One of the college students was Bernadette Devlin, who subsequently described the mood as they set out at seven o'clock of a bright August evening. "It was an event. It was the first civil-rights demonstration Northern Ireland had ever seen, and we all jogged along happily, eating oranges and smoking cigarettes, and people came out of their houses to join the fun. Marchers were dropping off at every pub on the way, and the whole thing had a sort of good-natured, holiday atmosphere, with the drunk men lolloping in and out of this supposedly serious demonstration." [13]

As they discovered when they reached Dungannon,

however, opponents of civil rights had managed to place a cordon of police across the road to prevent them from going through the town to the Market Square where they had planned to end their march with a rally. Dungannon has almost as many Protestants as it has Catholics, and its Protestant leaders had persuaded the authorities that this was a sectarian Roman Catholic march and, as such, was not entitled to pass through the Protestant section of town. This was the traditional means for deciding how to route marches either by the Orangemen or by a Catholic group. The leaders of the march succeeded in controlling the hotheads who were all for fighting their way through. They simply held their meeting on the road in front of the police cordon, then dispersed. Betty Sinclair tried to lead the crowd in "We Shall Overcome," but few knew the words and they broke instead into a Nationalist hymn. It was a mistake, establishing once more an identification of civil rights with what was in Northern Ireland a sectarian position.

What was really happening, although neither party seemed as yet to realize the fact, was that two hopelessly conflicting sets of assumptions were at work. The civil rights people were giving the law an absolute value. In that context it was both proper and logical for the people of Coalisland to march into the main square of Dungannon in which were located the local government offices responsible for housing in Coalisland. The public officials, the police, the B-Specials, and the Orangemen, who between them constituted the power structure in Dungannon, as elsewhere in Northern Ireland, started from a different position. For them there were two communities in Northern Ireland. One was dominant. It made the law and administered it. Basic to that law from time immemorial was the exclusion of the defeated and disloyal from the territory of the loyal victors. The Catholics of Coalisland could enter Market Square of Dungannon only one at a time and hat in hand to beg a favor. They could not come as equals to demand rights. To challenge that position meant challenging the monopoly of power of the victors, and the Civil Rights Association automatically declared its own disloyalty by doing so. The CRA leaders did indeed fight valiantly to break out of that trap, but they never succeeded, and their own followers did not help them. To establish their nonpolitical and nonsectarian character, they forbade any display of flags. Back in the ranks, however, someone would wave the tricolor of the neighboring Republic of Ireland (and also the official flag of the IRA) or the Plow and Stars under which the Socialist Citizen Army had fought in Dublin in the Easter Rising of 1916. Such acts had more meaning for the Unionists than the ineffective protests of the CRA leaders.

The importance of these contradictions would emerge later with the escalation of the official violence that followed logically from its own set of assumptions. As the marchers from Coalisland dispersed, their CRA leaders judged the experiment a total success. They had been able to march, and they had been able to control their followers when the crisis came. The publicity that resulted was tremendous. Those who had previously hesitated or doubted were being won over. They decided to march again, on October 5, this time in the city that brought out most fully the complexity and the depth of Northern Ireland's conflict.

Derry has for the two communities in Northern Ireland some of the meaning that Jerusalem holds for Jews and Christians. The Catholics who constitute two-thirds of its population still call it by the ancient name of *Doire Cholmcille*, the wood of Columba, so named because Saint Columba founded a monastery there in the sixth century. To the Protestants it is Londonderry, its official name since an English king in the early seventeenth century confiscated all the territory of the O'Neills and handed over this part of it to London's merchant adventurers. In 1689, the "Apprentice Boys" of Derry closed the city gates against King James and under the leadership of George Walker held out against overwhelming odds, even eating rats, until relief arrived 105 days later. Protestant Ulster's favorite slogan ever since has been Walker's defiant "No Surrender." Although the modern city is overwhelmingly Catholic, the holy ground inside the walls is held exclusively by Protestants. The Catholics are outside and below, still figuratively besieging it but always kept at bay. The Walker monument symbolizes Protestant determination, standing as it does on a high point of the medieval walls overlooking the Bogside ghetto. Here each year on August 12, anniversary of the relief of Derry, is held the most jingoistic of all Orange celebrations, with firing of cannon, blaring of bands, and singing of partisan songs to remind the more than 20,000 Catholics cowering sullenly below that they were and still are the vanquished.

The Derry Housing Action Committee, one of many civil rights organizations being formed all over Northern Ireland, took the lead in inviting the Civil Rights Association to demonstrate in Derry. Its members included a wide spectrum of anti-Unionist opinion, but its policy was similar to the official platform of the Civil Rights Association itself. Its simple and not particularly revolutionary program consisted of six points: one-man-one-vote in local elections; removal of gerrymandered boundaries; laws against discrimination by local government, and machinery to deal with complaints; allocation of public housing on a points system; repeal of the Special Powers Act; disbanding of the B-Specials. Other organizations which agreed to cooperate included the Derry branch of the Northern Ireland Labor party, the Young Socialists, and the Derry City Republican Club. The organizers felt it was important to challenge the image conveyed at Dungannon of the civil rights movement as sectarian. They accordingly picked a route that would take them inside the city walls, an area identified with Protestant custom and myth. The local Unionists immediately protested, and the Apprentice Boys, the local Orange organization, announced its own march along the same route for the same day. On October 3, the Minister of Home Affairs issued an order forbidding all processions within the city walls. At a long meeting the following day, the organizers decided to ignore the ban, thus escalating the civil rights protest to the level of civil disobedience. The issue, as they saw it, was whether the Stormont government could treat every protest against its policies as sectarian.

Advance publicity ensured the presence of a crowd of marchers estimated at about 2000, several Opposition members of the Stormont Parliament, several English Labor members of the British Parliament, and a strong contingent of newsmen and television cameras. The marchers soon found their way blocked. The police drew their batons and struck down the leaders, including two Stormont members who had to be hospitalized. As at Dungannon, an impromptu meeting was now held in the face of the police, with speeches, singing of "We Shall Overcome," and calls to the marchers to squat on the ground. The crowd was not yet familiar with what would soon be the quasi-official hymn of the movement, nor with the techniques of resistance by sitting in the road. The leaders urged the crowd to disperse, but they seemed much less inclined to do so than those at Dungannon. In any case, they could not have dispersed, because another cordon of police had cut off their retreat. Some began to taunt the police, and they charged the penned-in crowd from all directions, slashing with batons on skulls and genitals. Some broke through to a vacant lot and found stones to repel the attacking police. Water cannon were then brought up and used at close range to devastating effect. The police chased the fleeing marchers through the city streets, attacking every available target, including Saturday afternoon shoppers, in an undisciplined outburst, the water cannon smashing shop fronts and upper windows.

The televised police violence flashed on screens across the world produced major political results. As Bernadette Devlin, who had been there, put it: "Ireland was up in arms; you can slowly crush the Irish, you can take the ground from under their feet and they won't notice they're sinking down; but if you hit them, they will hit back. So the Unionist government did the civil-rights movement a favor. They gave it life in one day." [14]

The students of Queen's University, Belfast, some of whom had been in Derry, were particularly incensed. They marched in protest the next day to the home of the Minister of Home Affairs, and were doubly incensed when he greeted them as "silly bloody fools." The following day, 800 of them decided to carry the protest to the Belfast city hall, provoking a counterdemonstration led by Ian Paisley, and a three-hour sitdown in the city center where the police kept the two groups apart. Adopting procedures by this time well established among protesting students in American universities, the Queen's students began a series of marathon meetings, the outcome of which was the creation of another civil rights organization, People's Democracy. When People's Democracy decided to hold a protest march, they needed a signature on the form requesting a police permit, a signature that in Northern Ireland was certain to ensure a police dossier. "I've got nothing to lose," a young psychology student said. "I'll sign." That signature launched the diminutive Bernadette Devlin at 21 on her career in politics. People's Democracy played a significant part in the following months, forcing the pace by keeping up the pressure of demonstrations and demands when other civil rights groups showed a willingness to slow down in response to government promises of redress of grievances.

For the time being, nevertheless, Derry remained the main focus of attention. At a meeting a few days after the October 5 confrontation, a committee of 16 representatives of various viewpoints was set up as the Derry Citizens Action Committee. It included a Unionist, but he resigned to protest the committee's first decision. It was to stage a sit-down by the committee members in the location sacred to Protestantism and from which the October 5 march had been excluded. At the other extreme, a socialist leader of the Labor party declined the invitation to join a "middle-aged, middle-class, and middle-of-the-road committee." He was Eamonn McCann, a man who believed in revolution while working constantly to prevent violence. He would say that in Northern Ireland such reforms as "every man a job" and "every family a house" would constitute a revolution.

Even without McCann, the committee posted considerable achievements. A major march over the same route as that of October 5, although banned by the government, brought out 15,000 people, a human tide which the police did not attempt to stop when some breached the cordon and others made their way in small groups into the city and held the prohibited meeting. And from its membership emerged two moderates who would play a big part in the subsequent political events, John Hume and Ivan Cooper. The eldest of seven children of a Derryman who was unemployed for 20 years, Hume was for a time a Catholic seminarian and then a teacher, before going into business for himself. He helped to organize a credit union and a housing association in Derry and worked hard—though unsuccessfully—to have the new university located there. He was shortly to be elected to Stormont for Derry. At first he was highly regarded by Protestant moderates because of his unswerving commitment to nonviolence, but his support for rent and rates strikes later lost him that support. Ivan Cooper, a Protestant, would also be elected to Stormont, like Hume on a socialist ticket, and he would earn the bitterest enmity of his fellow Protestants by his total repudiation of the Unionist regime and equal commitment to the civil rights cause.

The rapid growth of the civil rights movement, combined with the multiplier effect of television and the other communications media, was having repercussions both inside and outside Northern Ireland. Deep divisions were showing within the Unionist party. Prime Minister Terence O'Neill continued to plead for moderation and to promise redress of grievances, while behind him an old enemy who was also a member of his cabinet, Brian Faulkner, was promoting a hard line, a line he correctly anticipated would catapult him into O'Neill's seat. Simultaneously, Minister of Home Affairs William Craig was using the police to reassert Protestant and Unionist supremacy in the traditional manner, by cracking the skulls of enemies. Craig's political formula was simple. "When you have a Roman Catholic majority, you have a lesser standard of democracy." The moral: get rid of them and keep true democracy. That there was wide support for the extremists was evidenced by the emergence of fascist types of organizations, the Ulster Constitution Committee, the Ulster Protestant Volunteers, and the Ulster Volunteer Force, all of them private armies whose parallel policies suggested a common origin and control. Unionist history was ready to repeat itself.

5

Violence Brings Polarization

If Ulster does not survive, then historians may well show that it was the Protestant extremists, yearning for the days of the Protestant ascendancy, who lit the flame which blew it up.
—TERENCE O'NEILL, former Prime Minister
of Northern Ireland [1]

As long as the Paisleyites—and Paisley is not necessarily one— believe their vision of history, act out their fantasies and fears in the street, then the people in the North are doomed to repeat themselves.
—J. BOWYER BELL [2]

The cracks appearing in the ranks of the Unionists in the late 1960s were still superficial; determination to maintain the 50-year monopoly of power remained as strong as ever. O'Neill insisted that his reforms would not weaken the bases of the state, and it was clear that he would have no substantial backing in any attempt at radical change. The big question for the Unionists was not their own will and ability to stand fast, but the readiness of the London government to support them. Labor was again in power in Britain, having won a narrow majority in 1964 and increased that majority substantially in new elections in 1966. So far it had honored the convention that the Westminster Parliament would not interfere in Northern Ireland's internal affairs unless a breakdown of law and order threatened. But its attitude remained one of tolerance, not of friendliness. Its interests and those of the Unionists were as far apart as ever. In addition, it was coming under embarrassing pressures, for the civil rights movement attracted world attention to the anachronism of civil strife based on religious affiliation in the second half of the twentieth century. It was particularly undesirable attention at a time when London was trying to break down France's resistance to British membership in the European Economic Community.

It had been a hard struggle for the civil rights movement to arouse public opinion in Britain. The British press, dominated by Conservative interests, had long adopted an attitude similar to that of the London government. It avoided any questioning of the decisions of Stormont. The picture it presented its readers was the official picture of a loyal majority constantly harassed by a disloyal minority. The blackout continued during the years of peaceful efforts by the civil rights leaders from 1964 to 1968. The little space that was given to events in Ireland was almost entirely from the slanted perspective of the Stormont government. Only when the conflict erupted into major violence was it deemed worthy of extensive coverage, and even then the reporting lacked depth and understanding. This was continued by the press in subsequent years, with the notable exception of two London newspapers, the *Sunday Times* and *The Guardian.*

It was television that first brought the social problems of Northern Ireland to the consciousness of ordinary people in Britain. From the middle of 1968 onward, in particular, every major clash was covered as fully as the similar events in the United States during the Martin Luther King marches and the subsequent violence in inner cities and on campuses. Television proved a catalyst. It took Northern Ireland into living rooms in England and around the world. The sight of peaceful, unarmed men and women being assailed not only by mobs but by the police spoke for itself. The Stormont leaders recognized this and it made them fear that London would yield to the pressures and take a more active hand in their affairs.

The views of the London government were already a matter of public record. Shortly before the 1964 general election which had brought him to the premiership Harold Wilson had written the Campaign for Social Justice. "We deplore religious and other kinds of discrimination," he said. "This should be tackled by introducing new and impartial procedures for the allocation of houses, by setting up joint tribunals to which particular cases of alleged discrimination in public appointments can be referred, and indeed by any other effective means that can be agreed." [3]

Near the end of 1968, Harold Wilson decided he could wait no longer. On November 4 he summoned Terence O'Neill to London and in a five-hour meeting told him there was a limit to Westminster's patience. Britain, he said, would back O'Neill on the reforms he had been promising but had so far hesitated to introduce because of opposition within his own party. The next day, Wilson repeated publicly in Parliament his determination to have reform implemented in Northern Ireland. If O'Neill and his ideals were rejected, he said, the British government would have to consider "a very fundamental reappraisal" of its relations with Northern Ireland. It was clear warning that the hands-off convention could be reversed.

On November 22, O'Neill announced his reforms. The gerrymandered Derry city council was replaced by a development commission. The Stormont government would see that local councils allotted houses on a basis of need and in accordance with a clear "points" system, the points being objective measures of need and priority. It promised a prompt reform of local government. The multiple vote given to big businessmen as property owners was to be abolished. However, a large number of men and women remained disenfranchised because they neither owned nor rented a home. Legislation would be introduced to create the post of ombudsman with authority to investigate all charges of discrimination. Finally, those parts of the Special Powers Act which were in conflict with international obligations would be withdrawn "as soon as the Northern Ireland government considered this could be done without undue hazard." [4]

Protestant extremists were outraged. Ian Paisley publicly denounced the police authorities for giving a permit for a civil rights march in Armagh for November 20. "You have lost control of Derry," he said. "If you don't stop the Armagh march, I will." The Ulster Protestant Volunteers, whose members pledge that "when the authorities act contrary to the Constitution, the body will take whatever steps it thinks fit to expose such unconstitutional acts," joined Paisley in preparing direct counteraction. Notices from "Ulster's Defenders" inserted in letter boxes in Armagh called on the people to board up their windows and evacuate their women and children from the city. A postscript added: "O'Neill must go." [5] Throughout the night preceding November 20 the Paisleyites occupied the streets. As the hour for the march approached, they were still in possession, armed with iron bars, lead piping, sharpened poles, and studded belts, and their numbers remained several times as many as the 350 police on hand. Instead of trying to disperse them, the police asked the 5000 civil rights marchers, who were unarmed, to withdraw. They protested that they had a permit from the Minister of Home Affairs, which the police should honor, but in the end they reluctantly submitted, and the day's only casualties were two British television crews. One had its equipment wrecked, the other its cameraman so badly beaten that he had to be hospitalized, both at the hands of the triumphant Paisleyites. Paisley was sentenced to three months in prison as the ringleader of the Armagh disorder, but this only served to raise his standing with the extremists, and he could still boast that he had demonstrated the effective way to deal with the civil rights protests.

Early in December, O'Neill repeated in a television program the undertakings for reform he had announced in November, strongly condemning the recourse to violence of the Unionist extremists and urging that "Unionism merely armed with strength" would be less secure than "Unionism armed with justice." At the same time he urged the civil rights groups to suspend further protests until he had time to implement his undertakings, and to indicate his goodwill dismissed his Minister of Home Affairs, William Craig, who had been openly identifying himself with the Unionist extremists and denouncing the civil rights movement as a cloak for subversion and treason. This initiative was well received by many Unionist supporters, and the Unionist party in Stormont gave O'Neill an overwhelming vote of confidence.

A majority of the civil rights groups also decided to suspend agitation, but the Young Socialists and the People's Democracy of Belfast's university did not agree. O'Neill, they argued, had said nothing about the most serious grievances, the Special Powers Act, the limited franchise for local government, and job discrimination by private employers. And while he had abolished the Unionist-controlled corporation in Derry, he had not carried his action to its logical completion by giving control of the city to the majority. They decided that something as dramatic as Martin Luther King's march at Selma, Alabama, was indicated: to assert their legal rights in parts of Northern Ireland which the Orangemen regarded as their strongholds they would undertake a march 75 miles across the state from Belfast to Derry, starting on New Year's Day 1969. The new Minister of Home Affairs tried to dissuade them, but when they insisted he agreed that he had no justification to use his powers to stop them. The marchers, 80 in number at the start, were constantly harassed by gangs of Paisleyites, and on almost every occasion the police took no action to protect them. But they pressed on, making many detours to bypass places where major opposition had been organized. "I am no moderate," Eamonn McCann told them, "but you will play into their hands if you attack or abuse them [the Paisleyites]. No, you must not attack these people. They are your proper and natural allies." [6]

Aided by massive television, radio, and press coverage, the number of marchers grew each day. On the morning of the fourth day, their number swollen to 500, they set out to cover the last ten miles to Derry, the route taking them over a river bridge at Burntollet about seven miles from their destination. It was a Saturday. The previous evening, Ian Paisley and others had addressed a "prayer meeting" in Derry and urged the audience not to tolerate the entry into "the city of the Apprentice Boys" people who were, as they put it, "no better than republicans"—that is to say, people committed to the destruction of the state of Northern Ireland and its absorption into the Republic of Ireland. News of the Paisley meeting spread quickly in the mainly Catholic city and a threatening crowd soon gathered around the meeting in the city hall known as the Guildhall. While most of the crowd obeyed its leaders' appeals to avoid violence, a few intransigents who remained after the others had dispersed burned an automobile owned by one of Paisley's lieutenants. Orangemen in the Guildhall then smashed the furniture to make clubs and sallied out in company with the police to disperse the troublemakers.

Following the "prayer meeting," the Orangemen who had participated in it carefully prepared an ambush. Truckloads of freshly quarried stones were distributed in piles spaced at 12-foot intervals on the side of a hill overlooking the route of the march close to Burntollet Bridge. Between the piles of stones were piles of empty beer and liquor bottles. In the morning, 200 men carrying iron bars and nail-studded clubs and wearing white arm bands for identification assembled in ambush on the hillside. Subsequent press photographs and eyewitness accounts identified about half of them as B-Specials out of uniform. Word of trouble ahead quickly reached the marchers. Before they left their camp site they were warned by their leaders of what lay ahead, and Eamonn McCann repeated the plea he had made in Derry the previous evening. "Our commitment to nonviolence," he said, "we must support to a lunatic extreme. We must agree that not one single person will retaliate even to save himself from injury. Physical intervention by a marcher must only be employed in order to save another whose life is in danger or who may suffer serious injury without your help. And even then your intervention must be confined purely to giving aid to those in danger, and not to retribution." [7]

The marchers moved out, police in personnel carriers and television cameras on trucks leading the way. As they approached Burntollet Bridge, three miles down the road, the police vehicles were still in front. Behind the police came a small group of Orange sympathizers provocatively waving a British Union Jack. A little earlier they had smashed the windscreen of an automobile carrying newsmen, but had been permitted by the police to participate as a counterdemonstration. Separating them from the marchers was a squad of steel-helmeted police equipped with riot shields and led by an inspector. More battle-ready policemen brought up the rear in personnel carriers. At the ambush site policemen were strung out along the fence, but they had no riot equipment and were chatting amiably with their B-Special friends as the latter prepared for battle. Bernadette Devlin has described what followed.

And then we came to Burntollet Bridge, and from lanes at each side of the road a curtain of bricks and boulders and bottles brought the march to a halt. From the lanes burst hordes of screaming people wielding planks of wood, bottles, laths, iron bars, crowbars, cudgels studded with nails, and they waded into the march beating the hell out of everybody.[8]

Many of the marchers were driven into the river, and others were beaten senseless. Eighty-seven were taken to the hospital for treatment and many others were less seriously injured. The police did not arrest a single attacker, nor were any of the B-Specials disciplined. Indeed not a single person was ever brought to justice, thanks to an amnesty conveniently declared by Prime Minister O'Neill a little later.

Those still able to walk broke their way through finally, and as they approached Derry their ranks were swollen to nearly 2000 by members of the Radical Students Alliance who came out to meet them. As they entered Derry, they were met once more by a hail of stones, bricks, bottles, and other missiles. As before, the police took no action against the assailants but insisted on rerouting the march so that it would not enter the walled city, the area sacred to the Orangemen whose ancestors had gallantly and successfully defended it in 1690. The march ended, accordingly, in the Guildhall square directly under the walls, and while final speeches and ceremonies were being held there, the Orangemen assembled above and showered down bottles, stones, and abuse.

A judicial investigation of "the causes and nature of the violence and civil disturbance in Northern Ireland," the Cameron Commission, set up by the government two weeks later, reported that the police had made a serious effort to protect the marchers at Burntollet Bridge, a conclusion rejected by most observers and students of the event. But even the Cameron Report did not attempt to defend the police behavior in Derry after the marchers completed their celebrations and dispersed. The police in uniform had begun to drink with the Orange demonstrators, and soon they had become fully integrated members of a riotous mob. "We have to record with regret," said the Cameron Commission,

that our investigations have led us to the unhesitating conclusion that on the night of January 4–5 a number of policemen were guilty of misconduct which involved assault and battery, malicious damage to property, to streets, in the predominantly Catholic Bogside area, giving reasonable cause for apprehension of personal injury among other innocent inhabitants; and the use of provocative sectarian and political slogans.[9]

What the commission was trying to say was that the drunken police and their fellow mobsters had swept out of the walled city down into the Bogside, banging their riot shields and shouting obscenities, smashing in windows and doors. Typical of their style was a shouted remark quoted by an English witness to the Cameron Commission: "Come out, you Fenian bastards, and we'll give you one for the pope." [10] How it looked to the people inside was described by one of them, Mrs. Sheila Donnelly: "At a quarter to three in the morning, a crowd of police in our street were shouting, 'Hey, hey, we're the Monkees. We'll Monkee you around 'til your blood is flowing on the ground. . . .' I looked out the window and one shouted, 'Come on out you Fenian, 'til we rape you.'" [11]

This civil rights march and the police riot it precipitated were of the greatest importance in clarifying the situation in Northern Ireland and determining the subsequent course of events. What the Catholics in Derry saw was a fully consistent policy carried out by the Orangemen, the B-Specials, and the regular police (RUC). It was a policy which equated civil rights with sedition and reacted to nonviolent protest with officially sanctioned violence. Burntollet Bridge confirmed decisively the long-standing and widely held belief that all sections of the police force were partial and sectarian. In the Bogside, tension was particularly acute after the night of terror. People built barricades in the streets to ensure that neither policemen nor mobs could again catch them unprepared. It was the first step in the creation of enclaves, soon known as No-Go areas, patrolled and defended by volunteers drawn from within the area itself, with entry barred to outsiders, including the police and other armed forces of the state. The signs erected at entrance points protected by antitank traps read: "You are now entering Free Derry." Technically, at least, it was open rebellion against the state, and the Orangemen became understandably incensed against the authorities when they decided not to attempt to force their way in. But the fact was that the Belfast government did not really have the trained men for such an attempt. Indeed, they had already written off the Bogside the previous year when they closed the one police station located within its boundaries. The only change now was that periodic armed patrols in peronnel carriers could no longer be continued. The incident was mainly significant as an anticipation of things to come, of a gradual dissolution of the state into self-regulating and self-disciplining "republics," some of them Catholic ghettos and others Protestant.

The day after the Bogside police riots, Prime Minister O'Neill proceeded to alienate the many Catholics who had hitherto been sympathetic to him by issuing an official statement which totally varied from the evidence provided by newspaper and television coverage. The guilty ones, he said, were the people who had marched. He did not add that they had done so with the permission of his Minister of Home Affairs and had shown heroic restraint under unprovoked attack. "Some of the marchers and those who supported them in Londonderry have shown themselves to be mere hooligans," he charged,

ready to attack the police and others. . . . The police have handled this most difficult situation as fairly and as firmly as they could. . . . Unless these warring minorities rapidly return to their senses, we will have to consider a further reinforcement of the regular police by greater use of the special constabulary [B-Specials] for normal police duties. . . . I think we must also have an urgent look at the Public Order Act itself to see whether we ought to ask parliament for further powers to control those elements which are seeking to hold the entire community to ransom. Enough is enough. We have heard sufficient for now about civil rights.[12]

O'Neill's credibility was further undermined the following September when the commission named by him under pressure of the London government and headed by Lord Cameron, a Scottish judge, gave the direct lie to his interpretation of the happenings at Burntollet and in the Bogside. By the time that report appeared, however, the situation had deteriorated so precipitously that its conclusions were mainly useful for correcting the historical record. No sooner had O'Neill announced, in mid-January, the creation of the Cameron Commission to investigate the causes and nature of the violence than some of his closest colleagues in government began to challenge his leadership. In February they precipitated a general election, which, while indecisive, left him slightly weaker than before. His hope of finding a middle ground on which moderates of both sides would support him was disappointed. He barely held his own seat against a challenge from Ian Paisley, and elsewhere the extremists on the Unionist side made inroads. The Catholics who would have backed him had been alienated by his inadequate response to the Derry violence, and showed their approval of the civil rights movement by electing three of its leaders, John Hume, Ivan Cooper, and John O'Hanlon, in the process displacing Eddie McAteer, the leader of the Nationalist party. Another important test came two months later in the form of a by-election for the mid-Ulster seat in the Westminster Parliament. Unionists were in a slight minority in this constituency, but they had managed to hold it in the past because the moderate Nationalists and extreme Republicans split the Opposition vote. This time they withdrew in favor of a civil rights representative, the diminutive but fiery 20-year-old college student, Bernadette Devlin. She represented the most radical wing of the civil rights movement, People's Democracy, and her success gave two of the twelve Northern Ireland's seats at Westminster to anti-Unionists. That her voice would be heard was made clear by the maiden speech delivered—flouting convention—the very same day she took the oath.

April 1969 saw further incidents of violence which were serious enough in themselves but even more serious because of the way in which the parties to the conflict interpreted them. The most significant ones centered again on Derry, which was clearly getting out of hand.

All the elements for an explosion had been so long present that people had stopped expecting it to happen. Before the creation of Northern Ireland as a separate state in 1920, the city of Derry had existed in a reasonably stable equilibrium. Its population at the most recent census (1911) consisted of 18,000 Protestants and 23,000 Catholics. The monopoly of wealth and status enjoyed by the Protestants more than compensated for the Catholic advantage in numbers. It was only in 1918 that Britain first gave votes to women, and up to that time it was universally accepted that in local government the voting system should be weighted in favor of the men of property who paid the bulk of the taxes. Protestant control in those circumstances did not create an intolerable emotional burden for Derry's Catholics, but the situation changed rapidly and progressively after 1920. The loss of the city's natural hinterland in Donegal to the west by the partition of Ireland started the economic decline. It was accentuated by the new state's economic policy of siting new industry in the area east of the River Bann, a policy for which economic reasons could certainly be adduced. A similar movement of population and economic activity occurred simultaneously in southern Ireland, drawing people from west of the Shannon to the vicinity of Dublin under the magnetic influence of the major British markets. In the north the economic inducement undoubtedly existed, but the trend was accentuated by the desire to favor the Protestant eastern part of the state at the expense of the Catholic hinterland. The result was that by 1961 the Protestant population of Derry city had remained stationary at 18,000, while the Catholic population had grown to 36,000. Yet in spite of the overwhelming majority in numbers now enjoyed by the Catholics, nothing else had changed. Gerrymandering had enabled the Protestants to maintain their control of the institutions of power and through them to ensure to their own group the benefits of good housing and access to desirable employment, while keeping the Catholics in their place. Derry remained for Protestants in Northern Ireland a symbol of the resolute Protestantism which had saved Ulster in 1689. The old walled city, the business center, continued to be a Protes-

tant bastion, sacred ground available only for professing loyalty to the regime. The Catholics were squeezed into the low
ground known as the Bogside, immediately below and to the
west, an area where they were forced to expand upwards in
high-rise apartments as their numbers grew, and from which
in the 1960s some 15,000 burst outward on the western edge
into the Creggan, slightly more middle class in its social
composition but still definitely part of the Catholic ghetto.

From its inception in the mid-1960s, the civil rights
movement had offered Derry as the major example of social
discrimination against Catholics. As each admission by the
Stormont regime that wrongs existed and would be corrected
was met by violent resistance on the part of the Orange extremists and a corresponding delay in implementation, the
emotional temperature rose in the Bogside and the Creggan.
Even such moves as the abolition of the city council were
greeted with suspicion and hostility. If the government recognized that the council was in the wrong hands, why not
transfer it to the right hands? It was saying that it could no
longer leave control in the hands of the local Protestant minority, but—by setting up commission rule—it was adding
that neither was it prepared to transfer control to the local
Catholic majority.

The spark that brought the explosion was struck in the
Bogside just two days after Bernadette Devlin's election
to Parliament, an event being celebrated by Catholics as
evidence they had finally united on the concrete, politically
attainable issue of civil rights. A civil rights march from Burntollet Bridge to Derry, announced for April 19, was banned
by the Stormont authorities as likely to cause trouble. Its
organizers accepted the decision but some of their followers
decided to stage a protest sit-down inside the walls of Derry.
Before long they found themselves involved in a fight with a
group of Orangemen who had decided to confirm for themselves that the ban on the civil rights march was being observed. As on other occasions when opponents of the civil
rights movement had clashed with demonstrators, the police

took sides, driving the Catholics out of the walled city and back into the Bogside. The people of the Bogside responded angrily to the invasion of their territory by a squad of riot police, helmeted, visored, carrying shields, pistols, and long riot batons, and dressed in bulletproof vests, police who according to the subsequent report of the official Cameron Commission committed "grave acts of misconduct."

The misconduct which had the gravest repercussions concerned Samuel Devenney, a 43-year-old man with a weak heart and a record of tuberculosis. He was at home with his wife and five children aged between 5 and 18 years, when a contingent of six police personnel carriers surprised a group of youths throwing stones at policemen. The youths dashed into the nearest doorway, which happened to be Devenney's, and disappeared, apparently bolting out the back. The police burst in after them and attacked the Devenneys with batons and boots. At an inquest held later on Samuel Devenney, his 16-year-old daughter Catherine is recorded as having testified that "her sister Anne was screaming that the witness [Catherine] was a girl and lay across her and asked the police not to touch her as she was only out of hospital, and the policeman said, 'I don't give a fuck where she's out of.' Witness sat on the floor with her knees up to protect her stomach because she had an operation. Her brother was crying." [13] Samuel Devenney's scalp was badly cut by a blow and he was hospitalized. Although it was never directly established that his death resulted from the beating, he did in fact die three months later; and as far as his Bogside neighbors were concerned, he immediately became a martyr for the cause of civil rights. The Cameron Commission's terms of reference did not authorize it to investigate this incident, but its report did recommend that it should be "probed and investigated." This was never done, and the reason why it was not illustrates the extent to which police discipline broke down in Derry on the night of April 19, 1969. It could not be probed because there were no police records. The desk log was not kept properly at the police station nearest the scene.

The police from Derry had been joined by police from outside the city, and all of them had operated as a mob without
interference from their officers. That much was known, and it
was enough to confirm the Catholics of Northern Ireland in
the views they had long held about the police.

Up to this time, the civil rights leaders had been extraor-
dinarily successful in keeping the emotions they had built up
in the Catholic community within the guidelines of nonviolence on which they had insisted as essential for success.
But the response to each expression of grievances, the repeated violence in which the police almost invariably joined,
was creating intolerable tensions. The breaking point came
the day after the second police invasion of the Bogside on
April 19, 1969. It came in Belfast 75 miles away, but as a
direct result of the previous night's events.

Telephone calls to civil rights leaders in Belfast from
friends in the Bogside started the process. The police are attacking us, they said, and the local police are being reinforced from other parts of the state. A diversion in Belfast
would force a redeployment of the police and take some of
the heat off the Bogside. An emergency meeting of the executive of the Belfast branch of the Civil Rights Association
was immediately summoned in a Belfast hotel. While sugges-
tions such as lying down as a group on the runways of the
nearby airport were being discussed, two members of the executive arrived back from Derry with a tape recording of
one of the Devenney children describing the ordeal her family had just been through. By now the news had spread rapidly and many sympathizers had crashed the meeting. The tape
recording inevitably inflamed passions. While the executive's
decision went no further than a call for immediate protest
rallies, some teen-agers from the Falls Road thought they had
a better idea. They dashed from the hotel, stole a car, gathered up milk bottles and proceeded to manufacture Molotov
cocktails, known in Belfast as petrol bombs. That night they
exploded 11 of them in small post offices scattered around

the city, the first less than half an hour after the meeting had ended.

There had been one major explosion before this date. Three weeks earlier, expert saboteurs had done over a million dollars of damage to an electricity transformer in Belfast, and an attack was made on high-tension transmission lines near Belfast at about the same time as the police in Derry were beating up the Devenneys. The night following the petrol bomb attacks on Belfast post offices, the outlet of a reservoir supplying three-quarters of Belfast's water was wrecked, and several more attacks on the city's water supply followed for over a week. Considerably later, after the London government had intervened openly in Northern Ireland and sent in a new police chief, several men were arrested and put on trial for damaging the Belfast reservoir. One of them, Samuel Stevenson, was by his own admission Chief of Staff of the Ulster Volunteer Force, an extremist Orange private army first organized in 1913—with the encouragement of Sir Edward Carson—to resist the granting of Home Rule to Ireland, and declared an illegal organization by the Stormont regime in 1966 after it was implicated in three killings in Belfast. Stevenson pleaded guilty and gave evidence against the others, creating a very strong presumption that the first of the bombings, of which Northern Ireland was to experience several thousand in the following four years, was the work of Orange agents-provocateurs seeking to arouse feeling against the other side.[14] While responsibility for the other incidents was never clearly established, many believe they were all part of a unified program. It is not without significance that the following October a uniformed member of the Ulster Volunteer Force killed himself accidentally while trying to dynamite an electricity station across the border in County Donegal.

At the time, however, the entire Unionist propaganda apparatus proposed a single, simple explanation. All the violence was the work of the sinister force which had been hiding behind the civil rights movement and manipulating its activities, and which now was finally emerging in its true colors. The hated and feared Irish Republican Army had once again declared open war on Northern Ireland. Whatever basis there might be for that assertion, the time had in fact come to move the IRA to center stage. However small the part it might have played up to this point, it was now and for the foreseeable future guaranteed a major role.

With the introduction of the IRA into the story, however, Northern Ireland in isolation ceases to be intelligible. The IRA draws its roots and sustenance from a notion of Ireland which antedates and transcends the division of the island into two states. It is the enduring symbol of the 800-year struggle of the Irish against the invader. For reasons which must now be explored, its continuing and projected roles can be appreciated only within that historical context.

6

The Historic Roots of Conflict

*Terrible things happened to people on both sides in the Civil
War, but there was no attack on Protestants as pro-British
agents or quislings. In spite of the history of absentee rack-
renting landlords during the time of the Protestant Ascendancy, it has been acknowledged that Protestants have played
a notable part in the cultural, civic and social life of Ireland—a
role which they continue to play.*
          —Denis P. Barritt and Arthur Booth [1]

The division of Ireland into two states in the 1920s, a
twenty-six-county Free State and a six-county Northern Ireland, did not reflect the will of either part of the country. In
the most recent elections three-quarters of the voters of all
Ireland had backed a party committed to full independence
of the entire island as a single state. The other quarter, concentrated in and around Belfast, also wanted to maintain the
country as a single unit but one that would continue as an integral part of the United Kingdom without any separate legislature of its own. This minority, however, had also made
clear that it did not under any circumstances want to be incorporated into a separate Irish state and was ready to fight if
coercion should be attempted.

The solution imposed by London gave the majority less than it wanted, the status of a dominion within the British Empire; and the minority more than it wanted, a separate state but one still constituting a part of the United Kingdom. As a further consolation to this minority group, London included in its jurisdiction not only the area in which its main strength was concentrated, but an additional area of approximately equal size. Although it lacked a majority in this peripheral area, its overall majority in the entire area of Northern Ireland taken as a unit was in the ratio of two to one.

Evolution of the constitutional situation of the dominions in the late 1920s, an evolution in which the Irish Free State played an important part, made it possible for the Free State to increase its autonomy without risking a renewal of British military intervention. In 1937 it adopted a new constitution, which changed its name to Eire (or in the English language, Ireland), and which in the intention of those who enacted it caused the state to be no longer a member of the British Commonwealth but merely associated with it in certain specified activities.[2] The United Kingdom government, whose main concern at that moment was the meteoric rise of Hitler's power in Europe, said that the Free State's unilateral action in its view changed nothing in the juridic relations of the two states.

Eire took a further step toward clarifying its international status in 1949 by proclaiming itself the Republic of Ireland. In the changed circumstances of the postwar world, with new states coming into existence almost daily, the United Kingdom finally reconciled itself to recognizing an obvious fact. It agreed that England's 750-year claim to sovereignty over Ireland—based originally on a grant by an English pope who wanted his countrymen to convert the barbarous Irish to Rome's ways—was dead as far as the 26 counties of the Republic was concerned. However, its Parliament at Westminster reaffirmed, in the Ireland Act of 1949, its sovereignty and jurisdiction over Northern Ireland. The boundary separating it from the Republic could not be changed, it said, without the consent of the subordinate Stormont Parliament, near Belfast. Moreover, it gave formal recognition to what had been a convention from the time Stormont had come into existence in 1921. The United Kingdom would not intervene in the internal affairs of Northern Ireland except to control a breakdown of law and order. This represented an enormous step toward autonomy for a region of the United Kingdom which had up to that time in legal theory been almost on the same level as Scotland or Wales, its Parliament enjoying in principle little more power than a county council or other unit of local government. However, it would emerge later that the jurisdiction reserved by Westminster for use in the event of a breakdown of law and order was no mere formality. Before long it would prove a decisive factor.

While reaffirming in 1949 its commitment to the Northern Ireland state, the government of the United Kingdom moved to restore the close working relationship it had long enjoyed with the part of Ireland that had now moved juridically out of its orbit. An exchange of treaties with the new Republic ensured to the citizens of each nearly all the benefits of citizenship within the territory of the other,[3] including the right to move, reside, and work without passports or other formalities. One important reason for this provision was the impossibility of setting up effective control machinery on the border between the Republic and Northern Ireland. That had been attempted and had failed much earlier. Even during World War II when Northern Ireland was a belligerent as part of the United Kingdom while the rest of Ireland was neutral, the controls on movement for security reasons were mainly between Ireland and Britain, not on the land border inside Ireland.

Unlike Northern Ireland, which came into existence with a large and intransigent Catholic minority, the Free State had a Protestant minority of under 10 percent. A few who formed part of or were emotionally identified with the previous British colonial system of government emigrated.

Those who remained quickly adjusted to the new regime and have always been entirely loyal to it. The Catholic majority has never seen them as a threat of any kind, which is understandable in view of their small numbers. Their spokesmen stress the generous treatment they have always received, noting a prominence far in excess of their numbers in government, the professions, and business.[4] Most Protestants deplore the laws which prevent divorce and ban the importation or sale of contraceptives as dictated by a moral and religious code to which they do not subscribe. However, they find little difficulty in evading either law if they wish to do so. What irks them more is a regulation made by the Roman Catholic church in 1908 which is still enforced strictly by nearly all bishops in Ireland, although substantially modified in most parts of the world. This regulation requires a commitment before marriage from husband and wife, when only one of them is a Catholic, that all children of their union will be raised in the Catholic faith. When a religious group is small, it is sociologically inevitable that many of its members will marry outside the group. A recent survey in the Republic shows that 30 percent of Protestant men and 20 percent of Protestant women in fact do so and raise their children as Roman Catholics. The result has been a decline to 5 percent in the Protestant proportion of the population, 3.7 percent Church of Ireland, 0.6 percent Presbyterians, 0.3 percent Methodist. An "all others" category of 0.5 percent includes Baptists, Mormons, Seventh-day Adventists, Jehovah's Witnesses, and those with no stated religion. Jews live mostly in Dublin (3000) and Cork (120). Spokesmen for the major Protestant groups project the disappearance of the remaining Protestants within a few generations, if the Roman Catholic bishops continue to insist on the present practice. Church of Ireland Bishop Donald A. R. Caird said in June 1972 that Church of Ireland membership in County Kerry was down from 6000 in 1900 to 906, mainly because of this Roman Catholic legislation. "Protestants are desperate," he said. "Many young men remain unmarried." [5]

It is frequently asserted that the Protestants of Northern Ireland belong to a race different from that of the rest of the Irish. Lloyd George, while British Prime Minister, said in 1918 that he would be no party to placing under Irish control a people "alien in blood, in religious faith, in traditions, in outlook, from the rest of Ireland." [6] William Whitelaw, named by London in 1972 to run Northern Ireland after Stormont had been suspended, while usually politically supersensitive in his public utterances, revealed himself to be as much a victim as Lloyd George of this basic English myth. It has, of course, no foundation in history, even for historians who claim to be able to distinguish one race from another.

Mesolithic man had reached Britain, which then was still connected by a land bridge to the European continent, by 7500 B.C. The land connections which joined Britain to Ireland when the seawater was taken up by ice in the Pleistocene epoch and which allowed animals to reach Ireland (but not reptiles, because of their inability to regulate their body temperature) had disappeared long before. It took Mesolithic man a further 1500 years to make the sea trip from Britain to Ireland.

From that time, as the two islands embarked on a process of warming up which is still in sluggish progress, they were periodically overrun by the masses of migrants who since the dawn of history have moved from east to west across the Eurasian land mass. Apart from a few adventurous Irishmen who reached Iceland early in the Christian era, they had nowhere farther to go until Columbus discovered America. So they ebbed and flowed across the islands and often back onto the European mainland, producing by centuries of slow crossbreeding a distinctive type, rather taller than most other Europeans, with pale complexion, light-colored eyes, broad bodies, large heads, pronounced features, brown hair. Black or blond hair was and still is rare. Red hair occurs four times in every hundred, being as common in Northern Ireland as elsewhere. By the beginning of the Christian era all the earlier settlers were absorbed culturally and linguistically into

the Celtic tribes who by then had fully occupied both islands. It was not until the fifth century A.D. that the Angles
and Saxons descended on the east coast of England from Germany and started to push the Celts and their language slowly
north and west. Much earlier, the northeastern part of Ireland
had been settled as the kingdom of Dal Riada by celticized
Picts who had probably come from Scotland where the Picts
had established themselves before the first invasions of the
Celts.

About the same time as the Angles and Saxons landed in
eastern England, the celticized Picts of Dal Riada were being
invited back into Scotland by a ruler who felt himself threatened by neighboring Picts and encouraged the Dal Riadans
to drive a wedge between the two groups of his enemies. This
they did so successfully that they were able to maintain a
single dynasty on both sides of the North Channel for a century and to populate a large part of the Scottish mainland and
islands facing Ireland. Frequent migrations between Ireland
and Scotland—in both directions—continued during subsequent centuries, with intermarriage of nobles and the hiring of mercenary soldiers from both areas, usually to fight the
English. Finally in the seventeenth century there came once
more to Ireland from what had been the kingdom of Dal
Riada in Scotland and from the border lands of southern Scotland the settlers since known as the Scots-Irish, a group indistinguishable by race or culture from the Irish whom they
came to subjugate. Now, however, they differed in religion
because the Scots had accepted the Reformation in its Cal-
vinist or Presbyterian form, and this new factor was seized
upon to create the conflict between the two groups which
still persists more than three centuries later.

How that conflict developed and persisted can be understood only within the framework of the historic relationship
between the two neighboring islands of Ireland and Britain.
Its greater size did not automatically free Britain from fears of
attack by its western neighbor. The irruption from the northeast in the fifth century which created the kingdom of Dal

Riada in Scotland was only one of many. Saint Patrick was probably brought to Ireland about the same time by a band of marauders who had landed near Bristol in southwestern England. Although the kings of England in the early Middle Ages were more interested in expanding their foothold in France, they were always conscious of the threat from the other side. Richard II was consequently happy to oblige, in 1179, when an Irish chieftain invited the king to support him in a squabble with his superior chief. That was the start of an effort of conquest which continued with varying fortunes into the twentieth century. The Anglo-Norman invaders enjoyed the benefits of a superior military technology, in terms both of weapons and of the arts of warfare, thanks in the first instance to the knowledge and skills imported into England itself by the Norman conquerors of that country in the eleventh century, and thanks subsequently to the greater size and affluence of England's economic base.

The Irish, nevertheless, had a secret weapon which long prevented the invaders from imposing their law, order, and way of life on the entire country, and which even after that goal was won denied them the peaceful enjoyment of the fruits of victory. As the English cultural historian Arnold J. Toynbee explains in *A Study of History*, Ireland had by the sixth century begun to develop what he calls the Far Western Christian Civilization which quickly shot ahead of the nascent Western Christian Civilization on the continent of Europe. It was a civilization developed by and centered on the Irish church. For several centuries the Irish church engaged in a program of cultural expansion, sending monks and scholars to all parts of Europe, and welcoming students from the Continent whom it fed, housed, and taught free of cost in the world's first recorded foreign-aid program. "The period of Irish cultural superiority over the Continent and over Britain," writes Toynbee, "may be conventionally dated from the foundation of the monastic university of Clonmacnois in Ireland in A.D. 548 to the foundation of the Irish monastery of St. James at Ratisbon *circa* A.D. 1090. Throughout

those five and a half centuries, it was the Irish who imparted
culture and the English and Continentals who received it."
In the parallel contest for power, however, "the Irish were
defeated . . . long before they lost their cultural ascendancy." They were beaten by a Roman church with traditions
of discipline and unity, whereas the Irish church "in its pe-
culiar isolation and security, had indulged, if not cultivated, a
libertarian genius." [7]

The part played by Rome in favor of the English in their
perennial conflicts with the Irish tends to be overlooked. At
the Synod of Whitby in the seventh century, Roman and English interests coalesced to isolate the Irish church as an institution and to prevent it from imposing its discipline and
structural forms beyond the island of Ireland and the western
part of Scotland. Although the Irish monks continued for several centuries to pour into England and onto the Continent,
they were always forced to adjust their practices and those of
their converts to the Roman discipline.[8] And during all that
time, as the Irish retained at home the religious customs they
might no longer export, Rome saw the English as its faithful
servants and the Irish as recalcitrant and doubtful subjects.
While Rome was building up the Constantinian church in
which the state accepted from the Church its social and
moral principles and used its legislative and police powers to
ensure that all citizens embraced and practiced them, in Ireland Church and state went their separate ways. Marriage
and divorce, for example, remained secular affairs determined by secular rules at open variance with the Church's
views. Ireland ignored Rome's pressures to change the ancient customs of married priests and bishops and hereditary
succession to Church offices. Historian Kenneth Nicholls says
that in no field of life was medieval Ireland's isolation from
the mainstream of Christian European society so marked as
in that of marriage.

Throughout the medieval period, and down to the end of the old
order in 1603, what could be called Celtic secular marriage re-

mained the norm in Ireland and Christian matrimony was no more than the rare exception grafted on to the system. Sir John Popham, attorney-general, writing in 1578 of the Munster gentry, declared that no more than one in twenty was married in church, but this may be an exaggeration. This secular marriage permitted easy divorce, and it was normal in late medieval Ireland for men and women of the upper classes to have a succession of spouses.[9]

For such reasons Rome blessed the Anglo-Norman invasion even before it began, and cooperated with the invaders in subsequent centuries in ensuring that only English-born clerics might become bishops in those parts of Ireland the English controlled at any given time. If the situation changed somewhat, though still often ambiguously, at the Reformation, it was not long until Protestant England—now a world power—managed to wield enough diplomatic influence at the Vatican to more than counter the distant voices of the Irish. By the nineteenth century and into the twentieth, the Catholic church in Ireland as an institution had bought the English viewpoint as fed to it from Rome. In all major issues—language, education, Home Rule, welfare, and land reform—its concern to protect its interests and to control the minds of Irishmen took precedence over other considerations.

The libertarian genius to which Toynbee refers affected not only the Church in the period preceding the twelfth-century Anglo-Norman invasion but also political life. Although the country's minor kings and chieftains were nominally subject to one high king, his authority was never effective. Constantly shifting groupings and alliances characterized civil life during both the period of cultural flowering and the subsequent centuries. Although the English invaders never succeeded in imposing their control over the entire island until the seventeenth century, they were always able to maintain a foothold by playing off one Irish group against another. Their principal problem was not Ireland's military strength but the ability of Irish culture to absorb all who came in contact with it. Like the first arrivals about whom Giraldus Cambrensis had complained, each succeeding wave of English invaders quickly became "more Irish than the Irish themselves." The problem would recur century after century until religion entered the picture to provide a new reference point.

It was not that England's rulers, while still Catholic, were less ruthless in their efforts to subjugate Ireland than the Protestants who followed them. From the beginning of the Anglo-Norman invasion, every effort was made to destroy the Irish system of learning and way of life. Fifteenth-century legislation known as Poynings Law provided that all acts of Irish parliaments were to be subject to review or abrogation by the English king and his council, and that the Irish Parliament had no control over the executive named for Ireland by the English king. In addition, it forbade the use of Irish law, Irish names, Irish dress, and the Irish language by the English settled in Ireland. From the outset the occupation was not merely intended to establish military control but to introduce colonizers, part of the movement of peasants which dominated the economic history of western Europe from the eleventh to the fourteenth century. Solid settlements of men of English descent were established on holdings small enough to ensure that most owners cultivated their property by their own labor and that of their family. The native population was usually sparse, so that the newcomers did not have to eliminate it. They simply chose the best land for themselves and let those they dispossessed move to the poorer parts.

By the middle of the thirteenth century, nearly two-thirds of Ireland was controlled by England. Irish rulers were, however, still in undisputed possession of most of Ulster and of small portions of the west and southwest of the island. The Irish fought back successfully for the following hundred years, helped by the assimilation of many of the English settlers, including their highest noblemen, into the Irish language and way of life. In 1315, Edward Bruce, a brother of Robert Bruce, King of Scotland, carried the war against England into Ireland. Supported by the O'Neills of

Ulster and crowned King of Ireland, he held the north for more than three years and raided widely into the English-held parts. He was killed in battle in 1318, which was about the time the plague known as the Black Death reached Ireland. It affected mostly the English settlers and left an infection which recurred for generations. By the fifteenth century, English government was effective only in Dublin and in the adjoining counties of Louth, Kildare, and Meath. Elsewhere, the Anglo-Irish lords had become wholly Irish and co-operated with the native rulers, while Ulster still remained almost untouched by the settlers.

From the time of the loss of France in the fifteenth century, the Tudor monarchs of England concentrated on Wales and Ireland, Henry VIII using the revenues of the suppressed monasteries to expand his control. He had himself declared head of the Church in Ireland, as in England, and he introduced in Ireland the same liturgical changes with one significant exception. Whereas in England the vernacular was substituted for Latin in all religious services, Latin was retained in Ireland. It was recognized that the vernacular, even in places in which the king's writ was otherwise unchallenged, was Irish, and the overriding official policy was to deny that language any status or recognition.

The Catholic Mary and her consort, Philip II of Spain, pursued the policy of reconquest and settlement of Ireland even more vigorously than their predecessors. To the two midland counties of Offaly and Leix, in which they planted settlers from England and expelled a large part of the previous occupants, they gave the names of King's County and Queen's County, in their own honor, names which persisted until the Anglo-Irish Treaty of 1921. During Elizabeth's long reign, covering the last half of the sixteenth century, England's effective control was expanded once more to the entire country outside Ulster. Although the Ulster chieftains were finally defeated in battle and forced to acknowledge British suzerainty, they still retained effective control of their homeland. It was during the reign of Elizabeth, also, that religion became the identifying mark of friend and foe. From that time on, to be a Protestant was to be loyal; to be a Roman Catholic was to be the king's enemy, an outlaw, a rapparee (freebooter), vermin to be destroyed on sight.

James I, Elizabeth's successor, decided to complete the conquest of Ireland by eliminating the surviving Ulster redoubt. His opportunity came when the two principal chieftains, the Earls of Tyrone and Tyrconnell, learned that plans were afoot to imprison them and fled to Spain. Their lands were declared forfeit to the Crown, and a "final solution" of the Ulster problem was decreed. A royal proclamation set out the particulars:

Whereas great scopes and extents of land in the several counties of Armagh, Tyrone, Coleraine, Donegal, Fermanagh and Cavan are escheated and come to our hands by the attainder of sundry traitors and rebels, we considered how much it would advance the welfare of that kingdom if the said land were planted with colonies of civil men and well-affected in religion; whereupon there was a project conceived for the division of the said land into proportions, and for the distribution of the same unto undertakers. . . .[10]

The offer was taken up by large numbers in northern England and southern Scotland. The Scots showed a particular readiness to colonize, and they formed a high proportion of the tenant settlers in Donegal, Down, and Antrim. They introduced a distinctive element into Irish society, differing both in race and in religion from the Englishmen brought in by a joint-stock company formed by the city of London, which received a grant of the city of Derry and changed its name to Londonderry. Whereas the English were Anglicans and identified with the Established Church of Ireland, the Scots were Presbyterians and quickly assumed the role of Protestant nonconformity. By 1640, there were an estimated 40,000 Scots in Ulster, at a time when the entire population of Ireland was probably less than a million.[11]

Twice more during the seventeenth century, Ireland was to experience large-scale warfare, and on both occasions the

Irish chose the losing side, a choice dictated by religion. They supported Charles I against Cromwell, and James II against William of Orange. By this time, with the destruction of their military strength, the Catholic religion had become their last means of self-identification as a separate people and culture. It was a religion significantly revitalized by clergy educated on the continent of Europe, a change which had been forced on the Irish church when its own seminaries and other schools were suppressed at home. One of the consequences was the ready acceptance of the reforms voted by the Council of Trent. For example, Irish law had previously countenanced a plurality of wives and easy divorce. In light of the contemporary criticism of the Republic of Ireland's constitutional prohibition of divorce, it is ironic that the pressure in favor of monogamy came in the seventeenth century simultaneously from the Council of Trent and from English Protestant rulers.[12]

In the seventeenth century, accordingly, the cause of Catholicism became identified with Irish freedom. Freedom, however, had even then a quite different connotation for two groups in Ireland, starting an ambiguity which has remained during the entire subsequent period. The Catholics of the eastern part of the country and of the towns of the south, in large part the descendants of early English settlers, meant by freedom a reestablishment of Ireland as a self-governing kingdom ruled by the same monarch as the neighboring kingdom of England. What they wanted was the repeal of Poynings Law, so that they would be free to write their own laws, including those governing the practice of religion. Catholics in others parts of Ireland, particularly in the north, understood freedom to mean a clean break with all things English. The notion of republicanism as understood today had not yet reached the world. They also wanted Ireland to be a kingdom ruled by a king, but he should be a prince from a Catholic country of Europe, free of pledges to England.

After Cromwell's campaign, it was decreed that all land-owners who had supported Charles should lose their property, and that even those innocent of rebellion against Parliament should retain property only in Connaught, which then included Clare. This decision left the tenants undisturbed, but they all came under Protestant landlords. When the monarchy was restored after Cromwell's death, Charles II made some small moves in favor of the dispossessed Catholic supporters of his father. The succession of his brother, a Roman Catholic, as James II, caused the Protestants to fear that these Catholics would return and oust them. After James II had been deposed by the Parliament in England in favor of William of Orange, who was married to James' daughter, Mary, James fled to Ireland and authorized the Dublin Parliament—consisting mostly of representatives of the "Old English" faction—to restore the land to those who had owned it before the Cromwellian confiscations. Ulster, strongly Presbyterian, resisted, the city of Derry holding out against James' besieging army for 105 days until relieved by a Williamite expedition from England.

William won victories at the Boyne, Aughrim, and Limerick, all of them entering the folklore of both Protestants and Catholics in Ireland, so that even today they continue to stir bitterness and division. The Boyne has long been the central celebration of the Orange calendar, marked by annual processions and vituperative speeches each July 12, while on August 12 the "Apprentice Boys" of Londonderry reenact the gallant defense of that city in 1689. Ironically, the Boyne was simply a rearguard action—and a successful one—to protect James' army while it withdrew to defensible positions, the decisive battle being that at Aughrim a year later. And doubly ironically, the sympathies of the pope were with William of Orange in his efforts to oust his father-in-law. But history has little bearing on myths which have acquired a life and dynamism of their own.

7

Religion Determines Civil Rights

*Its method of managing Ireland was the worst of all possible
expedients, that of endeavoring to inflame the animosities and
deepen the divisions between the Protestants and Catholics.*
— W. E. H. LECKY, historian

*Religious sectarianism originated not in Ireland but in Britain,
whose revolution was fought under the slogans of the Reformation. The final expropriation of the Irish tribal lands proceeded
under the only excuse which would justify naked robbery to
the British people. This was protection against the papacy, for
their practical purposes enshrined not in the spiritual power of
Rome but in the military designs of Spain and France.*
— C. DESMOND GREAVES [1]

The Williamite wars represented the final phase in the
completion of the military conquest of Ireland, and the following century saw the completion of the economic sub-
jugation of the Catholics. In the end they were left with only
one-seventh of the land, and that the poorest and most remote from the centers of wealth and power. The Bill of
Rights enacted by the English Parliament in 1689, and ac-

cepted by William and Mary as a condition of their ascending
the throne, made allegiance to the sovereign conditional on
his profession of Protestantism. Its provisions and implica-
tions, in addition, effectively stripped Catholics of the rights
of citizenship. In the half century that followed, it was reinforced by a series of laws, the so-called Penal Laws, the
purpose of which was to prevent the reemergence in either
Ireland or England of a Catholic property-owning class. They
did not seek to convert Catholics to Protestantism or even to
punish them for being Catholics as much as to exclude them
as a class from property, position, influence, and power.
Catholics were denied access to education, barred from public life, permitted only minimal facilities for worship, and
punished for having dealings with any priests other than
those registered with the authorities and certifiedly loyal.
Subjected as "dissenters" to many of the same limitations,
Presbyterians emigrated in considerable numbers during the
eighteenth century from Ulster to the United States where
they were in high demand as Indian fighters in Appalachia.

By the middle of the eighteenth century, a new social
equilibrium seemed well established. All former differences
among Catholics were submerged in the common poverty
and powerlessness to which aristocracy and peasants, native
Irish and Old English, had been reduced. Later it would
emerge that a difference in goals persisted between those
who favored autonomy under the English crown and those
who would break the English connection utterly; for the moment, however, both could agree on the immediate aim of
survival. Protestants, on the other hand, had become so secure in their monopoly of property and power that they felt
they could openly resist London's determination to run their
affairs. At the same time and basically for the same reasons
the American colonists proclaimed, they began to challenge
England's insistence on controlling their trade for its own
benefit. With the outbreak of hostilities in America, England
transferred most of the troops from Ireland. When France entered the war on the American side, a Protestant volunteer

force was created in Ireland, ostensibly to guard against a French invasion but in fact to give notice to London that times had changed. Within a short time, the demands of the Irish business community for abolition of restrictions on Irish trade were met, and in 1782 the English Parliament renounced its long-asserted claim to legislate for Ireland. The developing French Revolution, with its challenge to all conventional authority, was by this time stirring England to its depths. The direction events were taking in Ireland was particularly disturbing to the English government. It could no longer assume the automatic loyalty of Irish Protestants, and it decided to make overtures to the Catholics whose leaders were in total support of the papacy in its hostility to the French Revolution. An Act of 1793 abrogated most of the penal laws, although it retained the prohibition against Catholics being elected to Parliament. Two years earlier, a group of Presbyterians led by Theobald Wolfe Tone had founded in Belfast the United Irish Society, a radical organization inspired by the French Revolution and committed to "the principles of civil, political, and religious liberty." Wolfe Tone was also elected secretary of the Catholic Committee, an organization of emerging middle-class Catholics created in Dublin to press for an end of religious discrimination. It looked for a moment as if Catholics and Presbyterians would join in what promised to be an unchallengeable alliance.

The government, however, recognized the underlying difference of purpose between Presbyterians seeking an Irish republic based on the French model and Roman Catholics for whom the principles of the French Revolution were abhorrent, and it decided to exploit the differences between them, fomenting religious bitterness in Ulster, infiltrating spies and informers into the ranks of the United Irishmen, and giving the militia free rein for a campaign of terror throughout the country. A massacre of prisoners by the militia in County Wexford in May 1798 precipitated a premature insurrection by Catholics in the southeast of the country. When the news reached Belfast, a contingent of Presbyterians took the field and proclaimed the Irish Republic, the insurgent commanders dating their letters and instructions to "the first year of liberty." But a military base was equally lacking in north and south, and the government forces had no difficulty in stamping out the fires of revolt. The outbreaks were seized upon as excuse for a new wave of terror, preparing the way for abolition of the Irish Parliament and creation of the United Kingdom of Great Britain and Ireland in 1800.

The "union" thus established was no more a true union than was the later incorporation of Algeria into metropolitan France. Ireland was left with a separate administration named by and representing the interests of the imperial power, and the economic relationship became more fully than before that of a colony to the metropolis. The Catholics, however, who never had any representation in the Dublin Parliament, did not regard the Act of Union as making any significant difference in their circumstances. They concentrated in the first part of the nineteenth century, under the leadership of Daniel O'Connell, on the elimination of the remaining restrictions on their civil rights. Having won the right to sit in Parliament in 1829, O'Connell set out to recover for his Catholic followers the social and economic power which they regarded as their due. His demands were soon narrowed to the goal of repeal of the Act of Union. This would mean the setting up of a parliament in Dublin once more, but now a parliament dominated by the Catholic majority of Irishmen. For the Presbyterians, who previously had sought an alliance which would make them the spokesmen for disenfranchised Catholics, the demand created a new and disconcerting situation. They recognized that their deeds of ownership to Irish land were no stronger than those held by the members of the Established Church. If on coming to power Catholics demanded back the land taken from their ancestors, all Protestants would suffer alike. The threat was more than the fragile alliance could sustain. After a short period of uncertainty and internal debate, the Presbyterians threw in their lot with the Established Church and created the polarization of Protestant against Catholic which has ever since dominated the life of Ulster.

The Orange Order was the instrument which brought about this polarization and subsequently maintained it. The Order, established in 1795, found support for many years almost exclusively among members of the Church of Ireland. The people of Armagh, where the first lodge was founded, were of English rather than Scots descent. The purpose of the Order was avowedly to maintain the Protestant monopoly of power. The initiation oath stated:

I do solemnly and sincerely swear of my own free will and accord, that I will, to the utmost of my power, support and defend the present King George III, and all the heirs of the Crown, so long as they support the Protestant ascendancy, the constitution, and laws of these kingdoms; and I do further swear that I am not, nor ever was a Roman Catholic or papist; that I was not, nor ever will be, an United Irishman, and that I never took an oath of secrecy to that society. . . .[2]

The original objective of the Orange Order was to protect the poorer Protestant farmers and to terrorize Catholics who bid against them for land tenancies. The English government's program for the introduction of colonists from Scotland and northern England to Ulster in the early seventeenth century relied largely on merchant adventurers. They were granted ownership of large tracts on condition that they brought over reliable families and settled them as tenants. By the second half of the following century the growth of population was increasing the demand for land. The Protestant tenants in Ulster did indeed have more protection against arbitrary impositions of landlords than did Catholic tenants in the rest of Ireland. Nevertheless, their rights were limited, and the tendency of the courts and the administration was to construe them in an ever more limited way. This was part of a doctrine of the rights of property being developed among English economists and lawyers, a doctrine that would blossom into the Manchester school of laissez-faire. The property owner enjoyed unfettered rights. He could use every stratagem to increase his revenue. Tenancies were usually for a short term, and when it expired, the landlord gave the new tenancy to the highest bidder. The new economic thinking made it respectable for him to allow landless Catholics to enter the bidding. Formerly, those Catholics who had remained in the area in which their ancestors were once the landowners, could never hope to progress beyond the level of hired help. Their entry into the ranks of potential tenants created a crisis. Having lived so long in misery, they could outbid the Protestant competitors, for they were willing to live on less and would be no worse off than before if they overbid and were later forced to default. It was a technique of using the very poor to reduce the power and the share of benefits going to the less poor. Karl Marx in *Das Kapital* describes how English capitalists a little later used Irish laborers in England to squeeze the English workingman.

The Marquess of Donegal and other Protestant landlords were content in the name of progress to see their Protestant tenants forced to emigrate to the United States and be replaced by impoverished peasants who deep in their hearts still regarded as rightfully theirs the acres for which they now had to pay rackrents.[3] Soon, however, the Ulster tenant farmers decided to take the law into their own hands. It was an era of secret societies, and the Orange Order started as one among many, a union of men ready and equipped to use whatever force might be necessary to ensure that Catholics kept their mouths shut at land tenancy auctions. It was not yet the grouping of Protestants against Catholics which it later became. It was a grouping of poor Protestants to assert what they considered their rights against poor Catholics on the one hand and against rich Protestants on the other. In the 1820s, however, when the movement for Catholic emancipation led by O'Connell assumed national proportions, it broadened its perspectives. The decisive moment came when Henry Cooke, a Presbyterian minister descended from a Cal-

vinist who had fought on the walls of Derry in 1689, succeeded in persuading the majority of his followers to join in
opposing O'Connell's movement. It was not an easy victory
for Cooke. He was opposed by an equally famous Presbyterian minister, Henry Montgomery, two of whose brothers
had fought with the United Irishmen when they sought to
drive the English from Ireland and establish a republic in
1798.

The tradition of Belfast up to the time of the confrontation between Cooke and Montgomery had always been liberal and tolerant. But Cooke found a way to change that. He
insisted that every Presbyterian minister and seminarian had
to subscribe to the entirety of the Westminster Confession of
Faith (1645–1647), the most celebrated pronouncement of
English-speaking Calvinism. It was a direct challenge to
Montgomery who found repugnant its description of the
pope as "the anti-Christ" and its overall anti-Catholic bias.
Defeated in the theological conflict, Montgomery withdrew
and founded a separate Non-Subscribing Presbyterian
church. The triumphant Cooke drew into an alliance his own
church, the Orange Order, the landlords against whom that
Order had long fought, and the Established Church of
Ireland with which Presbyterian relations had previously
been hostile. It was the start of an era in which the aspir-
ing preacher's road to preferment was paved with denun-
ciations of the anti-Christ pope. (The tradition lives on in
such contemporary leaders as Rev. Martin Smyth and Rev.
Ian Paisley. The Catholic church remains for them "the scarlet whore of Rome," committed to overthrow of the Northern
Ireland state and to the physical annihilation of all Reformed
Christians.) "Our church is now in a melancholy condition,"
Montgomery observed at the height of his conflict with
Cooke. "Political and religious bigotry have mingled together; and those who foment the persecutions amongst us
have made it their policy so to conjoin the two principles that
scarce an individual is now held orthodox who is not also an
enemy to the civil or religious rights of his fellowmen." [4] He

was an excellent prophet, but even 150 years later still without honor in his own town.

Cooke's success in getting the main body of Presbyterians to join the Church of Ireland in the anti-Catholic Orange Order determined the future direction of Ulster. Belfast quickly became the home of bigotry and conflict. In 1835, the Orange celebrations ended in a riot in which the military used their sabres. A man and a woman were shot dead and many were wounded. Similar outbreaks of violence usually marked the annual processions of Orangemen celebrating the Battle of the Boyne in July and the siege of Londonderry in August. Under pressure from Parliament, the Orange Order was dissolved in 1836 and was not revived for a decade, but even after that date, various laws had to be enacted to prevent provocative parades and processions.[5] In 1867, William Johnston of Ballykilbeg was jailed for leading a banned march of more than 20,000 Orangemen on July 12. He gained so much popularity that he was elected to Parliament, where he helped secure the repeal of the laws restricting parades. Belfast had experienced serious sectarian riots in 1857 and 1864, and henceforth they were to form part of the pattern of its life, with major outbreaks in 1864, 1872, 1880, 1884, 1886, 1893, and 1898.[6] An official commission of inquiry in 1857 said that the celebration of July 12 by the Orange party was "plainly and unmistakably the originating cause of these riots." In 1864 another official commission, blaming the local police force for partisan support of the Orangemen, secured its abolition and the introduction into Belfast of the Royal Irish Constabulary. The Orangemen tried many times to have their own local police revived but were unable to do so until the creation of Northern Ireland as a separate state in 1920.

From early in the nineteenth century, Protestants could see that the power of the Catholics was everywhere increasing at a tempo that threatened their positions of privilege. During the 60 years preceding 1840, the population of Ireland doubled to 8 million, increasing enormously the demand for land. In pursuit of maximum profits, landlords fragmented the rented holdings. It was not only in Ulster that the Catholics, as the most impoverished group, were prepared to allocate a higher proportion of the projected crops to rent, thus coming into direct competition with Protestant leaseholders. Industrial capital, controlled by Protestants, was concentrated in the development of the Protestant city of Belfast which grew from 37,000 in 1821 to 349,000 at the end of the century. Excess rural labor, both Protestant and Catholic, spilled into Belfast in search of jobs, and the pattern of employing labor on a denominational basis was early established, the Protestants keeping for themselves the better-paying jobs. In the 1880s, when the Catholics in Belfast numbered 29 percent of a population of 210,000, a gang of Protestant shipyard workers, armed with iron nuts and rivets, attacked Catholic laborers at the docks. They forced many of them into the river, where one was drowned. It was a scenario that would be frequently replayed over the following century.

In spite of the enormous setback caused by the failure of the potato crops and the resulting famine in the 1840s, Catholic power continued to grow throughout Ireland. Elections to the Westminster Parliament in 1885 returned 85 Irish Nationalists who held the balance of power between England's two major parties, the Conservatives and the Liberals. The result was a commitment by the Liberals to repeal of the Act of Union and the restoration of a parliament in Dublin, a parliament that would now be controlled by the Catholics who formed some 75 percent of the population of Ireland. The Protestants, who had won some 20 Irish seats, mostly in Ulster, naturally lined up with the Conservatives to maintain the Union, in an alliance that still continues. The party's official title has since been the Conservative and Unionist party.

The threat of Home Rule roused the Orangemen to new heights of fury. Typical of their leaders was Thomas Drew, a Church of Ireland priest whose sermons were fanatical tirades against the Catholic church. "I learn by the doctrines, history and daily practices of the Church of Rome," Drew wrote on one occasion, "that the lives of Protestants are endangered, that the laws of England set at nought, and the crown of England subordinated to the dictates of an Italian bishop." Again he told his listeners how "of old times lords of high degree, with their own hands strained on the rack the limbs of the delicate Protestant women, prelates dabbled in the gore of their helpless victims. The cells of the pope's prisons were paved with the calcined bones of men and cemented with human gore and human hair." [7]

Powerful forces in England committed to maintaining the Act of Union encouraged sectarian divisions in Ireland. The motivation of some was crassly commercial. They benefited from the trade between the two countries and from manipulations of that trade which—for example—set the rates for rail and sea freight to favor English exporters at the expense of Irish consignors of goods, and which encouraged Irish banks to place their money in the London capital market rather than at home. Others were dazzled by the rapid and apparently endless expansion of England's wealth and power and became votaries at the shrine of an imperial destiny embracing the entire world, most of all and most obviously Ireland. The historian Macaulay could view with a certain equanimity the possibility that a visitor from New Zealand might one day sit on the ruins of London Bridge and reflect on the caducity of the great. But even this great Liberal became quite irrational when faced with the pigheaded insistence of the Irish to make it their own way. "The repeal of the Union we regard as fatal to the Empire, and we will never consent to it—never, though the country should be surrounded by dangers, . . . never till all has been staked and lost, never till the four quarters of the world have been convulsed by the last struggle of the great English people for their place among the nations." The Irish claim that the country would be better off with its own parliament than as an integral part of "the mother country" thus challenged the most basic assumptions of the empire builders. As for English public opinion, it counted for little. The English were content to leave to their rulers the problems of Ireland.

In all parts of Ireland, Protestants were the largest landowners, the wealthiest merchants, and the leading professionals. They also enjoyed a monopoly of posts in the government administration centered in Dublin Castle. For these favored ones, the Union was beneficial, at least to the extent that it protected their privileged position. But for the masses, including the many poor Protestants, it was costly. When Friedrich Engels made his first tour of Ireland in 1856, accompanied by his Irish wife Mary Burns, he wrote to Karl Marx of the "gendarmes, priests, lawyers, bureaucrats, squires in pleasing confusion, and a total absence of industry." It was hard to understand how all the "parasites" lived, he added, until he saw "the misery of the peasants." The police armed with carbines, bayonets, and handcuffs proved for him that Ireland was "the first English colony." Here, he concluded, "it can be clearly seen that the so-called liberty of the English citizens is based on the oppression of the colonies." It was similarly clear to Engels that those in power needed sectarianism for self-protection. If once the workers joined together, the Union could not long survive.

First among the impositions was a system of taxation which extracted from Ireland for the benefit of the English exchequer twice as much as from Englishmen, in proportion to the ability of the citizens of the two countries to pay. In 1896, a Financial Relations Committee said that Ireland had been mulcted of £325 million during the century. Then British industrial competition began to be felt seriously with the introduction of steam navigation in 1824. The number of workers in the Dublin silk trade fell from 6000 in 1824 to a few hundred 15 years later. Similar cuts in employment were experienced in the manufacture of cotton, leather, woolens, and hats, and the workers who survived were forced to work for less. Operatives in a major Dublin iron foundry, for example, had their weekly wage cut from 50 shillings in 1825 to

12 in 1836. Demand from the growing industrial centers in England kept agriculture buoyant in the first part of the century, with exports of wheat up nearly five times to 2,724,000 bushels between 1805 and 1822. Holdings were subdivided, and bog and mountain lands were reclaimed with spade, crowbar, and gunpowder. Exports of cattle had already begun, 25,000 head in 1801 and 98,000 in 1835. Nevertheless, the demands for land for tillage were so high that the cattle population remained low, a total of 1,863,000 at the 1841 census. The typical peasant farmer produced two crops, potatoes with which he fed his family, and wheat or other grain which he gave the landlord as rent and which the landlord exported to England.

When the potato crop failed in the 1840s, a prohibition of export of wheat would have ensured enough food to prevent famine. But the government insisted that economic laws were more sacred than lives. It repealed long-standing laws which had prevented the importation of grain to England from outside the United Kingdom while still allowing Irish landlords to continue to export their grain supplies to England. The result was a fall in the price of grains, to which Irish landlords responded by evicting the starving peasants and converting their lands to pasture and cattle raising. The value of land fell precipitously, and by 1871 the cattle population had grown to over 3 million. The average annual production of all food crops fell by 25 percent in 20 years from an 1850 level of 2.7 million starch tons, and it never regained that level, not even at the height of the campaign to grow more food during the First World War. But emigration caused the population to decline even more rapidly than the food supply, leaving an additional million starch tons available each year for animal feeds. Thus was developed the export trade in Irish store cattle for fattening and sale in England, a trade that still continues. The end result was to make England less dependent on Ireland than before, now buying a luxury food (beef) instead of the previous staple (grain). Ireland, however, had become more dependent on England by reason of its concentration on producing a luxury food for which there was no alternative market. Meanwhile, in typical colonial fashion, the Irish banks had become agencies for collecting capital and siphoning it off to the London money market where better and safer opportunities for investment existed. Landlords, also, followed their money to London, to which flowed each year millions of pounds from rents.

No event in Irish history was so devastating as this economic war launched under the cover of the potato famine of the 1840s, and none has so impressed itself on the Irish folk memory. "The famine left hatred behind," wrote Cecil Woodham-Smith in *The Great Hunger.* "Between Ireland and England the memory of what was done and endured has lain like a sword. Other famines followed, as other famines had gone before, but it is the terrible years of the Great Hunger which are remembered." [8] For the victims and their descendants there could never be peace while Englishmen had any control of their destiny. Unfortunately, however, the impact of the Famine had been felt principally by the Catholic peasants of the south and west of the country. It was consequently possible for the English Conservatives opposed to this first step in the dismemberment of Empire, to represent the separatist movement as a threat to all Protestants. And that is precisely what Lord Randolph Churchill did in 1886 when Liberal Prime Minister Gladstone accepted office with the support of Parnell's Irish party, promising Home Rule in return. In his own words, Churchill "played the Orange card," delaring that "Home Rule is Rome Rule," and that "Ulster will fight and Ulster will be right." At a mass meeting in Belfast, he said that "Mr. Gladstone asks for time to show whether all these ceremonies and forms which are practised in your Orange lodges are really living symbols or idle and meaningless shibboleths." His speech, in which he urged the Orangemen to use force, if necessary, against the government, had the precise effect he had sought. "From that moment, the excitement in Belfast did not subside," wrote his son Winston.

"Eventually dangerous riots, increasing in fury until they almost amounted to warfare, occurred in the streets between the factions of Orange and Green. Firearms were freely used by the police and combatants. Houses were sacked and men and women killed. The disturbances were savage, repeated and prolonged." [9]

The Churchill tactic succeeded. Nearly a hundred Liberal members of Parliament deserted Gladstone to defeat the Home Rule bill and precipitate a general election. But even if the bill had passed the House of Commons, it would never have succeeded in the House of Lords in which the Conservatives had an overwhelming majority. As this fact became clearer in 1893, when the Commons passed a Home Rule measure only to have it killed by the Lords, the Irish party pushed ever harder with the Liberals to end the veto power of the nonelected and unrepresentative House of Lords. This the liberals undertook to do in 1906 when they again returned to power and in 1911 the Parliament Act stripped the Lords of their veto power. That Act was accepted by the Lords under the threat that the Prime Minister would have the king create enough new peers to override their opposition if they did not accede to it.

This radical change in the English constitution had taken place against the background of rapid world change. The British Empire was still at the height of its power, yet subject to serious threats. Most obvious of these was the growing might of the German Kaiser, determined to expand the bridgehead he had established in Africa and building up a war machine at home that boded ill for England's allies, France and Russia. England had defeated the Boers at the turn of the century but felt it necessary to give them Home Rule in 1906 and to enlarge their autonomy by creating the Union of South Africa as a self-governing dominion in 1910. At home, Conservatives and Liberals were engaged in a see-saw struggle for control of the organs of domestic and imperial power, a struggle in which the two parties were distinguished less by policies than by personalities, and in which both sides were willing to pay generously for votes. From the viewpoint of the Irish party this was excellent, especially because the election of 1910 had once more given it the balance of power between Conservatives and Liberals.

The situation inside Ireland had, however, also changed significantly. For the first time labor was emerging as a significant force under the leadership of James Connolly and James Larkin. Both were sons of working-class Irish emigrants, Connolly having been born in Edinburgh in 1868 and Larkin in Lancashire eight years later. Connolly was an intellectual without schooling, who taught himself to read, went to work at the age of 11 and in due course graduated to his father's job, a manure-carter. A committed socialist, he founded the Irish Socialist Republican party in Dublin in 1896 but enlisted few followers and went to America in 1903. It was only after his return to Ireland in 1911 that he succeeded in building a solid base for his ideas. Meanwhile, Larkin, a great hulking man of extraordinary eloquence, had begun in 1907 to tap the biggest pool of industrial labor in Ireland, Belfast's unskilled workers. Very much aware that sectarianism was ultimately a device of the power structures to keep Catholic and Protestant workers apart, the labor leaders offered a socialist ideology which would transcend religious differences and recognize the reality of class conflict. The Orangemen quickly recognized that their power was being threatened, and through their lodges they succeeded in persuading the Protestant workers that they were preparing their own destruction if they allowed Catholics to join with them on terms of equality. Defeated in Belfast, Larkin next sought to organize Dublin's dockers and transport workers. This time, the employers persuaded the Catholic church to denounce the socialism of the labor movement as anti-God. In a direct test of strength in a general strike in 1912, labor was once more defeated.

Its power was, nevertheless, by no means broken. Convinced that social reform would never come to Ireland while its affairs were decided in London, and that the kind of

Home Rule for which the Irish party was willing to settle
would also make no real change in the power structures, the
labor leaders now set their sights on a workers' republic and
joined openly with the extremist political groups who were
simultaneously starting to surface. Most uncompromising of
these was the Irish Republican Brotherhood (IRB), the secret
society deriving from the Fenians of the previous century
which was committed to physical force as the only way to
drive the English out of Ireland. The IRB gradually penetrated a large number of public movements organized for
more limited purposes but all committed in principle to an
independent Ireland in which the country's distinctive culture could once more flourish. These included the Gaelic
League and Sinn Fein.

The Gaelic League had been founded in 1893 by
Douglas Hyde, a Protestant who was later to become President of Ireland from 1938 to 1945. Its objective was the restoration of the Irish language, which had withstood all the
English efforts to destroy it, from the fifteenth century when
the Poynings Law was passed down to the middle of the
nineteenth century, but which in the second half of the nineteenth century had collapsed in the wake of the Famine and
disappeared as a vernacular except in a few isolated areas,
mostly in the south and southwest. In 1899, Arthur Griffith,
an Irish journalist of Welsh descent, had begun to promote
the expression "Sinn Fein," Gaelic for *ourselves,* as a slogan to signify commitment to the Irish language and culture.
Sinn Fein emerged in 1905 as a political organization, but
its appeal remained limited. Its candidates for election to
Parliament were consistently defeated. Ireland continued to
be represented at Westminster by the Irish party and the
Unionist party, the former returning three-quarters and the
latter one-quarter of the approximately 100 members allocated to Ireland.

The Home Rule bill for which the Irish party was prepared to settle passed in the House of Commons in 1912. It
conferred on a Dublin Parliament a very modest measure of

autonomy. Westminster would retain control of foreign affairs, the army, and taxation. It would, however, give Dublin—after an interval—control of the police force, a provision which was immediately seized upon by the Orange intransigents as proof that England was about to hand them over to Rome rule. Under the Parliament Act, the House of Lords could delay enactment of the measure for two years, and the Orange leaders set out to create in these two years a situation which would make it impossible to put the measure into effect. With the aid of leading English politicians and military men, they embarked on a bold program of challenge of the authority of Parliament. Its leaders were Sir Edward Carson, a Dublin-born lawyer who had already held office in a Conservative government and who would return to the cabinet in the coalition government formed shortly after the outbreak of World War I in 1914; and a stockbroker named James Craig, who would much later be raised to the peerage as Lord Craigavon after many years as Prime Minister of Northern Ireland. Their supporters in England included the most powerful and prestigious elements in the society, almost all the proprietors and publishers of newspapers, the aristocracy, wealthy businessmen, and members of the professional classes. The higher commands in the army and navy fomented civil war and pledged themselves to support it. Sir Henry Wilson held one of the most confidential posts in the War Office. Lord Roberts was head of that office and as such the final civilian controller of the armed forces.

The campaign concentrated on two objectives: an attempt to get Parliament to modify its decision, and a preparation for sabotage and war if this failed. For the first time the issue of partition of Ireland became a practical one. The Unionist leaders recognized that they could not hope to control the entire country, and the discussion narrowed down quickly to the question of how much they could control. The first option was to take over the historic province of Ulster, consisting of the nine counties of Donegal, Londonderry, Antrim, Down, Armagh, Monaghan, Tyrone, Fermanagh, and

Cavan. It was quickly recognized, however, that a Unionist majority could not be guaranteed in Ulster. A by-election in the city of Londonderry in 1913 confirmed this. The seat was captured by the Irish party, reducing to 16 the number of Unionist members sitting for Ulster, with 17 on the other side. The Unionists then proposed that Home Rule should be limited to the rest of Ireland, leaving the whole of Ulster under direct rule from Westminster in the same way the entire country had been ruled since 1800. London, however, refused to consider that solution. Presumably it feared that a region in which half the inhabitants were opposed to the basic assumption on which it would have to be ruled was ungovernable. If the country was to be partitioned, it should be into two parts, each of which would stand in the same relationship to the central government in London.

The solution, as formulated in the Government of Ireland Act of 1920, was a measure so unsatisfactory to all the parties concerned that not a single Irish member of the Westminster Parliament, Unionist or Nationalist, voted for it. The act provided that both parts of partitioned Ireland would remain as integral parts of the United Kingdom, and that "the supreme authority of the Parliament of the United Kingdom would remain unaffected and undiminished over all persons, matters and things" in the area of jurisdiction of the Dublin and Belfast parliaments. They were furthermore specifically debarred from legislating on the Crown, peace and war, the armed forces, treaties with foreign states, treason, naturalization, trade with any place outside the jurisdiction, radio, air navigation, lighthouses, coinage, weights and measures, copyrights, and patents. This meant that they lacked control of the post office, the savings banks, and about 90 percent of their own taxation. They were, however, given control of the administration of justice, including the police, and of housing, powers which the government of Northern Ireland was to use very effectively to benefit one section of the population at the expense of the other. Authority in fiscal matters would be closely restricted, with revenue derived mainly from taxes imposed and collected under the authority of Westminster. Revenue collected in or attributable to the region would be put in a separate fund, and the regional parliament could use this money along with the small amount it might raise on its own authority to pay the costs of the local government. The regional parliament also was to pay an agreed share of the costs of common expenditure, such as for the armed forces, foreign affairs, and other general purposes of the kingdom. Northern Ireland did in fact make such a contribution to London in the first years of its existence. But the economic depression of the 1930s hit it harder than Great Britain as a whole, and subsequently the cost of government grew enormously, especially with the development of the welfare state. In consequence, Northern Ireland has been subsidized for many years, and it is agreed it cannot in the foreseeable future maintain the British level of social services without continuing British aid.

By 1920, however, when London finally decided to implement a form of Home Rule comparable to that proposed in the 1914 Act (implementation had been postponed for the duration of the First World War, and then simply forgotten), the balance of forces in Ireland had shifted radically. The Nationalist movement, which the vast majority of Irishmen had backed for more than a century, was based on the assumption that it was possible to find a permanent solution to Ireland's problems within the British constitutional framework. Its goal was not separation of the two islands but a simple adjustment of their relations so that each might manage its own affairs within a common citizenship and subject to a single ultimate sovereign authority, the Parliament at Westminster. That assumption was shattered by the British response to the appeal to arms made by the Orangemen when it became clear in 1911 that the veto power of the House of Lords would soon be curbed and that it would then no longer be possible to depend on the Lords to prevent Home Rule. Hitherto it had been agreed on all sides that the issues were to be settled by democratic means and within the framework of British constitutional conventions and procedures. The Orangemen were first to repudiate that assumption, when the methods of British "democracy" ceased to be automatically manipulable, making physical force not only respectable but ultimately the only option for all parties.

The first step in support of the new strategy was a visit to Belfast by Sir Edward Carson in 1911, where James Craig welcomed him with a 50,000-man Orange parade. Carson told his listeners that they must prepare themselves to assume the responsibility of governing "the Protestant province of Ulster." The response was the creation of a commission to prepare for a provisional government of Ulster, followed by the reorganization of the armed blacklegs who had been used in 1907 to disrupt the trade-union activities of James Larkin. The Conservatives in England immediately espoused their cause for several reasons. They were committed to the preservation and expansion of the British Empire, and they feared the negative impact in India and elsewhere of the withdrawal of the first colony, the one which had longest shared the benefits of membership. If the Empire could not even integrate a neighboring island inhabited by people of the same race and speaking the same language, how could it justify itself to Asians and Africans? They were also influenced by a residual anti-Catholicism, now more cultural than theological. The 1689 Bill of Rights and the Act of Settlement had not only transferred ultimate sovereignty from the king to Parliament but had made allegiance to the Crown conditional on the maintenance of the Protestant political ascendency. Home Rule would put an end to the Protestant control of the administrative machinery in the area to which it applied, and that meant jobs held by relatives, friends, and supporters of the Conservative leaders. Finally, and perhaps most importantly, the Conservatives saw Ulster as an issue which would destroy the Liberal party, the bunch of radical upstarts who were set to tear down that happy combination of traditions and conventions which constituted the English way of life.

England split, accordingly, on party lines. Winston Churchill, who had started his political career as a Conservative but at this point was a Liberal, agreed to join the top Nationalist leaders at a rally in Ulster Hall, Belfast. When he got there, however, he quickly realized what his father had done when he "played the Orange card." Not only Ulster Hall but every hall in Belfast was closed to them, and they had to settle for a football field in the Catholic ghetto. Bonar Law, leader of the Conservatives, next showed up in Belfast with a retinue of 70 members of the Westminster Parliament and pledged to a crowd of 100,000 his support for their threat to defy Parliament. Later Bonar Law added that he could imagine no extreme of resistance to which the Orangemen might go that he and the overwhelming majority of British would not support. To which Carson added that he didn't mind if it was treason, because in the struggle "the best in England" would be with them. Frederick E. Smith, later Lord Birkenhead, a leading lawyer, said that "there is no length to which Ulster would not be entitled to go, however desperate or unconditional." 10

As the Home Rule bill went forward, so did the open training of a militia force, the Ulster Volunteers. They were equipped with modern rifles brought in illegally from Germany under the noses of the authorities, and Carson assured them that he had pledges from "some of the greatest generals in the army" to come over from England and lead them. Bonar Law, recalling the repudiation of King James II in 1688 in favor of William of Orange, publicly called on the officers of the British army to disobey orders if directed to enforce Home Rule. King George V added his support behind the scenes, warning Asquith that a danger of army mutiny existed if the government went ahead with Home Rule. That danger became a reality in 1914, when 50 officers stationed at the main British army base in Ireland, the Curragh, announced their intention to resign their commissions rather than lead their troops against Ulster. After a period of vacillation, the War Office yielded to the ultimatum, assuring the officers that British troops would not be employed to force the Ulster Volunteers to accept Home Rule.

The Curragh mutiny occurred in March, less than five months before Germany would invade Belgium and precipitate World War I. The German generals, already pushing forward feverish war preparations, were elated. They assured the Kaiser that he could proceed safely with his expansionist plans. Even if England were to join France and Russia against him, they said, it would be paralyzed by internal conflict and civil war in Ireland. Historians tend to believe that this German reading of the events in Ireland did in fact influence Germany's decision to embark on the bloody venture. Those events and the British response to them certainly played a decisive part in reversing the policy of peaceful agitation to which most of the Irish had been committed since Daniel O'Connell's unarmed victories in the British Parliament nearly a century earlier. Henceforth, violence would be respectable. Or as Patrick Pearse, a young schoolteacher who would shortly proclaim a republic under arms and pay for the gesture with his life, put it: the Orangeman might be ridiculous insofar as he believed incredible things, but not in his willingness and ability to fight for what he believed.

8

Sinn Fein Opts for Physical Force

*No people hate as we do in whom the past is always alive.
There are moments when hatred poisons my life and I accuse
myself of effeminacy because I have not given it adequate expression. . . . My hatred tortures me with love, my love with
hate.*

— WILLIAM BUTLER YEATS [1]

The dramatic success of the appeal to force by the
Orangemen and their highly placed English allies had a traumatic impact on the rest of Ireland. The previously dis-
credited extremists immediately moved to center stage. They
had a magnetic spokesman in Patrick Henry Pearse, a bilin-
gual poet, dreamer, and schoolmaster in his mid-thirties, son
of an English father and an Irish mother. Tall and dignified,
he neither drank nor smoked. A quotation from Cú Chulainn,
hero of Irish saga, emblazoned on the walls of his school, expressed perfectly his belief in his destiny. "I care not that I
am only one day in the world, provided I am famous." [2]
Pearse urged all seeking Home Rule to set up their own militia. In words and images drawn directly from the prophets

who had reawakened Israel from its deepest degradation and despoilment, he plucked at the heartstrings of Ireland.

> My mother bore me in bondage,
> in bondage my mother was born,
> I am the blood of serfs;
> The children with whom I have played,
> the men and women with whom I have eaten
> Have had masters over them,
> they have been under the lash of masters.
> And though gentle, have served churls. . . .

> I am flesh of the flesh of these lowly,
> I am bone of their bone,
> I have never submitted. . . .
> I say to my people that they are holy, that they are august,
> despite their chains
> That they are greater than those that hold them,
> and stronger and purer.
> That they have but need of courage,
> and to call on the name of their God,
> God the unforgetting, the dear God that loves the peoples
> For whom He died naked, suffering shame.

> And I say to my people's masters: Beware,
> Beware of the thing that is coming, beware of the risen people
> Who shall take what ye would not give. . . .[3]

The thing that was coming was rapidly taking shape. In 1913, Larkin and Connolly created a Citizen Army to protect meetings of trade unionists which were being broken up by hired goons, and a little later Eoin MacNeill started the Irish Volunteers. Born in the Glens of Antrim just north of Belfast, in an isolated area that had never lost the Irish language or its ancestral loyalties, MacNeill was like Pearse in that he projected a dreamy otherworldliness, which the Irish regard highly in their leaders. A founder in 1893 with Douglas Hyde of the Gaelic League dedicated to the revival of the Irish language, he was an eminently respectable professor in the Dublin college of the National University, an expert in the sophisticated Brehon system of laws and institutions which had governed Ireland before the Anglo-Norman invasion. His associates in the Volunteers included members of Sinn Fein and of the Irish Republican Brotherhood (IRB), of which Pearse was a member but not the more moderate MacNeill. A women's auxiliary, the Cumann na mBan, served as a nursing corps and performed courier and other noncombatant services. It was led by such women as Countess Constance Markiewicz, a cousin of poet William Butler Yeats, who would enter Irish folk history for her prowess as a rifleman during the Easter Rising of 1916, and Madame Maud Gonne Mac-Bride, whom Yeats described—quite correctly—as the most beautiful woman in the world.

The Citizen Army was well trained and disciplined, but small in numbers. It was headed by James Connolly, a dedicated socialist, an iron-willed man who believed in equal rights for women. By the middle of 1914 it was claiming a thousand members. The Irish Parliamentary party headed by John Redmond gained control of the Irish Volunteers in early 1914. Recruitment soared, so that by the outbreak of World War I in August there were 180,000 men with some basic training but few arms. With war came new complications. In response to the upsurge of national feeling in Britain, both the Parliamentary party and the Orangemen pledged their respective armies to fight for the Empire, the former for the promise of Home Rule, the latter for the postponement of implementation of the Home Rule law until the end of the war. The original founders of the Irish Volunteers succeeded in regaining control of the organization in September, and they repudiated the agreement to send the Volunteers to fight in France, demanding as their price for this favor the immediate implementation of Home Rule.

The overwhelming majority of the Irish public still supported the Parliamentary party, however, and this was reflected in the split which quickly followed in the Volunteers. Only 12,000 of the 180,000 in training accepted the decision of the new executive. The others were reformed as the Irish National Volunteers, the government promising to

equip them and to recognize them as a separate expeditionary force, as it had done both for the Ulster Volunteers
and the volunteer units from various Commonwealth countries. The War Office in London, however, always obsessed
with the fear that Irish arms would in the end be turned
against England, refused absolutely to carry out the under-
taking and insisted that any volunteers from Ireland—other
than the Ulster Volunteers—be incorporated into existing
units. For the Sinn Feiners this was yet another example of
England's perennial duplicity, and they used it to slow down
the rush to join the forces. Nevertheless, by the end of the
war an estimated quarter of a million had joined up from the
south of Ireland and a further 60,000 from the six counties
which were later to become Northern Ireland. The Ulster
Volunteers suffered enormous losses at the Battle of the
Somme in 1916, a day enshrined in Ulster folk memory with
the Battle of the Boyne and other memorabilia of Orangedom.
The undeniable gallantry of the Orangemen at the Somme is
contrasted with the perfidy of the Fenians who that same
year stabbed the Empire in the back by their Easter Rising in
Dublin. What such limited folk memory omits is that propor-
tionately heavier losses were sustained with equal gallantry
by their brothers from the south. By the war's end in 1918,
Irish combat deaths were 49,400, of which 10,000 were men
of the north.[4]

    The groups who refused to fight England's war either ab-
solutely or until Home Rule had first been granted found
themselves in an extreme minority position after most of the
original Irish Volunteers decided to follow the Irish Parliamentary party. By this time, some newspapers were beginning to identify these groups collectively as Sinn Fein.
Although the Sinn Fein organization was only one of many,
the name stuck; and it ultimately enshrined Sinn Fein in history as the nucleus of the separatist movement. Within the
group there were members of several political persuasions, ten-
dencies which have a continuing importance because they
were carried over into the subsequent political life of Ireland.

On the left was the Citizen Army, its leaders committed to socialism and seeing themselves as part of a world movement
to free the workers from the injustices of capitalism. Among
themselves they were ideologically divided on the issue of
support of Irish nationalism. The majority, led by James Connolly, took the position that the political aspirations of the
Irish must first be satisfied before they could be persuaded to
deal with the more basic issue of class exploitation. Others
rejected all forms of nationalism, as being part of bourgeois
society; one being a still little-known playwright in his middle thirties, Sean O'Casey. He felt so strongly on the issue that
he resigned from the Citizen Army and withdrew unhappily
to the sidelines. Yet he continued to brood about his former
companions and their motivations. The shams, the crudity,
the pettiness, the greed, and the violence of Dublin life
enshrined in the ever-popular *The Plough and the Stars* indicates O'Casey's lifelong obsession with the society he
loved and his radical vision for it. In addition to the ideological conflict within the Citizen Army, tension was increased
by the fact that practically all the members were Roman
Catholics and hesitant to break radically with the policy of
the Church, which at that time condemned all forms of socialism.

On the right wing was the numerically strongest element, people ideologically committed to the capitalist system
and unsympathetic to the growing demands of labor for recognition. Their spokesmen included Eoin MacNeill and Arthur Griffith. Prepared to go to almost any lengths to avoid
condemnation by the Church, they argued that in a self-
governing Ireland the Church would have more support for
its objectives than within the existing system. The regime
they sought was little different from that for which the Irish
and Anglo-Irish had opposed Cromwell in the seventeenth
century. They were willing to remain in the British Empire, provided only that they were allowed to run their own
affairs. Their concept of social change was limited to disman-
tling the structures biased in favor of Protestants which En-

glish governments had created and protected over several centuries.

Between these two extremes was the group which contained the most dynamic and persuasive leaders, Patrick Pearse, Thomas MacDonagh, and an old Fenian named Thomas Clarke. Their aims were, like those of the right, primarily political rather than social. But they wanted a total break with England, an independent republic in the tradition of Wolfe Tone and the French Revolution, though always within a Catholic framework that created many tensions and ambiguities for them. It was this group which pushed the idea of armed rebellion while the war was still undecided, recalling the maxim of a nineteenth-century Fenian that England's difficulty is Ireland's opportunity. The right was willing to go along, but reluctantly, and subject to the condition of receiving German supplies of arms and equipment in sufficient quantity to give some assurance of success. With news that German arms were on the sea, an uprising was planned for Easter 1916. Learning at the last moment that the arms ship had been intercepted and sunk and that the Irish envoy to Germany had been captured after landing on the Irish shore from a German submarine, MacNeill canceled the orders. Pearse and his friends decided, however, to make a token stand. Joined by Connolly and 220 members of the Citizen Army, they assembled 1,000 Irish Volunteers and some members of the youth and women's auxiliaries. On Easter Monday they seized the central post office and other buildings in Dublin, and proclaimed Ireland an independent republic. The English authorities replied with massive infantry and artillery attacks which destroyed a large part of the city and caused heavy casualties before the survivors surrendered the following Saturday.

The initial Irish Nationalist reaction to the Easter Rising was overwhelmingly negative. The vast majority of Irishmen remained convinced that the best way to secure self-government was to cooperate with the British, as the Parliamentary party advocated. The British authorities, however, were in a vengeful mood and decided to make an example of the men who had, as they saw it, stabbed them in the back. One by one they court-martialed and shot all the top leaders of the rebellion, including the 58-year-old Clarke. Connolly, mortally wounded during the insurrection, had to be carried in a chair to face the firing party. It was a capital blunder. The national revulsion was total and immediate. Even those who most opposed all Connolly stood for were outraged. Meanwhile the British increased their repressive activities. In addition to the men who had surrendered, large numbers of others were rounded up and interned in England. In the jails and internment camps, however, the prisoners reorganized, as did their supporters outside. Lloyd George, the wily Welshman who became British Prime Minister in December 1916, recognized that the repression had been counterproductive. One of his first acts in office was to release the internees, and six months later he also paroled those serving court sentences. They included two men who would head the new leadership, the 32-year-old Eamon de Valera, the highest officer to escape execution after the Easter Rebellion, and a youth of 27, a civil servant named Michael Collins. De Valera had been born in New York, and his reprieve was generally credited to the anxiety of the British government not to offend United States sentiment which was turning steadily toward the Allied cause. De Valera was the unchallenged heir to the mantle of the executed leaders. Collins became Director of Organization of the Irish Volunteers. He played a key role during the following critical years, particularly because of his genius in espionage and counterespionage.

The country's new mood was established in February 1917 when the Sinn Fein candidate, the father of an executed 1916 leader, was decisive victor over the candidate of the Parliamentary party in a by-election for the British Parliament. He set a new style by boycotting Parliament as a usurping authority. The British government, anxious to avoid additional trouble in Ireland while the war was still in doubt and sensitive also to United States opinion, made further efforts for a compromise. But it was hopelessly out of touch with the changing mood of Ireland. An attempt to bring all the competing factions together in an Irish convention was aborted by Sinn Fein's boycott. Even the older politicians who attended felt the need to escalate their demands in response to the changed expectations of the public. While some would still settle for Home Rule, provided it applied to the entire island as a unit, others were now insisting on the much wider autonomy enjoyed by Canada, Australia, and the other self-governing dominions.

The British alternated the stick with the carrot. They arrested the principal Sinn Fein leaders early in 1918 on the pretext of a German plot, and, at about the same time, Parliament decided to extend conscription to Ireland, a move that resulted in an unprecedented unification of Nationalist elements in a covenant to resist conscription by all nonviolent means. In spite of the loss of face, the government was forced to scrap the conscription law.

The decisive showdown came in December 1918 when a general election to the British Parliament was held just a month after the war had ended with an Allied victory. It was the first election held under universal suffrage, with one vote for every man and woman over 21. Sinn Fein put up candidates pledged to boycott Parliament if elected. Their platform called for measures to secure the international recognition of Ireland as an independent Republic. Their social program, though still cautious, called for a guaranteed living wage for workers and better housing. The Parliamentary party, sensing the national mood, now wanted dominion status rather than Home Rule. The Unionists remained opposed to any change in the existing political status of Ireland as an integral part of the United Kingdom ruled directly from London.

Sinn Fein won an unprecedented victory, securing 73 of the 105 Irish seats, this in spite of the fact that most of its candidates were in jail. In Ulster the Unionists won 18 of the 35 seats, a number corresponding almost exactly to the ratio of

Catholics and Protestants in that province. The Parliamentary party was practically wiped out. The Sinn Fein deputies who were not in jail met in Dublin on January 21, 1919, to reaffirm the continuing existence of the Irish Republic which had been proclaimed by the Fenians in 1858 and reproclaimed by the Provisional Government established in Dublin in 1916 during the Easter Rising. They set up a government organization to collect taxes and administer justice. It included a defense department which assumed responsibility for the Irish Volunteers, now officially renamed the Irish Republican Army (IRA). These were not purely formal or technical steps, for they had an immediate political significance within the context of Irish Catholicism. Previously, any group committed to physical force, or binding its members by secret oaths, was automatically condemned by the Church in pursuance of a policy established in the previous century. Many had found ways to live with their consciences, but few were comfortable in their conflicting allegiances. Henceforth, the IRA was the official army of a sovereign state, the Irish Republic, and that meant that one of the most serious handicaps which Irish separatist movements had suffered was eliminated. Henceforth, the Church would bless Irish arms and condemn as usurpers those who fought on the other side.

Within a short time, the British administration outside Ulster had ground to a halt. Justice was administered in Sinn Fein courts, and the IRA executed the judgments. People stopped paying taxes to the British administration, and many handed at least part of the money instead to Sinn Fein. The success in the elections to Parliament was paralleled at the county and city levels. Soon the local administrations across the country were controlled by Sinn Fein and executed its policies.

The British government, still headed by Lloyd George, replied with a two-pronged strategy: a political policy calculated to woo the people away from Sinn Fein by granting a part of the Nationalist demands, and a military policy of repression of Sinn Fein. The policy of repression was primarily carried out by the Black-and-Tans and the Auxiliaries, two paramilitary bodies recruited mainly in England, in large part among the demobilized veterans of the recent war. The Black-and-Tans, whose barbarities have enshrined them permanently in Irish folklore just a notch above Cromwell, got their nickname from a uniform combining police tunics with army pants, an indication of the haste with which they had been assembled. The principal political gesture was the already mentioned Government of Ireland Act of 1920 which provided for two administrations in a divided Ireland, one embracing northeast Ulster with a two-to-one Unionist (Protestant) majority, one for the rest of the island with an overwhelming Nationalist majority and more than 90 percent Roman Catholic.

As subsequent historical investigation has established, the various British governments involved during and after the war never approached the issues on the basis of the wishes of the Irish people but always in terms of their political struggles at home and the interests of the British Empire as they conceived them. At the same time that they were giving mutually contradictory assurances to Arabs and Jews regarding the future of Palestine, they were making comparable promises in Ireland. Lloyd George assured the leaders of the Irish Parliamentary party that exclusion of six Ulster counties from the jurisdiction of an all-Ireland Parliament would be only temporary, while telling Sir Edward Carson, the Unionist leader, that the north would never be allowed to join the south even if it wanted to.

The Unionists won 40 of the 52 seats in elections held in 1921 for the newly established state of Northern Ireland, and King George V opened the Parliament in June. With massive help from British troops the activities of the IRA within the state's borders were kept under control, and the process of developing the administrative organs, including a police force, went forward vigorously. Soon, however, a new threat developed. As mentioned above, the Anglo-Irish Treaty signed in December 1921 by representatives of the British government and of Sinn Fein stipulated that the whole of Ireland would come under the overriding jurisdiction of an all-Ireland Parliament envisaged by the treaty, unless Northern Ireland voted against it within six months. It further provided that, if Northern Ireland did vote against it, a joint commission would be set up by the Westminster, Stormont, and Dublin governments to redraw the partition line "in accordance with the wishes of the inhabitants, so far as may be compatible with economic and geographic conditions." Since the city of Derry, the counties of Tyrone and Fermanagh, and the southern halves of Armagh and Down—all of them situated along the existing border—had Catholic majorities, this clause constituted a threat that the area of Northern Ireland might be shrunk to half its size, left only with the city of Belfast and its immediate surroundings.

Northern Ireland opted out without delay, but the issue of the border commission remained unsolved for several years, with consequent unrest in the areas which might be affected by the commission's decision. The Stormont government decided that delaying tactics were in its interest, refusing to name a member to the proposed commission on the ground that it was not bound by a treaty it had not signed. As things turned out, it had no cause for worry. The British government used its reserve powers to name the Stormont representative as well as its own, and the two proceeded to gang up on the Irish representative, arguing that the overriding condition was the economic one, that is, that the economic viability of Northern Ireland would be furthered by the inclusion of some additional territory rather than by giving up part of what it already had. The Dublin government was in a particularly weak position. The treaty had been approved by a bare majority of the Sinn Fein Parliament, and an ensuing general election confirmed that the country was hopelessly split on the question of whether or not the Irish should settle for dominion status within the British Empire rather than the Republic for which the Anglo-Irish War had been fought. A large part of the IRA, contending that its oath of allegiance to the Republic still bound, refused to accept the legitimacy of the successor Free State government, and a bloody civil war ensued in 1922 and 1923 that left the Free State an economic shambles, unsure of itself and bitterly divided. In these circumstances, its leaders felt they had secured the best possible deal when they agreed to accept the existing border as definitive in return for remission by Britain of some of the debt obligations the Free State had assumed in the Anglo-Irish Treaty. But neither they nor their followers, and still less the Republican opponents they had just defeated in the civil war, felt the decision was anything more than yet another form of English aggression. Maps could now be printed without fear that they would soon have to be scrapped, but the Irish Question still lacked an answer. And because it lacked an answer, the IRA would continue for the foreseeable future to enjoy the respect and support of large numbers of Irishmen, even though it was now proscribed in the Free State as well as in Northern Ireland. Why it still enjoyed this support and how it used it will be told in the following chapters.

9

Enter the IRA

In Ireland there are two acceptable reactions to a crisis. The first is to get down on your knees and pray to God. The second is to go down on one knee, lift a gun and try to shoot the head off your opponent.

—Rosita Sweetman [1]

The Irish attitude to violence has long been ambivalent. For 200 years and more, the leaders of the Roman Catholic church in Ireland, as in Italy and many other countries, have been economically and emotionally tied to the monied interests. They have, in consequence, been inflexibly opposed to those violent world movements which threaten the status quo—that is, their own material and spiritual power and that of their friends. They lumped together French revolutionaries, Garibaldi's *carabinieri*, Bakunin's anarchists, and Marx's Communists, as forming part of the worldwide conspiracy impiously proclaiming equal rights for all, "levellers," as Pope Pius IX called them.

The British government was definitely sympathetic to Garibaldi and made no effort to keep Karl Marx out of the British Museum, the resources of which were so necessary to him as he wrote *Das Kapital*. But it liked the way the bishops in Ireland warned their devout flocks to shun all enemies of the social order that had been immutably ordained by God and was upheld in Ireland by the most respectful, albeit heretical, armed forces of His (or Her) Majesty's government.

The Lord Lieutenant and the Home Secretary never passed up an opportunity to encourage a bishop to recall Rome's direct prohibitions and excommunications in readiness for whomever endangered his own eternal salvation by joining oath-bound secret societies plotting against Church or state. Such warnings were not taken lightly by Irish Catholics accustomed to blind obedience to priest and bishop and heirs of a tradition of reverence toward Rome.

And yet there were stubborn facts. You couldn't deny what your bishop proclaimed in a solemn pastoral letter. But neither could you deny a fact. One such fact was that British rule in Ireland was unjust, resting on no other foundation than power, the power that had robbed Irish Catholics of their property and given it to heretics, the power still being used in favor of heretics against Catholics, or—as George ("AE") Russell once put it so well in a response to imperial poet laureate Rudyard Kipling—"ever quick to defend the strong against the weak." Neither could you deny the fact that British power was such that counterforce could be built up only in absolute secrecy, and British duplicity such that the most binding oaths were hardly adequate to protect the conspirers from infiltrators.

Such facts were so stubborn as to overcome the scruples of many Irish Catholics in every generation. The tension, nevertheless, always remained. Often it drove the oath takers to cast off other restraints along with their obedience to Rome. And thus developed the myth of the gunman, the first of those "freedom fighters" whose popularity spread around the globe in the second half of the twentieth century, a man committed to the simple ideal of freeing his country from its oppressors, authorized to use all available means for that end, seeking no glory other than martyrdom, faithful in his own way to a Church that did not understand him. Watered with his blood, as with the blood of those who had gone before, the seed of freedom would sprout from the ground and bloom at the moment least expected. Such is the myth and the mystique of the IRA. Its strength and endurance will be understood only when it is realized that some considerable part of this curious emotional mixture exists in every man of Irish blood and background who has ever in any way identified himself with the national dream of an Ireland free from foreign control and manipulation. As the IRA man is ambivalent toward his Church, so other Irishmen are ambivalent toward him. If they cannot support him, they must do violence to themselves to oppose him. So it has been at least as far back as the creation of the Irish Republican Brotherhood, otherwise known as the Fenian Society. Michael Doheny and John O'Mahony, two survivors of the minor insurrection engineered by the Young Irelanders in 1848, started it in New York on Saint Patrick's Day, 1858. They were already in touch with James Stephens, another 1848 veteran, who had returned to Dublin from Paris in 1856, and he undertook to recruit members for them in Ireland. The "organization," as its members usually called it, was quickly banned by the Irish bishops. "Those who engage in and encourage secret plots and conspiracies," said Archbishop Paul Cullen of Dublin, "may think they are patriots, but they are the worst enemies of their country." [2] The Fenians thought of themselves as having a single military role, namely, to expel the English from Ireland, and they avoided formulating any social program that might distract the members from that purpose. The only concession they made to the mood of potential recruits was a general expression of commitment to agrarian reform envisaged as a return to its rightful owners of land usurped by "an alien aristocracy." [3]

In the light of later history and contemporary conflicts within the IRA, it is significant that the original Fenians lacked an ideology. The social novelties then flying around

Europe, from Karl Marx's *Communist Manifesto* to Bakunin's anarchism, the utopian socialism of Robert Owen, and the reforms proposed by the British Chartists, scarcely touched them. Their program started and ended with violent national revolution. All of Ireland's problems could be solved with a gun, the gun that would chase the British out of the country.

Thanks to the ban of the bishops, a ban reinforced in 1870 by a papal decree of condemnation, Fenianism never acquired a mass following in Ireland. It was limited mostly to small groups in the towns and cities, and was for a time more successful in the United States, where hatred of England was the dominant emotion of the immigrants from Ireland and where the social control of the Church was less pervasive. A convention in Cincinnati in 1865 decided to attack the British in Canada, and the following year General John O'Neill led 800 men—most of them Civil War veterans—across the Niagara river and captured Fort Erie.[4] Cut off by United States troops, he was forced to retreat toward Buffalo, where most of his men were arrested. Several other border raids were similarly unsuccessful. At most, they increased the tension between Britain and the United States at the end of the Civil War, and they had the indirect effect of encouraging the confederation of Canada as a measure of defense against expansionist designs from the United States. Thereafter, Fenianism declined on both sides of the Atlantic. An attempted rebellion in Ireland in 1867 mostly demonstrated its weakness. A few policemen sufficed to deal with the handful of ill-armed and ill-trained revolutionaries who answered the call.

The movement, nevertheless, did not die out entirely. Under the alternative name of the Irish Republican Brotherhood, a few of the faithful continued their dreams and their schemings, mostly in the United States but always with contacts in Ireland. The revival of a sense of Irish nationalism at the end of the nineteenth century and the start of the twentieth, expressed in the movement to restore the Irish language as the vernacular, in the Sinn Fein program of self-respect and self-reliance, and in the literary movement centered on the Abbey Theater, was not the work of the IRB but it quickly redounded to its benefit. When elements within that movement decided that physical force was a necessary part of a program to free Ireland, it sought its roots in the tradition that went back to the republicanism of the eighteenth century and continued through Wolfe Tone and the United Irishmen, Robert Emmet in 1803, John Mitchel in 1848, and finally the Fenians and the Irish Republican Brotherhood. Returning to Ireland from New York in 1907, Tom Clarke set out to bring together in the IRB the more extremist of the emerging new leaders and fashion them into a secret top-level decision-making group. He seemed an extraordinary choice for this vital task. At 49 he was in poor health as a result of 15 years spent in English jails and was out of touch with the changing Irish scene because he spent the following 9 years in America. Even his appearance was unimpressive. As he stood every day and all day behind a counter, he looked exactly the role he had chosen as cover, the seedy proprietor of a small tobacconist shop in Dublin, receding hairline, with a drooping moustache and cheap eyeglasses. But the constant stream of customers did more than buy their smoking supplies: they transmitted information, contacted key people, and quickly built up the network Clarke needed. A report to the 1912 convention in Atlantic City of the parallel United States organization, Clan na Gael, gave IRB strength as 1660 in Ireland and 367 in Britain.[5] Patrick Pearse, the visionary poet, was one of them, and they gave full support to his efforts to create the Irish Volunteers in 1913 and to infiltrate the top leadership of the 11,000 or 12,000 volunteers who refused the following year to join Britain in its war against Germany. The decision to come out in arms against the British, which led to the Easter Rising of 1916, was made at an IRB meeting soon after the war began in August 1914. The IRB in New York immediately approached the Germans as potential allies, sending a retired member of the British Foreign Service, Sir Roger Casement, a Protestant from County Antrim, to negotiate in Berlin for an expeditionary force and a shipment of modern arms. The German arms, as noted earlier, were intercepted at sea by the British. Casement was captured and hanged.

Concurrently with this phoenixlike rebirth of the IRB to assume a leading role in the freedom movement came a re-evaluation of that movement itself from the viewpoint of Irish Catholicism. Here again the man most responsible was Pearse. He succeeded in blending the ideals of Irish nation-alism and religion so that the hesitant Church leaders were finally persuaded that the way of salvation for Church and country alike called for the blood sacrifice of gallant men, a sacrifice constantly likened by Pearse to that of Christ. The depth and extent of the impact of these ideas is seen in the works of the most popular of Irish novelists of the first quarter of the twentieth century, Canon P. A. Sheehan, a country parish priest. His *The Graves of Kilmorna*, written in 1912 and 1913 and published in 1914, is the story of an old Fenian who idealizes the Irish revolutionary tradition and deplores the supine worldliness of contemporary Ireland. Ireland in Fenian times had kept the Ten Commandments, while modern Ireland—dragged down by the Irish Parlia-mentary party—was the victim of and engulfed in vice, avarice, and materialism. Elitism was a dominant principle for Sheehan, as it was for Pearse and the IRB. Even though the mass of the people supinely accepted the domination of the oppressor, the nation survived in the chosen few who retained faith and hope. As with "the remnant" in the Old Testament, it was the few rather than the many who were the nation's spokesmen and saviors. In the words of a character in *The Graves of Kilmorna:* "The reign of democracy set in with the French Revolution; and its elephantine hoofs have been trampling out all the beauty and sweetness of life since then. . . . Democracy has but one logical end—socialism. So-cialism is cosmopolitan—no distinction of nationalities any longer; but one common race. This means antimilitarism, the abolition of all stimulus and rivalry."

The concepts may well have been suggested to Sheehan

by the publication *Sinn Fein,* in which had been written in November 1911: "Imperialism and socialism—forms of the cosmopolitan heresy and in essence one . . . have offered man the material world—nationalism has offered him a free soul." Sheehan in turn may have helped Pearse develop his idea of the value of blood sacrifice to redeem a people, a dominant element in Pearse's efforts to promote the Easter Rising. The thought is expressed by several characters in *The Graves of Kilmorna:*

I have never thought of anything higher or greater than to strike one smashing blow for Ireland, and then lie down to die on some Irish hillside. . . . We may also have to teach from our graves. . . . It is the fools who do all the world's great work. . . . If no blood is shed, the country will rot away. . . . As the blood of the martyrs was the seed of saints, so the blood of the patriot is the sacred seed from which alone can spring new forces, and fresh life, into a nation that is drifting into the putrescence of decay.

In a poem in Irish, Pearse prayed: How I would thank the God of mighty deeds—even if we were to live for only a week after—to see Mother Ireland and a thousand warriors issue a challenge to the English." One of his best-known poems in English, "The Fool," is a mosaic of scriptural references:

> Ye shall be foolish as I;
> ye shall scatter, not save;
> ye shall venture your all,
> lest ye lose what is more than all;
> ye shall call for a miracle, taking Christ at his word.[6]

The rationalization of elitist revolution presented by Canon Sheehan does not mean that Irish churchmen had suddenly abandoned their rigid conservatism. The overriding consideration of the bishops remained, as it had always been, to keep their monopoly of the allegiance of the Irish Catholic masses. They had welcomed the Act of Union in 1800 and supported the Union in the years that followed because they believed they could exercise more influence over a London administration than over a Protestant-dominated Irish administration. But London had disappointed them in many ways, particularly in its refusal to provide a new university totally under the bishops' control, thus ensuring the education of an Irish elite on whose orthodoxy and commitment they could always count. Their desire to control education had become an obsession. They chose to leave the administration to Protestants, on whom they could exercise political pressures, rather than accept the secular university which London was willing to concede, a university which might produce Irish Catholic administrators taught to question the universal wisdom of bishops. The bishops had made various alliances with the Irish Parliamentary party but had never secured the basic commitments they sought. That party was much too dependent on the liberals in England, friendly to the dangerous new ideas coming from the Continent, and not at all anxious to give the bishops control of education. Although forced to give lip service to the notion of Home Rule, the bishops had long since decided that it held more threats for them than did the continuance of the Union.

In this mood of frustration with both the existing administration and the proposed Home Rule alternative, Irish churchmen began to be touched by the romantic dream offered by Pearse and his friends. An Ireland returned to its heroic past and purged free of all the vices and errors of the modern world could be both Catholic and Gaelic, both Gaelic and Catholic. It was not that the bishops had been converted to the cause of a free Ireland. Their concern was simply that Ireland should remain Catholic in the sense in which they understood the word. If this involved freedom, then let freedom come—that was immaterial. The bishops were further influenced to accept this line of thought by the growth of popular sentiment in favor of Sinn Fein. Like all realistic leaders, they knew when to join what it would be folly to oppose.

Typical of the change is the evaluation of the Easter Rising of 1916 by Bishop Edward O'Dwyer of Limerick who 25 years earlier had been identified as a pro-Unionist or "Castle bishop." In 1887, O'Dwyer had written that "the spirit of general resistance to civil authority . . . has been growing in Ireland, and if encouraged will produce the same results to religion that the revolution has produced in every country in which it has triumphed." By 1915, he was openly denouncing John Redmond, head of the Irish Parliamentary party, for urging Irishmen to fight for England against Germany. "What have they or their forebears ever got from England that they should die for her? . . . The war may be just or unjust, but any fair-minded man will admit that it is England's war not Ireland's." [7]

A year later O'Dwyer was defending the Easter Rising. His defense was an extraordinary one for a churchman, opening up justifications which were warmly welcomed by the gunmen of the time as a belated recognition of their virtue, and which have ever since continued to reverberate in Irish minds when confronted with the problem of the lone individual who pits his judgment against that of the majority. Referring to the young men who had died in Dublin, O'Dwyer said:

Was I to condemn them? Even if their rebellion was not justifiable theologically, was I to join the gang of renegades who were throwing dirt on Pearse and MacDonagh and Colbert, and the other brave fellows whom Maxwell had mercilessly put to death? Was I to join the condemnation of the men, and women too, who—without trial— were deported by thousands? The Irish Volunteers were too few for the enterprise, but that perhaps is the worst that is to be said against them. Rebellion to be lawful must be the act of the nation as a whole, but while that is true, see the case of the Irish Volunteers against England.

First of all, England had been guilty of "tantalizing perfidy" on the Home Rule issue. It had treated Ireland in ways that the young men of any nation could not be expected to bear patiently. The rebels were "the true representatives of Ireland, . . . the exponents of her nationality. . . . Sinn Fein is, in my judgment, the true principle, and alliance with English politicians is the alliance of the lamb with the wolf." The following year O'Dwyer was still developing the same argument. The Easter Rising, he insisted, was "a reaction against weakness and stupidity and corruption. But hopeless as it was, it has not been fruitless. It has galvanized the dead bones of Ireland and breathed into them the spirit with which England has had to reckon."

Other prominent churchmen accepted this interpretation and expanded it. Monsignor M. O'Riordan, head of the prestigious Irish College in Rome, for example, asserted that England had by its misdeeds lost the right to govern and to be obeyed. "Wrong is not less a wrong because it is decreed by a legislature; and illegal resistance or evasion became the natural protection against immoral laws. And so the Catholics of Ireland rightly disowned what force made them endure." [8]

The response of the IRB and its associates was understandably enthusiastic. As Dr. Patrick MacCartan, a member of the IRB supreme council wrote to an associate in the United States, "They have redeemed the Catholic church in the eyes of Nationalist Ireland of the stain caused by the attitude of some priests and bishops in the days of Fenianism." It was now possible not only to envisage but to organize a mass movement dedicated to physical force without fear of clerical anathemas. And that was precisely what happened. Although the military command structure in Dublin had been destroyed in the Easter Rising, within a year the entire country had been reorganized, with enthusiastic companies of Volunteers in practically every parish. By now the Volunteers were starting to be known as the Irish Republican Army, although the origin of the title remains obscure. Dr. J. Bowyer Bell, the American historian who has authored the definitive book on the IRA [9] says that a green flag inscribed with the letters IRA was used as early as the abortive Fenian invasion of Canada in 1866. Pearse identified himself as commander of the forces of the Irish Republic in *Irish War News* on April 25, 1916, the day following the proclamation of the Republic and the formation of a provisional government as the first action in the Easter Rising. In a manifesto on April 26 he was named as the Commander-in-Chief of the Army of the Irish Republic. The letters IRA were found on a blackboard in the College of Surgeons, one of the buildings occupied during the Rising, and prisoners soon began to place them after their names in their letters home.

Whatever doubt may have previously existed, the Irish Volunteers definitely became the Irish Republican Army in January 1919. A general election to the British Parliament had been called the previous month, just five weeks after the end of the First World War. In Ireland Sinn Fein won an overwhelming victory of 73 seats, leaving the Irish Parliamentary party with only 6. The only opposition was in northeast Ulster, where the Unionists won 26 seats in and around Belfast. The Sinn Fein candidates had announced in advance that they would not attend the British Parliament at Westminster. Instead, those who were not in prison or on official missions, 27 in all, assembled in Dublin on January 21 to constitute themselves as Dail Eireann (the Parliament of Ireland), to reaffirm the proclamation made at Easter 1916 of the Irish Republic, and to vote a constitution, a declaration of independence, and a program of social and democratic rights. The rulers of Britain, who had just emerged victorious from the greatest war in history, thought it all slightly ridiculous, typically Irish. But for the Irish, the gesture was important. There was now in existence a government elected by and responsible to the Irish people. It had an army already in existence, Irish Volunteers, and this was now the Irish Republican Army, owing and professing allegiance to the one lawful government in Ireland. The most rigid requirements of Catholic theology had been met. All actions, including the taking of life, were now unquestionably lawful for members of the IRA acting under orders. The last hurdle had been jumped.

The first of the guerrilla actions, which would soon become known as the Anglo-Irish War, took place the same day
as the Dail met. An IRA column in Tipperary killed two policemen protecting a load of explosives. As attacks continued, the
police were concentrated in the larger barracks, leaving the
countryside and the villages under the control of the local
IRA. The Dail moved rapidly to create all the agencies of a
government, utilizing the existing structures to the extent to
which they could be controlled or penetrated. Republican
courts were soon functioning in much of the country, and Republican police and tax officials were installed. Most of the
local government bodies had Republican majorities and took
orders from the Republican department of local government.
Payments of taxes and land annuities into the British exchequer declined enormously.

The British government poured troops into the country
and expanded the police force with emergency units hastily
recruited in England, heavily armed and little trained. They
were frustrated by the guerrilla tactics of the IRA, which was
everywhere, yet invisible, its gunmen ordinary members of
the community, farm workers, bus drivers, store assistants,
who slipped away for a few hours in their civilian clothes to
mount an ambush, attack a police barracks, or wipe out a spy
ring. To meet what they saw as terror tactics, the British resorted to counterterror, never officially sanctioned but obviously tolerated and often encouraged by the officers in
charge of the various forces. The pattern was to continue. For
two years the barbarities exercised on the general population
increased. Homes of suspects were destroyed, entire towns
looted and burned down in retaliation for attacks on police
and soldiers, and individuals seized and shot in cold blood
by disguised men subsequently certified by coroner's juries
to have been members of the armed forces of the British
Crown. When Thomas MacCurtain, Lord Mayor of Cork and
commanding officer of the First Cork Brigade of the IRA, was
seized in his home and shot dead in front of his family, the
general headquarters of the IRA ordered the execution of

several of the policemen it judged responsible, including an inspector named Swanzy. The order was carried out in due course. Even Swanzy did not escape, although his superiors had quickly transferred him to the relative safety of Lisburn near Belfast.[10]

The IRA were particularly successful in placing their agents in key positions for collection of information about their opponents—in the civil service in Dublin and London, in post offices, on trains and buses. When the British tried to counter by importing a group of experienced secret service agents, the IRA went one morning to the "safe houses" in which the agents had been installed in Dublin and killed 14 of them. The response of the Black-and-Tans was to take out 3 IRA prisoners and execute them while "attempting to escape," and to open fire on a crowd at a football game in Dublin, killing 12 spectators and wounding 60. By this time, the war of words had risen to such a pitch that neither side could deal objectively with any issue. The British allowed Terence MacSwiney, successor to MacCurtain as Lord Mayor of Cork, to die after a hunger strike of 74 days. The long-drawn-out ordeal produced a blaze of anti-British publicity around the world and ensured MacSwiney a permanent place among Irish martyrs along with MacCurtain, the 12 football spectators, and an 18-year-old medical student named Kevin Barry, who was hanged for his part in a raid in Dublin. The British lost the sense of proportion which is normally their final saving grace. For example, the chief architect of the hard line in Ireland told the House of Commons that the people of Cork had burned their own city. What had happened was that the Auxiliaries had run amuck after losing 19 men in two ambushes: first, they set the city ablaze, then they cut the hoses of the firemen who tried to extinguish the fires. Destruction was estimated at $15 million.

By 1921 the British forces deployed in Ireland included nearly 40,000 troops, more than 6000 regular police, and an equal number of Black-and-Tans, 1500 Auxiliaries, and a new police force in the north of Ireland drawn from sections of the population bitterly opposed to the IRA which would soon grow to 3000 full-time and 50,000 part-time armed men. Against them was ranged an invisible army estimated by British intelligence at between 100,000 and 200,000 men. From the military viewpoint, however, they constituted a rabble and not even a rabble in arms. The vast majority had no training other than some formal drill periods, often with wooden guns, and a few route marches. Few had ever come under fire or fired a shot in anger. Ammunition was so scarce that many had not fired even a practice shot. Between them they possessed some thousands of rifles and pistols of many makes and sizes, and only a small amount of supplies and explosives. The only heavier weapons were a few machine guns, most of them seized from the enemy in ambushes and raids on police barracks. By June 1921 they had received from friends in the United States 50 of the new Thompson submachine guns, but even with these, their offensive potential was limited. To keep a thousand men on the move in flying columns and raiding parties was about the most they could attempt.[11] The result was a no-win situation. No matter how many IRA men the British captured, tried, and executed as murderers, there were more to take their place. Each house of a suspected IRA sympathizer burned by the Black-and-Tans was matched by a Unionist's house burned by the IRA. Day by day Irish opinion hardened.

When the British Parliament in 1920 finally passed a Home Rule measure dividing Ireland into a predominantly Catholic region, called Southern Ireland, and a predominantly Protestant area consisting of the six counties around Belfast, called Northern Ireland, the solidly Sinn Fein supporters ignored the move as an irrelevance. The British called elections for the new parliaments in May 1921. Sinn Fein, by now an illegal organization, used the British electoral machinery to vote for a second Dail Eireann, a body that had also been outlawed by the British. Its candidates won every seat in Southern Ireland except for four seats allotted to graduates of the predominantly Protestant Trinity College.

In Northern Ireland, the Unionists won 40 of the 52 seats. Anticipating Sinn Fein success, the British had provided that if there were more than 50 percent abstentions in either Parliament, its area would be governed as a Crown colony. The northern Parliament met and inaugurated the new regime. Only the four Trinity representatives appeared when the southern Parliament was summoned to meet in Dublin. From the viewpoint of Sinn Fein, Ireland as a whole had given it an unshakable mandate to govern the entire island Republic. To underscore that position, the IRA burned down Dublin's customhouse, the seat of nine British administrative departments, including the taxation department and the local government board. Without the mountains of paper consumed in the holocaust the administration could no longer function.

The British generals, like generals everywhere, had a solution. They could restore law and order in a reasonable time and with reasonable casualties if given another 100,000 troops and the authority to carry out mass relocation of the rebel population, to set up blockhouses to control movement, and to prevent reinfiltration of undesirables. (It was a classic technique which would be resorted to again for the pacification of Vietnam 50 years later.) But for British politicians the political costs were too high. Lloyd George, in particular, head of a shaky government and determined not to founder on the Irish Question like everyone of his predecessors who had tried to deal with it, saw compromise as his only hope. His concern was perhaps not so much what the rebellious people of Ireland might do as what the Irish in America had already done and threatened to carry, if necessary, to unforeseeable lengths.

The Irish in the United States, divided before and during the First World War, had formed a solid and deeply committed unity afterward behind the separatist forces for whom Sinn Fein spoke in Ireland. They had engaged in a bitter conflict with President Wilson because he had ignored a resolution passed by the House of Representatives proclaiming Ireland's right to self-determination and ignored

Irish demands to place the issue of Irish freedom on the agenda of the Versailles peace conference. They had rallied American opinion against membership of the United States in the League of Nations. The Friends of Irish Freedom spent vast sums on newspaper advertisements opposing League membership during the presidential campaign of 1920. In that election, the Irish helped ensure the success of Harding as the anti-League candidate.

Lloyd George saw that he could not win a decisive military victory in Ireland as long as millions of sympathizers were organized in the United States to provide arms and supplies. He knew that the continuing aid and high-level support of the United States needed by Great Britain would be in jeopardy as long as the passions of the Irish in the United States remained inflamed. He decided, accordingly, to swallow his pride. Eighteen months after he had assured the world that the British had "murder by the throat," he wrote to the head murderer in June 1921 proposing a peace conference. The leaders of Sinn Fein, the Dail, and the Republic surfaced in Dublin to sign a general truce on July 8 with the British Commander-in-Chief in Ireland. Its terms provided for the gradual withdrawal of most British forces, even before the signing of a treaty of peace, their place to be taken by the IRA.

10

The Free State

*As are many other aspects of Irish society, the Catholic
church there is ultraconservative, . . . a force for conservatism, not on the basis of preserving Catholic doctrine or preventing the corruption of her children, but simply to ward
off threats to her own security and influence.*

—BERNADETTE DEVLIN [1]

Historians still disagree as to who or what won the
Anglo-Irish War, or indeed if there was a winner. But in July
1921 the Irish people had no doubts. The IRA had done it.
From the half-world of stealth and secrecy, the heroes
emerged into the spotlight of glory, gradually acquiring
slouch hats, Sam Browne belts, and green-gray uniforms. The
IRA accepted all the honors as their due. They had proved
Daniel O'Connell wrong and Patrick Pearse right. The only
way to talk to the English was with a gun. As one of their
most imaginative leaders later expressed it in his memoirs,
they had by their guerrilla tactics "prevented British authority from functioning in Ireland, laid its administration in
ruins, driven out or under cover the British minions, necessi-
tated a large and costly army of occupation, humiliated Brit-

ish military power, caused the name of Britain to stink in the
nostrils of all decent peoples, and inflicted sufficient casualties on their soldiers to seriously disturb a government finding it difficult to supply reinforcements." [2]

The treaty discussions in London dragged on until December. By that time several political changes were clearly
established though still ignored by many of those affected. A
separate state had been brought into existence in the area
described in the 1920 Government of Ireland Act as Northern
Ireland. It was a state dominated by the Orange Order and
controlled by the police and B-Specials, who were backed up
by an Ulster Volunteer Force of 100,000 men and assured of
all needed cooperation from Britain. What the truce had
brought in this area was intensified warfare by all the forces
of the state against an IRA whose right to exist they denied, a
warfare in which the IRA guerrillas were not on top and the
friendly people whom they needed as a sea in which to swim
were being methododically driven from their homes and
jobs. As for the rest of Ireland, the protracted discussions behind closed doors were obviously not concerned with something so straightforward as the kind of relationship to be
established between the British Commonwealth and an
independent Irish Republic. A compromise for something
less than a republic had to be in the making, and that was
what Lloyd George offered the Irish negotiators on December 6, 1921, in the terms of an ultimatum. Either they
signed that same day, he told them, or the negotiations were
ended, to be followed immediately by a resumption of war
to the death.

The document they reluctantly signed offered vastly
more than the most liberal of earlier Home Rule proposals.
Ireland acquired the same status as the self-governing dominions of Canada and Australia. But "Northern Ireland"
would be free to opt out, something it was obvious it would
do. However, to soften that blow, if Northern Ireland insisted
on partition, a commission would be created to adjust the
boundary in accordance with the wishes of the inhabitants,

so far as economic realities might permit. It was the formula under which the Versailles Peace Conference was at that very time redrawing Europe's borders after World War I. The Irish were confident the agreement would transfer to the south half the area and a third of the population of Northern Ireland, making what was left unviable as a separate state. The most galling clause of all was the stipulation of an oath of allegiance to the British Crown, an explicit rejection of the Republic for which so many had suffered and died.

Publication of the treaty immediately split Sinn Fein down the middle. For acceptance were many of the original Sinn Feiners who had much earlier sought a settlement along the lines of the prewar Austro-Hungarian empire, a dual monarchy, the separate kingdoms of Great Britain and of Ireland being united by their common allegiance to a single Crown. With them now were many pragmatists who would accept dominion status as a forerunner of full independence, and who considered the oath an unimportant "scrap of paper." On the other side were not only the ideological Republicans but a more moderate group led by Eamon de Valera who were willing to accept what they called "external association," a proposed new form of Commonwealth membership which would permit the country to function internally as a Republic and leave open the issue of allegiance. The British were not yet ready to accept this subtlety, to which they became reconciled only after World War II as a device to retain some vague hold on India and other former possessions around the world.

The division within Sinn Fein was mainly along social lines. For the treaty were people of property; the Unionists living in the area of Southern Ireland, few in numbers but influential as bankers, insurance men, stockbrokers, accountants, and landowners; the profoundly conservative bishops and upper clergy of the Roman Catholic church; the business community; and many professionals. Ranged against them were the small farmers and shopkeepers, along with urban and rural workers. But the choice of sides, far from being automatic, demanded excruciating decisions from those whose class identification was weak and whose emotional commitment had built up in the years of heroic struggle. Brother divided against brother, family against family, neighbor against neighbor, village against village. The Dail vote in favor of the treaty was a bare majority, 64 for to 57 against.

For nobody was the issue more excruciating than for the IRA. From the time the choice of sides had to be taken, after the signing of the truce, the IRA had gradually developed the organization appropriate to the official army of a recognized state, but its leaders were well aware of the uncertainty of the future. A truce was not a treaty. Even though the British were withdrawing, they still had bases throughout the country and were increasing their strength in Northern Ireland. Training and discipline were accordingly stressed, and weapons were smuggled into the country from abroad. When the treaty came, the high command of the IRA split, just as the Dail cabinet did and also the Dail itself. Ironically, the weight of the IRB, traditionally the most extreme element, was on the side of the treaty. Michael Collins, IRA Adjutant General, described it as "a stepping-stone to a republic." Collins had reorganized the IRB a few years earlier and many of his friends served on its executive.

Field commanders of the IRA, however, opposed the treaty violently. They belonged to the same social stratum as their men, small farmers and urban and rural workers. And they found it easy to rationalize their opposition. It was the army that had proclaimed the Republic in 1916, and it was the army that had made it possible for the Dail to proclaim it again in 1919 and to make that proclamation a reality during the following years. It was those who remained faithful who were entitled to judge the others. Any attempt by the Dail to vote away the Republic was *ultra vires* and automatically caused the Dail itself to cease to function as the legislature of the Republic.

The IRA was still technically under the control of the Defense Minister named by the Dail, but that control became daily more ambiguous and uncertain. The defense ministry set out to create a regular army, uniformed and living in barracks, starting with IRA units willing to accept its authority. That move, however, quickly alarmed those opposing the treaty. They called an army convention in Dublin in March 1922. Although the Defense Minister forbade attendance by any officer who recognized his jurisdiction, it assembled 223 delegates representing 16 divisions with a listed strength of 112,650 men. Resolutions calling for a military dictatorship or declaration of war on the Free State fell just short of a majority, and the final decisions avoided an open break. It was clear, nevertheless, that this army did not regard itself as subject to the Free State authorities or to the Dail which had transferred its allegiance to the Free State.

An arrangement was made for cooperation between the two armies, that of the Free State and that of the Republic, in a campaign against Northern Ireland where pogroms had flared to new heights. Some units actually moved north and crossed the border, to be driven back by British troops supported by artillery. Meanwhile, Britain increased pressure on the Provisional Government of the Free State to assert effective control over all armed units within its jurisdiction, especially after the Chief of the Imperial Staff—a bitter foe of Irish nationalism—was assassinated in London. Equipped with British artillery, supplies, and funds, the Free State army attacked the IRA headquarters in the Four Courts, Dublin's central law courts. The magnificent building was extensively damaged in a three-day bombardment. When its defenders surrendered, the Free State army proceeded to shell other IRA strongholds in Dublin, repeating the destruction of much of the city center which had just been rebuilt after a similar bombardment in 1916. But the IRA still held most of the country and outnumbered the Free State army by five to one.

For reasons never fully clarified, however, the IRA kept strictly on the defensive, allowing the Free State army to expand to 60,000 and to obtain artillery, armored cars, and other material from Britain. The Free State military and political leaders, on the contrary, acted vigorously and ruthlessly. Soon they had captured all cities and important towns, driving the IRA to the guerrilla tactics it had earlier used against the British. The bishops also moved to the support of the Free State, declaring that the IRA lacked moral justification for resistance to lawful authority and that its members were to be denied the sacraments. It was a bad blow, but by this time the arguments of Pearse, Canon Sheehan, and Bishop O'Dwyer had helped most IRA members to consider their stand legitimate. For them, the bishops—like the Dail—had turned from the straight road and consequently had lost the moral authority to judge actions performed by the IRA on behalf of the Republic.

The Free State now pushed through a law more repressive than any enacted by the British. It provided the death sentence for possession of a weapon, and it was applied literally to make it clear to the other side that the government would stop at nothing. Erskine Childers,[3] an English-born upper-class Protestant who had started life as a Conservative but later had thrown in his lot wholeheartedly with Sinn Fein and become a cabinet minister in the Dail government, was executed for being in possession of a small pistol, an ornament rather than a weapon, a gift from Michael Collins. The Free State government had the sentence carried out while an application for habeas corpus was before the law courts. When the IRA replied by shooting two of the deputies (one fatally) responsible for what they called the "murder bill," the Free State cabinet selected four IRA leaders being held in custody and shot them without any pretense of legality.

By April 1923, such ruthlessness had convinced the IRA leaders that they could not win, and Eamon de Valera was named to negotiate terms. The Free State government refused to negotiate, continuing its military pressure and jamming the jails with thousands of prisoners. The IRA leadership finally decided that active operations had to be

suspended. On May 24, de Valera sent a message to the
men in the field:

Soldiers of the Republic, Legion of the Rearguard: The Republic
can no longer be defended successfully by your arms. Further sacrifice of life would now be vain and continuance of the struggle in
arms unwise in the national interest and prejudicial to the future of
our case. Military victory must be allowed to rest for the moment
with those who have destroyed the Republic. Other means must be
sought to safeguard the nation's right.

The message was followed by an order from the IRA
leaders to all units to hide their arms and disperse.

Large-scale conflict was at an end, but the atmosphere of
bitterness and conflicting claims would weigh on Irish political life for years to come. The IRA had not surrendered, did
not turn in their arms, and had abandoned none of their
claims to be the only legitimate government in Ireland. The
Free State government continued to round up every identified or suspected IRA man it could lay its hands on, passing
additional legislation to hold suspects without trial notwithstanding the *de facto* end of hostilities. In August the Free
State government called general elections, relying on its monopoly of power to ensure a decisive victory at the polls. It
was now headed by William Cosgrave, a veteran of the Easter Rising, Michael Collins having been killed in an ambush
and Prime Minister Arthur Griffith having died of a heart attack three days apart a year earlier. It had some 60,000
soldiers deployed with heavy equipment and in effective
control of almost the entire country. It had the financial and
military support of Great Britain and the backing of the entire
press and the bishops. Ten thousand of its opponents were in
jail and any leaders still free were in hiding. When de Valera
appeared—as announced—to address a pre-election meeting
in Clare, the county which by electing Daniel O'Connell in
1829 had wrung Catholic emancipation from Britain and
which de Valera had represented since 1917, soldiers with
fixed bayonets seized him and placed him in solitary confine-

ment in Dublin. Despite this and other pressures, Sinn Fein did surprisingly well. It polled 286,000 votes, as against 415,000 for the government, winning 44 seats to the government's 63. Clare polled 80 percent for Sinn Fein. The government made the most of its majority, but the IRA leaders were elated at their surprising support. They read the results as showing that a very high proportion of the people, perhaps even a majority if one took all the handicaps into account, would not be happy until the Republic proclaimed in 1916 was again a reality.

The Free State government had other problems too. Northern Ireland had opted out of the dominion established by the Anglo-Irish Treaty of 1921. It had then built up a strong force of armed police and an unofficial but officially approved and supported force of 100,000 territorials to defend its territory from the revision envisaged in that treaty. When it refused to participate in the revision commission, Lloyd George sided technically with the Free State while substantively backing Northern Ireland. He described the boundary problem as "only a minor sectarian problem in a corner of Ireland" and claimed that the treaty signers had intended merely to exchange a few parishes, with the north benefiting as well as the south. By 1924, de Valera and most of the other prisoners were again free, and de Valera entered the political fray to reject Lloyd George's interpretation and to criticize the Free State government when it finally accepted defeat and agreed to leave the border where it had been placed in the 1920 Act.

Throughout 1924 and early 1925 Sinn Fein steadily increased its proportion of the votes cast in a series of by-elections to the Dail. Some leaders were talking about the day when more than half the members elected to the Free State Dail would choose their own meeting place and reestablish the Republic. Until then they would continue to boycott the Free State Dail, as they had done from its inception. For them, the lawful government was still that of the Dail as constituted before a majority of its members early in 1922 accepted the treaty signed in December 1921. Nevertheless, opinion was growing inside Sinn Fein that the realities of politics and power demanded that the deputies take their seats to fight the Free State system from inside. The Free State government, for its part, was determined to give them no alternative. In April 1925 it introduced a Treasonable Offences Act to counter the proposed Sinn Fein strategy of a counterparliament. The measure proposed the death penalty for waging war on the state and specified penalties for usurping executive authority or parliamentary functions, as well as for creating a military force. The government moved to isolate the opposition further by insisting on the oath of allegiance for all public offices, and it exercised its control of the administrative machinery to ensure that only supporters of the regime got any kind of work paid from the public purse. The years of turmoil had played havoc with the economy and left a high level of unemployment. Hunger was forcing Sinn Fein supporters to emigrate. The writing was on the wall. If Sinn Fein was to survive, a strategy had to be devised to allow its Dail members to take their seats—and that involved the hated oath of allegiance to the British Crown—with a maximum of political benefit and a minimum loss of face.

That was how the politicians saw it. But the military leaders of the IRA, never politically sophisticated and still simplistically equating force and power, were far from any such conclusion. As the rumors grew, they called together a general army convention in November 1925. Its agenda concerned the mechanics of creating a powerful secret military organization in England to carry the war to that country if it again attacked Ireland. The appropriate date for starting another revolution was discussed but not determined. And, anticipating the danger that the Sinn Fein politicians might defect, the convention passed a resolution directing that "the army of the Republic sever its connection with the Dail and act under an independent executive," and that "such executive be given the power to declare war when, in its opinion, a suitable opportunity arises to rid the Republic of its enemies." [4]

While the IRA was preparing to go its own way, Sinn Fein split once more over a proposal by de Valera, who was still its president. He proposed that its deputies enter the Free State Dail, provided the oath of allegiance was waived. He insisted that even though the oath was in the 1922 Treaty and in the constitution enacted in accordance with that treaty, the Dail could decide that its members need not take the oath, and he urged a public campaign to persuade the Free State government to amend the law accordingly. For many members of Sinn Fein, the oath was not the sole issue. They wanted no part of the system of government imposed by England on Ireland, a system that included partition of the country. When the annual assembly failed to reach a consensus, de Valera and his followers withdrew in April 1926 to organize a new party. *Fianna Fail* (Soldiers of Destiny) would enter the Free State Dail, once the oath was removed, and work inside by constitutional means toward an all-Ireland Republic.

These developments confirmed the IRA leadership of the correctness of the decision to break with the politicians and return to the Fenian and IRB tradition of seeing the army as custodian of the national sovereignty, a position now more tenable than previously because the Irish people had openly endorsed it in the elections of 1918 and 1921. The new Chief of Staff went off to the United States to ensure a continued flow of money from Irish-Americans, who had long constituted the main financial support of Irish extremism. De Valera, New York-born, had close relations with most of the leaders in America, and many backed him in his latest move. But the still-powerful, although declining, Clan na Gael, remained open to the argument for physical force, and continued to send money and arms.

Back in Ireland, the IRA had gone through yet another reorganization and emerged as still a force to be reckoned with. It could count on 20,000 to 25,000 members, spread

throughout the country and learning to survive the constant
surveillance of the Free State army and police intelligence.
Most of the leaders kept their traditional distance from politics. The function of the army was to free Ireland, they said,
and the entire people would then decide without outside interference the kind of social and political system they
wanted. But an issue that would subsequently loom larger in
IRA councils was starting to emerge. One member of the
Army Council, Peadar O'Donnell, was encouraging a campaign to withhold land annuities. These were payments by
small farmers, former tenants, who were buying their holdings over a period of years from the government agency
which had already bought out their landlords. O'Donnell was
a committed socialist, a position that could be advanced only
with the greatest circumspection because of Church opposition. Several times during the political fever of the previous
years, especially before the 1922 Anglo-Irish Treaty, a movement had arisen spontaneously among the small farmers and
landless laborers to force the division of the big farms, especially those owned by absentee landlords. Their attempts to
speed the process by threats or by squatting on the land, although favored by the majority of the IRA who themselves
came from the land-hungry classes, were quickly denounced
by the Church and repudiated by the Sinn Fein leadership,
which was almost entirely middle class and as such un-
responsive to the social needs of its supporters. Two-thirds of
the members of the first Dail elected in 1918 were urban professionals and white-collar workers, a further quarter were
capitalists, and only 10 percent were farmers, not all of them
by any means small farmers.[5] Subsequent leadership re-
flected the same pattern.

   In 1926, however, O'Donnell discovered a way to promote his socialist ideas without a direct clash with the
Church. The Free State government had made a secret agreement to hand over to the British exchequer payments made
by farmers who were buying their holdings under a govern-
ment-financed program of land reform. The British argued

that it was they who had advanced the purchase price with the land as guarantee for its repayment, that the debt was a simple commercial one. Not so, said O'Donnell, when it became public knowledge that the annuities were being sent to London. The exchequer which advanced the money was the common exchequer of the United Kingdom of Great Britain and Ireland, and it was a recognized fact—verified by British commissions of inquiry—that since the Union of 1800 Ireland had paid far more than its equitable share into that exchequer. It was Irish money the exchequer had used to make the advances, giving it no continuing claim for reimbursement.

O'Donnell was editor of a weekly political newspaper financed by the IRA, and he used its columns to urge the farmers to withhold payment of annuities and force a decision on the morality and legality of the British claim. His campaign quickly became popular, especially in the west and northwest of the country. He then challenged his associates in the IRA leadership to join him on this issue. It would, he said, provide once again a broad popular base to sweep away the British-installed regime in Dublin and restore the Republic. Most of them hesitated. Some were unwilling to renew so soon the civil war which they felt was an inescapable part of the process of returning to power. Others entertained the soldier's contempt for politics and his fear that he could not win in that dirty game. The upshot was that de Valera took over O'Donnell's crusade and used it to carry his new party to power constitutionally in 1932.

Before achieving power, however, de Valera had first to get inside the Free State Dail, a move which his opponents were determined to make as difficult as possible. However, the general election in 1927 left things more confused than before. The government won 47 seats to Fianna Fail's 24. Sixty-two were spread among small parties and independent candidates. When the Dail was summoned, de Valera tried to force his way in without subscribing to the oath but was prevented by the Clerk of the Dail who locked the doors. He then initiated the proceedings for a referendum to amend the constitution; but before he had gone very far, the political situation was radically changed by the assassination of Kevin O'Higgins, Minister for Justice, on his way to Mass one Sunday. A talented but bitterly partisan politician, O'Higgins was widely regarded as the man most responsible for the harshness of government policy during the civil war, including the shooting of hostages without trial. The government reacted to his killing by arresting every IRA leader in sight. It also introduced three bills in the Dail: one limiting further the rights of the citizen, including the right to jury trial; one providing that every candidate for election to the Dail had to take the oath of allegiance when nominated; and one limiting the constitutional right to demand a referendum to those Dail members who had taken the oath of allegiance.

De Valera was finally forced to a pragmatic step in the interest of political survival. He led his men into the Dail, announcing that he was not taking an oath but merely putting "my name down in this book in order to get permission to go into the Dail." He then immediately challenged the government, and the Dail divided 71 to 71 on the vote of confidence. The government won on the Speaker's tie-breaking vote but recognized that it did not have a working majority and called an immediate general election. Sinn Fein did not put up any candidates and the IRA refused to endorse Fianna Fail, limiting itself to an informal call to vote against the outgoing government. That government did, however, win a working majority of seven, which gave it another five years in power.

They were to be difficult years for the IRA. The great majority of the Irish people had decided by their votes in the 1927 election that the future lay with the government set up under the Anglo-Irish Treaty of 1922, a government incompatible with the Republic which the IRA was committed to restore. Many of the members of the IRA had left to join de Valera in his defection. In addition, the Cosgrave government was elated by its success in finally forcing de Valera and his supporters to recognize its legitimacy. Sinn Fein had shown its weakness by failing to put up a single candidate at the 1927 election. Only the IRA remained, and they had been badly shaken by the defections to de Valera and by stepped-up police action after the assassination of Kevin O'Higgins. Helped by some money and arms from the United States, the leadership nevertheless held together and kept enough units scattered throughout the country to continue skirmishes with the police that resulted in an occasional death.

There was still no prospect of an immediate major revival of popular support for the IRA to justify a renewal of guerrilla warfare, and pressures grew for some radical political activity simply to hold the supporters together and encourage young people to join. Peader O'Donnell was still the spokesman for this strategy, and support for him grew rapidly when the country began to feel the impact of the Great Depression of 1929. In spite of all the political unrest, the Cosgrave government had scored significant economic successes during the previous years. It had created a national electricity grid supplied by the Shannon's hydroelectric generators. It had established agricultural standards to expand the profitable markets in Britain. Industry was growing and the rate of emigration was decreasing. But the economy had long been unable to provide minimum living standards for all the people, and the onset of depression quickly exposed the shallowness of the prosperity. The decline in British demands for Irish exports as well as the decline in the demand for Irish labor in Britain and the United States had rapid and extreme repercussions. Hungry men began to band together into all kinds of radical organizations, the Republican Council, the Working Farmers' Committee, the Irish Tribune League, the Workers' Defence Corps, the Friends of Soviet Russia, the National Unemployed Movement, the Women's International League for Peace and Freedom. Peadar O'Donnell had a hand in most of them, and the IRA was well represented in the membership. O'Donnell had finally convinced the central executive that here was a way to restore the IRA fortunes. In February 1931 they agreed to throw their support to an umbrella political organization known as Saor Eire (Free Ireland), an association of Irish workers and farmers committed to the overthrow of British imperialism and Irish capitalism and the establishment of an independent socialist republic.

For the government the challenge was serious. With little economic expertise, and most of that distorted by laissez-faire theories imbibed from British mentors, it had failed hopelessly to marshal its limited economic reserves in a way calculated to lessen the impact of depression. The power and daring of the extremists was growing visibly. Police and jurymen were being threatened and even assassinated by IRA gunmen. A new political movement to the left of Fianna Fail might temporarily weaken de Valera but would in the end isolate the Cosgrave party at the extreme right. And even there it was being challenged by people who were turning to Mussolini's Italy for a solution to Ireland's problems and starting a movement that would soon occupy center stage for a brief dramatic moment. If the Fascists could make Italy's trains run on time, some were saying, maybe that was what Ireland needed.

The Cosgrave government decided to undercut Saor Eire and its IRA backers, and to do so in a way that would simultaneously embarrass de Valera and his Fianna Fail. They had always enjoyed an extremely close and almost invariably cordial relationship with the Roman Catholic bishops. The conservatism of a government composed of and representative of the monied classes, bankers, big business, commerce, and industry was matched by the conservatism of Ireland's churchmen. Insofar as the politicians and higher civil servants had a philosophy, it tended, at the level of theory, to derive its inspiration from British liberalism, with its stress on the rule of law (which in practice they had no difficulty in violating), parliamentary democracy, and private enterprise. They were convinced that the social order, at the apex of which they happened to be, was eminently just. By ensuring the wealth of capitalists and ranchers they were involved in a moral enterprise which would guarantee as much well-being as was good for them to small farmers and workers.

Churchmen, trained to accept without question not only Rome's dogmas but its every mood, and convinced that this allegiance was the surest protection of their authority against interference of Protestant English bureaucrats and upstart Irish politicians alike, had an even more reactionary outlook. The heirs of those who in 1870 had sent Irishmen to fight for Pius IX against Garabaldi and Victor Emmanuel continued to view the world in the black-and-white simplicity of an open struggle between good and evil. As Pius IX had done nearly a century earlier, they were still condemning socialism as a revolt of "levellers" proclaiming equal rights for all, a world-wide conspiracy against "kings and princes," a challenge to the immutable order established by God. In that order each man had his rank and status and corresponding rights. The bishop lived in a palace and the farm laborer in a shack by God's dispensation, each of them gaining merit and ensuring salvation by joyful acceptance of his lot. With Leo XIII they condemned Communists and other nihilists for refusing to obey constituted authority, for advocating collective property, and for proclaiming the absolute equality of all men. When Pius XI said that communism was evil not only because it was socialistic, but also because it was atheistic, they took his word for it. But in their minds the real objection was always over the program to destroy one social order and create another in defiance of the immutable order of nature established by the Creator. Such a program was to them a personal insult, a challenge to their own established place in Church and in society.

In practice the philosophy of the Free State government and that of the bishops dovetailed very comfortably. The regime welcomed the Church's support and was willing to pay for it. The Irish revival of the first part of the century had coupled faith and fatherland, and as the Sinn Fein mystique rose to its triumphant climax after the Easter Rising of 1916,

the country experienced a parallel wave of religious enthusi-
asm. Church publications flourished. Thousands joined pious
confraternities and associations. Vocations were plentiful
both to the priesthood and to the religious life as monks and
nuns. Missionary congregations sprang up to build a spiritual
Irish empire in China and Africa.

The establishment of the Free State gave the bishops the
long-desired opportunity to consolidate their control of social
life by creating appropriate institutions. A period of puritani-
cal regulation set in. Some bishops put an end to all dancing
in their dioceses, a ban which they then had the power to enforce, and everywhere dances and similar amusements came
under strict regulation. It was "an occasion of sin" to allow
social contact between boys and girls and even between men
and women without strict supervision. The traditional separation of schoolchildren by sex and by religion was strengthened, and the bishops exerted strong and usually successful
pressures to prevent participation by Catholics in civic associations open to members of other denominations. Thus, the
Red Cross was left to the Protestants, the Catholics forming
their separate St. John's Ambulance Brigade. The Baden-
Powell scouts were similarly left to the Protestants, and Catholics created their own scout organization. The ban on
attendance by Catholics at Dublin's Trinity College was
reinforced, guaranteeing separate education at all levels. And
so it went across the board. The state cooperated by censor-
ing films and publications. The law banning books incorporated the words of canon law to define its object. A book "in
general tendency indecent" had to be prohibited. Amateur
canonists on the board of censors interpreted the mandate so
rigorously that books were forbidden for an objectionable
sentence or two. The importation or sale of any device for the
"unnatural" prevention of conception was prohibited by law
under strict penalties. Some would have gone farther. It was
suggested that cathedrals and churches taken over by the
Protestants at the Reformation should revert to Roman Catholic ownership, as they did for a brief period in the seven-

teenth century during the Cromwellian wars. Some urged positive state action to reduce the proportion of Protestants in key positions in banking, insurance, accounting, and big business, arguing that their preponderance was the result of centuries of official discrimination against Catholics, as in fact it was. But in these areas, saner counsels prevailed. Some reacted to the open discrimination of the Orange-dominated regime in Northern Ireland by urging like treatment for Protestants in the south. The dominant view, nevertheless, was that the proclaimed national objective of ultimate reunification of the country would best be served by generous treatment of the Protestants already within the state's jurisdiction. This was easy, since they were numerically so few that they could not pose a threat, under any circumstances, to the majority. After 1922 there was a small Protestant emigration, mainly of those career members of the British "establishment" or those so closely identified with it that they regarded themselves as part of the British presence. Those who stayed integrated quickly into the political and social structure. Their presence in economic affairs that they long dominated is still considerably in excess of their proportion of the population, but their preponderance has gradually diminished.

When civil war broke out in 1922, a few individual bishops sympathized with the Sinn Fein, or Republican, side, but the episcopal body came out strongly on the side of the Free State government. In October 1922 they condemned its opponents as conducting not a war, but "a system of murder and assassination." [6] They denied the sacraments to active opponents of the government, which for the average Irish Catholic was the ultimate punishment, since it placed his soul in everlasting jeopardy. For reasons already explained, however, the bishops' ruling was not automatically accepted. The civil war went on, and the IRA and other Republican groups continued to maintain considerable strength after it ended. The bishops had demonstrated to them for the first time that the allegiance of the masses could no longer be taken for granted. The growth of Saor Eire with its socialistic teachings alarmed them, and the Cosgrave government understandably played on their fears, urging them to speak out once more in defense of the "Catholic principles" on which Church and state alike rested.

Saor Eire held its first convention in Dublin in September 1931 and voted itself a constitution. The document was far from radical, indeed deliberately vague. The organization would unite farmers and workers in a program based on that offered by the leaders of the Easter Rising in their proclamation of the Republic. The most specific commitments were to public ownership of transport and cooperative control of land. The government and the press immediately began a campaign of denunciation of the communist threat to Ireland's religious and cultural ideals. The Catholic bishops met and issued a statement to be read in all churches. It was a specific condemnation of Saor Eire and of the IRA: "the two organizations . . . whether separate or in alliance, are sinful and irreligious, and . . . no Catholic can lawfully be a member of them." Simultaneously, the government rushed a constitutional amendment through the Dail authorizing a military tribunal to supersede the courts in "political" cases. The amendment gave new discretionary authority for search, arrest, and detention without trial, and for declaring an organization to be illegal.

For the de Valera party, this red-baiting was embarrassing. Most of its leaders had been excommunicated during the earlier civil war and they understandably still nursed a grievance against the bishops who had taken that action. But precisely because of that earlier conflict with the bishops, they felt they must lean over backward in order not to alienate them again when they were so close to achieving a majority in the country and taking office. Yet to give the government these emergency powers was to hand it a new lease on life. Fianna Fail felt trapped. It opposed the government proposals in the Dail, but mainly with theoretical and peripheral arguments. The government, for its part, lost no opportunity to identify Fianna Fail with the organizations condemned by the bishops, thereby hoping to detach enough support to swing the upcoming elections. And as soon as the constitutional amendment became effective, it banned not only Saor Eire and the IRA but a dozen related organizations such as the Friends of Soviet Russia and the Workers' Defence Corps. The police intensified their harassment of known IRA sympathizers, not only the leaders but the rank and file. Tension mounted, as demonstrations revealed widespread sympathy and support throughout the country for the proscribed groups. Rumors of a renewal of open or guerrilla warfare flourished. IRA leaders, on fund-raising visits to the United States, discovered that members of Clan na Gael were also deeply sympathetic to the new revolutionary ideas and maintained wide-ranging contacts with international extremist groups. After the Saor Eire convention in Dublin in September 1931, an appeal was made to the Clan leadership in New York to ship immediately as much equipment as possible. The word was quickly passed to other groups in the United States, producing a flurry of fund raising. Much of the money went into the purchase of arms, especially Thompson submachine guns. Men who had emigrated from Ireland after the civil war began to make preparations to return for the new round of fighting they were promised would not be long in coming.[7] But the IRA executives continued to hesitate and to defer a decision. Many of its members were arrested and given prison sentences under the new emergency powers legislation. Finally, it was decided that the odds against a successful military operation were too long, and all units were instructed to let the storm blow over. In addition, the Church was intervening from a new direction to lessen tension. Much earlier it had prepared elaborate plans to celebrate, in June 1932, Saint Patrick's arrival 1500 years earlier. The climax of the festival was to be an international Eucharistic Congress that would assemble a million people in Dublin. Not even the IRA could risk disturbing this unique event.

Tension had eased so dramatically by late 1931 that the Cosgrave government decided on a general election in January 1932. The religious climate was probably the determining factor. The recently reaffirmed Church ban on radical movements, including the IRA, paralleled exactly the government moves—by now obviously successful—to root out these same movements. The de Valera party was in the ambiguous position of maintaining lukewarm support for the Church's stand and lukewarm opposition for that of the government. Even if it now was the official opposition in the Dail, it had never fully removed the stigma carrying over from the civil war; many still questioned its religious orthodoxy. To the government it seemed unthinkable that a majority of the Irish people would place in jeopardy the success of the celebrations for Saint Patrick, including the Eucharistic Congress, by transferring power at this moment to a party without previous experience in government, a party whose attitude to the state was hostile and still ambiguous, a party whose relationship with the bishops was far from cordial.

The Cosgrave party was undoubtedly correct in judging that its chances of retaining power for a further five years were better now than in October, when elections would be mandatory. They had, nevertheless, a difficult task ahead. For two years they had floundered around helplessly in the face of the depression. Cost paring had been their sole answer. They had cut pensions and the salaries of teachers and the police. Women teachers were forced to resign if they wanted to marry. Yet unemployment had continued to grow, and with it social tension. Fianna Fail played relentlessly on all these failures and promised a series of attractive economic changes. Self-sufficiency would be encouraged both by expanding industry and by shifting from cattle raising to intensive production of food crops. Instead of being turned over to the British exchequer, the land annuities would be used to modernize farming. In addition, the oath of allegiance to the British Crown, the issue on which the civil war had been fought, would be dropped.

For the IRA the choices were not very attractive. The banning of Saor Eire and the yearlong campaign of harassment and coercion had made it impossible to present candidates for election or seize the moment to topple the regime. But the obvious determination of the Cosgrave government to wipe out not only the IRA but all progressive Republican movements had made one point clear. The IRA leadership might not like de Valera, but Cosgrave had to go. After considerable discussion within the IRA leadership, this stand was made official. The order forbidding IRA men to vote or to work on behalf of candidates was withdrawn. Specifically, they should try to defeat the Cosgravites. Since de Valera was the only alternative, many interpreted the instruction to mean that the IRA should work and vote for his party. The level of cooperation varied from place to place, but the overall impact was significantly favorable to Fianna Fail.

Mr. de Valera himself, moreover, managed the kind of balancing act which was always his trademark in politics. In 1917, Sir James O'Connor, a spokesman for the small group of wealthy pro-British Irish Catholics, had told Cardinal Logue, then head of the Irish bishops, that de Valera was "a high-minded and sincere Catholic." [8] He did not want physical force, O'Connor said, and was totally unsympathetic to the radicals and social reformers who sought to upset the class order ordained by providence. He succeeded in retaining some of that image even during the civil war. He kept carefully in the background, leaving major decisions to others; he insisted convincingly that he was a devout and committed Catholic even when the bishops ruled to the contrary. In that complicated role he was helped in part by his own ability in making subtle theological distinctions, in part by the support of sympathetic priests, most of them members of international religious orders with headquarterss in Rome who claimed canonical exemption from the rulings of mere bishops.

In the 1932 election campaign, de Valera again emerged as the man of moderation and propriety. While encouraging the IRA and the other radicals to believe that deep down he still shared all their dreams, he carefully explained to the Church and the business community that he would do absolutely nothing to rock the boat. As for the oath, he insisted that although the Anglo-Irish Treaty included a form of oath which members of the Dail might take, it did not require them to take it. As regards the land annuities, the lawyers had established that a clear legal question was involved. The annuities would be collected and placed in a special account until that question was decided by an international court to which both parties, Britain and Ireland, would give binding jurisdiction. The de Valera tactic was successful. His party elected 72 of its candidates to Cosgrave's 57. The support of seven Labor deputies gave him a working majority in the Dail.

11

De Valera in Power

Let it be made clear that we yield no willing assent to any form or symbol that is out of keeping with Ireland's right as a sovereign nation. Let us remove these forms one by one, so that this state that we control may be a republic in fact.

—EAMON DE VALERA [1]

For the IRA the immediate results of the Fianna Fail victory were excellent. No sooner had de Valera formed his cabinet than two of its members visited IRA men sentenced to imprisonment by the military tribunal set up a year earlier. The prisoners were quickly released, and the government suspended the special powers it enjoyed under the constitutional amendment, though without annulling the legislation which would permit it to reinvoke them.

Encouraged by such gestures, the IRA leaders felt it was time to demand more substantive changes. Their expressed hopes ranged from assurances that Fianna Fail would move without delay to reestablish the Republic along lesser ideological concerns such as rewarding those who had kept the faith in the ranks of the IRA, and punishment of the renegades who had persecuted them. De Valera was contacted

directly by two old friends, one representing the ideologically moderate or strictly political wing of the IRA, the other
the socially radical wing which had produced Saor Eire. De
Valera assured them that Fianna Fail would now be the vehicle for the assertion of all of Ireland's rights and would move
as rapidly as possible toward the goals they all shared. But
his timetable and sense of priorities differed from theirs.

De Valera had never insisted, for example, on a radical
break with England or the British Commonwealth. With the
oath out of the way, he believed, they could reach a mutually
beneficial relationship of equality. He had to face the fact
that partition of Ireland was fully institutionalized in two
governments with practically nothing in common. Insistence
on the name of a republic would add one more obstacle to
reunification. Worst of all, he saw no further function for the
IRA. Constitutional and diplomatic means would henceforth
suffice. The constitutional evolution of the British Commonwealth during recent years had eliminated whatever
doubts existed in 1922 regarding the full sovereignty of the
member states. The 1931 Statute of Westminster had even acknowledged explicitly their right to secede.

De Valera might have decided that the IRA had no further function. The average Irishman, nevertheless, thought
differently. He did not see how a Fianna Fail government
could establish a satisfactory relationship with the army
created in 1922 to crush the movement they had been leading. Sooner or later, it must in self-protection incorporate the
IRA into the defense system. In anticipation of this move,
recruits poured into the IRA. The suspension of the special
powers, the release of prisoners, and other signs of official
benevolence caused the police to stop interfering with IRA
meetings, training of members, or demonstrations. Arms
were again flowing from the United States.

This new IRA, however, had a weakness which few yet
saw. It was losing its identification and its sense of purpose.
Instead of formulating an independent policy, it was waiting
for signals from Fianna Fail. Saor Eire, its recently created

political arm, collapsed as fast as it had grown. The reason was not simply the Church's condemnation, though that played a part, but the growing belief that Fianna Fail would carry out the purposes for which Saor Eire had come into existence. This belief was strengthened by two actions the leadership of Fianna Fail had quickly taken in fulfillment of election promises. It abolished the oath of allegiance, and it suspended payment of the land annuities to the British exchequer. The British replied by imposing additional duties on imports from Ireland calculated to replace the revenue the land annuities had been providing. The British then offered to submit the issue to an exclusively Commonwealth tribunal. Remembering how the Free State had fared with a Commonwealth tribunal over the redrawing of the boundary with Northern Ireland, the Irish government insisted on an international tribunal, meanwhile passing legislation to impose compensatory duties on imports from Britain. The economic war was on.

It seemed hopelessly one-sided. Ireland sent 92 percent of its exports to British markets, while Britain depended on the Free State for only 7 percent of its imports. In addition, the depression had reduced the Irish economy to desperate straits even before this new pressure was applied. But Fianna Fail showed itself surprisingly innovative. It gave bounties to tillage farmers, introduced price controls, offered free meat vouchers to the unemployed, and pushed industrial development, setting up several state bodies to expand production of cement, fuels, and other basic items of which Britain had previously held a monopoly. Then there was the major intangible. Many who disagreed strongly with de Valera still responded with atavistic determination to British aggression, as they saw it. Here was Goliath making his old taunts against David. Inevitably, the IRA quickly found a role. They instituted a boycott of British goods, especially ale, often adding the violent destruction of supplies to the more conventional weapons of the boycott. They also challenged the Cosgrave party and others who denounced the

Fianna Fail moves as treaty violations and defended the British actions as a logical and proper response to de Valera's mistaken policies. As was the case with Italy's Fascists and Germany's Nazis, the more conservative elements felt threatened and began to form paramilitary bodies as a counterweight to the IRA, finally uniting as the Blueshirts in 1933. The Brownshirts had just brought Hitler to power, and some fanatics in Ireland aspired to a similar *coup d'état.* When in August Fianna Fail reinvoked the special powers voted by its predecessor two years earlier and banned a Blueshirt march in Dublin, the IRA activated 3000 men and located them along the proposed route just in case the government forces might be unable or unwilling to enforce the ban.

Skirmishing between IRA and Blueshirts continued for two or three years, while de Valera insistently repeated that Ireland no longer needed private armies of either the right or the left. Simultaneously he pressed a low-key but ultimately effective program to return the IRA to the sidelines. A new detective branch recruited several hundred prominent Republicans to keep tabs on the Blueshirts, thus depriving the IRA of leaders and potential leaders. As for the Blueshirts, de Valera took them less seriously, being correctly convinced that they were too removed from Ireland's traditions to flourish for long. A militia force was created to provide an alternative outlet for youthful enthusiasms of many who would otherwise have joined the IRA. Pensions were voted for injured men and compensation for property damage for those on the losing side in the civil war, only the winners having previously been taken care of. Institutions and ceremonies related to the Free State's membership in the British Commonwealth were eliminated or downgraded, de Valera promising that this was but a first installment. When Edward VIII abdicated in 1936 to marry Wallis Warfield, de Valera used the crisis to complete the elimination of the British Crown from the Free State's constitutional framework. Britain and the other dominions accepted Edward's abdication and transferred their allegiance to his brother, George VI. The Dail, however, merely accepted the abdication, then passed enabling legislation to authorize the executive to utilize for such purposes as it deemed appropriate. The king was recognized by the Commonwealth nations "as the symbol of their cooperation" for "the appointment of diplomatic and consular representatives and the conclusion of international agreements." [2] The link was still essential for these purposes. Foreign states would not accept Free State ambassadors or ministers unless accredited by the British Crown. It was not until the decolonization era following World War II that international recognition of new states became routine.

Of course, the partition issue also counseled prudence. To break all ties with the Commonwealth would further widen the emotional gulf between north and south, a consideration that undoubtedly weighed with de Valera. But quite apart from that reason, the Free State was not then in a position to launch out internationally on its own. Even upstarts like Hitler and Mussolini had still too much respect for the British Crown and the conventions of diplomacy.

With "external association" thus fully established, de Valera moved rapidly on another project that he felt would further undermine the IRA and establish himself definitively as the guardian and repository of national sovereignty. He drafted a new constitution designed to eliminate any possible restrictions on Irish self-identity inserted by English insistence in the constitution of 1922. No major change in the philosophy or system of government resulted. The administrative system based on British practice, with which Ireland was long familiar, was retained.

What was innovative was the attempt to formulate in some detail the social principles which should underlie and inspire national policy. The 1930s were a particularly bad time to make such an attempt. The depression had generated worldwide ideological confusion, with communism, nazism, fascism, and other "isms" finding fanatical supporters and opponents. To the liberal-democratic principles going back to such political theorists as Montesquieu and Tocqueville, de

Valera thought it necessary to add an overlay of what were then being touted as the definitive Roman Catholic teachings on the social order.

The political benefits of this line seemed overwhelming at the time. De Valera knew he could never get a majority in a referendum to enact the new constitution without the support of the Church, many prominent members of which continued to be distrustful of his party and himself. His opponents continued to harp on the civil war condemnation. A book published in 1937 was still insisting that neither he nor his associates had ever repented of their disobedience to the Church.[3] And nobody seemed to have the least anticipation of the long-term result of creating in one part of Ireland a series of social attitudes, assumptions, and ultimately laws deeply different from those governing society in the other part.

Many profound ironies were involved. The constitution of 1922 enacted by the Cosgrave government had been totally secular and had established the principle of separation of Church and state, this in spite of the fact that the Cosgrave party was in basic ideological agreement with the Catholic church and needed its active support to legitimate the new regime and enable it to survive its many enemies. One reason for the reserve on the part of the state at that time and for the Church's acquiescence in it was that the future of partition was still quite uncertain. To show partiality to Roman Catholicism would have predetermined the decision—which the north took in any case—to go its own way.

De Valera, while personally devout and a regular communicant, had much less cordial relations with the Church as an institution in Ireland. It had turned against his side in the civil war, visiting its excommunications on all active members of the group of which he formed part. As president of the League of Nations in 1935, he exerted all his influence—successfully—to have that body condemn Mussolini's invasion of Ethiopia, a project with which many of the Irish bishops sympathized. He insisted in 1936 on strict Irish neutrality in the Spanish civil war, again following the League of

Nations ruling, and banned the efforts openly encouraged by the Irish cardinal and many bishops to raise a volunteer expedition in Ireland to fight for General Franco.[4]

The politician in de Valera decided as usual to steer a middle course. There had developed in the country a considerable volume of opinion or feeling in favor of more explicitly "Catholic" social institutions, a mood summed up by Edward Cahill, a popular Jesuit lecturer and writer, when he deplored what he called "the strange anomaly of a profoundly Catholic nation devoid of many of the external features of a Catholic civilization, and suffering from all the material and very many of the mental defects which usually result from an un-Christian social regime." [5]

At de Valera's request, Father Cahill drafted a preamble and a series of "social" provisions, drawing from the Polish constitution of 1921 and the Austrian constitution of 1934, as well as from papal encyclicals and other Catholic sources. The result was more than de Valera had bargained for, and he turned to a personal friend, John McQuaid, for a formulation more in keeping with Irish conditions. It was a particularly unhappy choice. McQuaid, who was to become Archbishop of Dublin in 1940 and retain that prestigious position for 32 years, was the most obscurantist Irish churchman of the twentieth century, his public statements and actions doing more than those of any other single individual to widen the gap between the Protestants of Northern Ireland and their fellow countrymen. McQuaid's recommendations reinforced those of Cahill. They expressed the world view of Pius VII and other nineteenth-century popes allied with the last remnants of feudalism in its dying struggle against the Enlightenment, the French Revolution, and all the liberating movements which proclaimed the equality of men and women of every condition and sought to put human rights before those of property and other vested interests.[6]

All of this was a long way from de Valera's personal views, and he tried to tone the language down as best he could. The result was a mishmash which recognized the family as "the natural primary and fundamental unit group of society, and as a moral institution possessing inalienable and imprescriptible rights, antecedent and superior to all positive law," promising to protect mothers against having to go out to work "to the neglect of their duties in the home," prohibiting divorce, acknowledging man's "natural right, antecedent to positive law, to the private ownership of external goods," favoring private initiative in industry and commerce, and recognizing "the special position" of the Roman Catholic church as "the guardian of the faith professed by the great majority of the citizens."

Having made these high-sounding concessions, de Valera proceeded to turn them into window dressing by hedging them with limitations. The special status of Roman Catholicism was pralleled by a recognition of the Reformed churches, Jewish congregations, and other religious bodies existing in the state. Freedom of conscience and religious practice was guaranteed. The state undertook not to endow any religion or to discriminate in giving aid to education or otherwise, and to protect the right of each denomination to its property. The exercise of rights by citizens could be regulated by the state in the public interest. The principles of social policy enunciated in the constitution were stated to be for the guidance of the legislature and not capable of enforcement in the courts of law. It was a typical balancing act, but it achieved its purpose. Cardinal Joseph MacRory described the result as "a great Christian document." Even the Roman Catholic extremists who had been plugging for a medieval theocracy were silenced when Pope Pius XII went out of his way to pay a tribute during a visit by de Valera to Rome.

The treatment of the relationship both with Britain and with Northern Ireland was similarly nuanced. Within the Free State, henceforth to be known simply as Ireland (or Eire, the equivalent in Gaelic), the British Crown was stripped of all function and symbolic status. But the constitution avoided using the word *republic* to describe the state, and it did not abrogate the right of the Crown to perform certain external functions. The British, in consequence, decided that the constitutional relationship between the two countries was unchanged and the king continued to accredit Irish representatives abroad. As for the partition of Ireland, "the whole island of Ireland, its islands and territorial seas" were affirmed to constitute the national territory. But the fact of partition was acknowledged by the added clause specifying that—until further notice—the laws enacted by the Dail would have "the like area and extent of application" as the laws heretofore enacted by the Free State.

De Valera achieved his short- and middle-term objectives. The people approved the constitution. The isolation of the IRA was promoted by removing the last trappings of the imperial connection and reaffirming the integrity of the national territory without a direct confrontation with Britain. It was not until very much later that the cost would become generally apparent, namely, a deepening of the emotional gulf between north and south by the blunt repudiation of the legitimacy of the Northern Ireland regime and the positive institutionalization of Catholic attitudes and assumptions as the exclusive expression of Irish ideals and values.

The list of wrongs which constituted the IRA's justification for its refusal to accept the de Valera step-by-step approach and go out of business was to be significantly further shortened the following year. Growing British concern at the political deterioration on the continent of Europe, where Hitler continued to build up his military machine and to swallow his neighbors one after another, caused London to end the economic war and restore cordial relations with a neighbor whose contributions of food and fighting men had long been important in Britain's wars. For one lump-sum payment equal to two and a half times the annual installment at issue, Britain surrendered all claims to the disputed land annuities. It also withdrew its garrisons from three ports in which it had kept them under the Anglo-Irish Treaty of 1922 and surrendered all claims to port facilities in wartime specified in that treaty. For de Valera it was a tremendous coup, making neutrality a possibility in the war which daily came ominously nearer. Only the issue of partition now remained, and when war broke out in September 1939, de Valera proclaimed neutrality on the ground that Britain must render justice by returning Northern Ireland before it could claim to be waging war on the side of justice. The most London would offer was a statement affirming its support of the principle that the Irish should settle their differences and get back together. De Valera did not judge it worth the price and maintained neutrality to the end. At times it seemed that the British would violate it, but they decided that a benevolently neutral Ireland was better than an occupied one. So Ireland supplied food, soldiers, and industrial workers in return for minimum rations of gasoline, tea, and other products in short supply. It also took in nearly 100,000 British refugees and provided many other services to the British and later to the Americans.[7]

By the late 1930s the leaders of the IRA were left with only the single issue of partition to justify their continuing existence, and they lost many activists and supporters as the de Valera strategy produced one striking result after another. There were, nevertheless, enough men left to maintain an organization which reached into every part of Ireland and had abundant contacts and sympathizers in England, Scotland, and the United States. Money continued to arrive from the United States, and there was still a determined belief that only force could overcome the final obstacle and reunite the country. Within the organization, however, there was deep division over tactics and strategies. Some were strongly in favor of the radical policies urged by Peadar O'Donnell which would commit the IRA not only to break all connection with England but reorder society for the benefit of workers and small farmers. Against this policy on the ground that it was a distraction from the IRA's specific and primary function, and also divisive of Irishmen who were all needed for the fight for freedom, were many strictly military men, who suspected politics and politicians and believed in the supreme power of force. The one who now emerged as spokesman for this viewpoint was Sean Russell. As far back as 1923, Russell had gone to Russia to buy arms, but his interest in that country had always remained purely practical. To the extent that it was against England, it was a friend of Ireland. That was all.

Russell had few enemies. Even those who least approved his views never doubted his honesty. In 1934, he won a round against O'Donnell, presiding over a court-martial which expelled O'Donnell from the IRA. The charge was that he had participated in a Republican congress which had openly criticized the IRA for lack of a social awareness. Two years later, Russell had a clash with Sean MacBride, son of Maud Gonne MacBride, a lawyer, and an active radical politician. MacBride had become Chief of Staff of the IRA, and his legal concern for precision caused him to question accounts presented by Russell, who had been Director of Munitions ever since the 1923 order to dump arms at the end of the civil war. Everyone knew that Russell's entire life was committed to accumulating and storing the weapons with which he hoped one day to renew the fight, but record-keeping was not his forte. On MacBride's insistence, he was court-martialed for misappropriation of funds and penalized by exclusion from the inner circle of command. Many of his friends, quite sure that he had not benefited personally, were deeply offended, and they decided to retaliate by promoting the idea of opening a new war front in England. The issue was fought back and forth for two years, until an IRA convention in 1938 elected an executive in which Russell was named Chief of Staff and in which the majority backed him and his program.

The action did not produce an open split, but it caused many senior and important members to withdraw officially and others to drift away. Russell had been in the United States during the period of his eclipse, and he had gained the support of many members of Clan na Gael for his idea. They now stepped up the needed flow of funds. But Russell and his men lacked the vision and the expertise to develop a plan that might have caused serious injury to Britain, for example, organized sabotage of the war industries which in early 1939 were in full production in the effort to be ready for Hitler's anticipated war moves. Instead, they settled on a campaign of minor destruction, small fire bombs in postal boxes and department stores, along with a few more or less symbolic attacks on power lines, generating stations, and similar targets. Before moving, however, they went through a ceremonial designed to establish the "legality" of their proposed move, something that has always been important to the IRA and which helps to explain its continuing appeal. They requested the surviving members of the Second Dail, that is to say, those of the members who had been elected in 1921 and refused to accept the Anglo-Irish Treaty signed later that year, to authorize them to declare war on Britain. The response was favorable and led to a decision by the Dail group to transfer to the Army Council of the IRA the right to set up a government of the Irish Republic. This the IRA accepted as giving them the moral and legal right as such government to declare war, thereby salving the consciences of the many members concerned about ecclesiastical condemnation of illegal organizations.

The next step was a formal ultimatum to the British Foreign Secretary demanding the withdrawal of all British soldiers and civilian representatives from every part of Ireland. Unless it acted within four days, the ultimatum said, the British government must take the consequences. Four days later, explosions started in England, and the campaign continued all through the spring and summer. In August, Britain enacted emergency legislation which authorized tight control of immigration, the right of deportation, the registration of all Irish living in Britain, and the detention of suspects. A month later the Second World War had broken out, and de Valera undertook even stronger measures against the IRA within his jurisdiction than those recently taken by Britain. He realized that Irish neutrality could not possibly be maintained if his country were permitted to become a base for sabotage against a Britain at war.

Before long the pressures mounted to an intensity that forced the IRA back on the defensive at home and ended the campaign of sabotage in England by cutting off men and supplies. Yet the nucleus of the IRA held together for the entire war, engaged in cat-and-mouse tactics with the Irish police and armed forces and involved in bizarre negotiations with Nazi agents, from whom they sought arms and money but who were more generous with advice on how the IRA could reorder their priorities for the benefit of the Nazi war effort. Internal dissension further weakened the nucleus of the faithful as various top leaders fell under the suspicion of being agents working for the Dublin government, for the British government, or for the Nazis. The purposes of the organization seemed to be lost as its members wasted their energies on coups and countercoups. The lesson for many IRA members and sympathizers in Northern Ireland was that they should stop looking to the south for help and instead determine their own policy and plan their own means to implement it. It was an ironic development. The *raison d'être* of the IRA both north and south had been to end the partition of Ireland. Partition as an institution, however, had become so entrenched that it was now threatening to extend to the IRA itself.

12

The IRA in Northern Ireland

*If you think you're not confused, you just don't understand
what's going on.*

—Belfast saying

The problems of the IRA within the territory of Northern
Ireland had always been considerably different from those of
the units on the other side of the border. Relations with the
Dublin government had often been bitter and always uncertain, but the clash was a family one over means rather than
over ends. Relations with the Belfast government and its supporters did not exist at all. For them, the IRA was an enemy
with whom any accommodation was unthinkable. It was to
blame for the disruption of the unity of the United Kingdom,
forcing the British government to allow a part of it to secede
and form the Free State. It continued to deny Northern Ireland's right to exist and was ready to use all available means
to destroy it.

The logic of the Belfast regime called for every possible
effort to wipe out the IRA, but at the same time it incorporated a contradiction which made the task impossible. The
regime had decided at its inception, as a matter of policy, to

identify political loyalty with Protestantism and to treat all Catholics as at least potentially disaffected. The inevitable response of the Catholics was to polarize in self-defense around the IRA, thus providing the sea in which the gunmen could swim in relative security in spite of the best efforts of the security forces. Official policy similarly forced the police to regard every action of the Catholic community as inspired by the IRA and in consequence a threat to the safety of the state. The publicity ensured continuing support of the IRA but the identification prevented normal political evolution. If the Catholics wanted anything, it had to be automatically opposed, and by force if other means failed to suffice.

After the pogroms in Belfast in 1920 to 1922 and the building up of strong local defense forces to counter a possible armed attack from the Free State, the IRA in Northern Ireland found itself reduced for many years to the task of holding the organization together. Hope of help from the south declined with the outbreak of the civil war there, and it fell further when the protreaty party won that war and shortly afterward acquiesced in accepting the earlier established boundary as permanent. Pressure from the Northern Ireland police never let up. It was necessary to burrow deeper and deeper in order to survive. At the same time, within the Catholic community there were fewer of the political and social conflicts which affected the Free State. The IRA in the south might decide that Cosgrave was worse than Lloyd George, and later that de Valera was worse than Cosgrave. But the perspective in the north was different. The governments in Dublin were composed of sincere Irishmen who were agreed in their opposition to partition even when in conflict about how to end it. For Catholics in the north the main issue was to get rid of a bigoted government which trampled on all of them alike. Even if some did not think the IRA approach was the best one, they were all glad to know a few armed men were somewhere on their side when trouble threatened. Within the IRA, similarly, there was no conflict between men of different social trends. The immediate need was for arms and training for the fight. Such subtleties as those which in the south pitted Sean Russell against Peadar O'Donnell would have to wait.

The early 1930s seemed for a moment to offer the Catholic community the possibility of escaping from the sectarian web. With unemployment running at 30 percent in Belfast, Protestants as well as Catholics were starving, and for a time the poor began to organize across denominational lines. A hunger march on Parliament was decided upon in 1932, and when the government banned it, crowds began to demonstrate in the city. The police followed their usual practice of treating the Catholics as the instigators. They charged the demonstrators on the Catholic Falls Road, and when the news reached the Protestant Shankill nearby, the workers there came out to support their Catholic fellow workers, precipitating a riot in which property was wrecked and burned, and in which two men were killed. But for once, the riot had not been a sectarian one.[1]

The dangers lurking in such a development had, however, already become apparent to the Orange leaders. A little earlier, in fact, they had organized the Ulster Protestant League. They maintained that the rise in unemployment made it more important than ever to deny jobs to Catholics. All good Protestant employers, they urged, should not employ Catholics, and all good Protestant workers should refuse to work alongside Catholics. In that way, there would be enough jobs for Protestants and their enemies alone would suffer. The Prime Minister and other cabinet ministers endorsed this policy, and it was preached incessantly from Orange platforms. The campaign reached a crescendo in 1935 with a wave of murders, burnings, and lootings. The government banned all parades and demonstrations but backed down in the face of Orange demands that the traditional celebrations in July must not be called off. These celebrations sparked off three weeks of sectarian rioting in which a dozen people were killed and hundreds injured. It was a hopelessly one-sided contest. Evidence in subsequent court cases, in which victims sought damages for malicious injuries, established that 514 Catholic families, numbering 2241 persons occupying 430 dwellings, had been expelled from their homes.

One major purpose of all the riots was to drive back into the ghettos those Catholic families which in times of peace had ventured outside into neighboring streets. The claimants who were granted compensation by the courts were almost entirely Catholic; and all but three of the few Protestant claimants were in court not because they had been attacked in their homes by Catholic mobs but because Protestant mobs had damaged property they had rented to Catholic tenants. The victims in claims resulting from death or disablement from gunshot wounds numbered 43, of whom 26 were Catholics and 17 Protestant, this in a city more than two-thirds Protestant. As for the partisanship of the police, it was established that the 120 police on duty on a night during which 56 houses occupied by Catholics were burned or wrecked arrested only 4 rioters. In all of this, the IRA lacked the strength to offer more than token resistance. Nevertheless, the people were convinced things would have been worse if the IRA had not been around, and in consequence the IRA emerged from the riots with considerable prestige. In addition, their contention that attempts to make peace with the regime were futile had been proved to the satisfaction of most.[2]

The revival of the pogrom, which it had been generally assumed was a thing of the past, created a new concern among people in the Free State. In principle they were all opposed to partition and refused to imagine that it could last for any length of time. In practice, nevertheless, they had become more and more reconciled to the fact, and their professions of concern sounded ever less convincing to the Nationalists in the north who for years had been watching them make their own political and social decisions without the slightest concern for the impact such decisions might make on the other side of the border.

After the pogroms of 1935, however, some of the old bitterness, always latent in the south against the partisan
Orange regime in the north, was expressed again. Many
organs of opinion and individuals in the south backed an approach to the British government made by the Roman Catholic bishop of Belfast and other members of the Catholic
community in the north. The bishop and his associates had
failed to obtain from the local government the impartial inquiry they had requested into the disturbances; the Stormont Prime Minister had replied by charging that the
Catholic community was itself to blame. The origin and circumstances of the riots, he said, were to be found "deep-
seated among a certain section in our national life who are
disloyal to the throne and the constitution of these realms." ³

The approach to the London government succeeded in
enlisting the backing of many members of the Westminster
Parliament, which, under the Act of 1920 creating the Northern Ireland regime, retained "unaffected and undiminished"
its "supreme authority" over "all persons, matters and
things" in Northern Ireland. British Prime Minister Stanley
Baldwin, however, told Parliament that "this matter is entirely within the discretion and responsibility of the government of Northern Ireland, and for fundamental constitutional
reasons the possibility of holding an inquiry by the imperial
government is completely ruled out." ⁴

To most Irishmen this decision was not only evasive but
a deliberate distortion of the facts. For the IRA in particular it
confirmed their thesis that the only thing the English lis-
tened to was force, and it had a definite impact on the decision of the IRA to move ahead with the policy of renewing
open war which Sean Russell was then recommending. It
also guaranteed a more favorable reception for that policy
from many moderate Irishmen who in other circumstances
would not have countenanced it. Indeed, as an alternative to
Gilmore's plan for carrying the war to England, a third party
within the IRA led by Tom Barry of Cork urged that the "immediate and terrible war" against the British be waged not in

England but in Northern Ireland, and an IRA convention in 1936 actually carried Barry's resolution by acclamation. Some who thought the decision unwise resigned from the IRA and made their way surreptitiously to Spain where they formed the 400-man James Connolly battalion of the Abraham Lincoln Brigade to fight with the Spanish Loyalists against Franco. Forty-two of them were killed, 12 captured, and 114 wounded. But Barry pushed ahead with his plans, not for a guerrilla war in Northern Ireland, but for one big blow from the outside to test the enemy strength and the people's reaction. The blow was to be an attack on the Armagh military barracks by a 26-man unit from Cork. The Northern Ireland IRA was all in favor, having always been on the side of Gilmore and the direct-action people, and opposed to Peadar O'Donnell and the others who, in their view, distorted priorities by getting mixed up in politics and social philosophy. Just as the men were about to set out, however, they discovered that their supposedly secret plans were common knowledge among IRA men and sympathizers in various parts of the country, and they prudently canceled the project, fearing the police might also be privy to the supposed secret. Actually at that moment the northern IRA was almost without top leadership, for its central group had been seized at a meeting in circumstances for which the supreme executive in Dublin was largely to blame. The impact of the two incidents was to persuade the Northerners that the more they depended on themselves, the better chance they had of surviving and progressing.

When Russell returned to power in 1938, nevertheless, the IRA in the north did not want to be left completely on the sidelines, and they suggested that the campaign against Britain should be preceded by a tryout in Northern Ireland. The targets selected were the customs posts along the border. These posts are under direct British control, customs being a service reserved to London, and their destruction would have high symbolic value as a direct attack on the British-manned division of the country. As on many other occasions, the preparations were poorly made. A bomb exploded on its way to its destination killing the three men in charge of it and alerting the northern police. Although some border posts were destroyed, the main result was to arouse the police to renewed concern, and it enabled them to seize more of the IRA leaders in Northern Ireland—as well as many sympathizers—at the outbreak of war the following year. By that time, the Belfast activists had lost perhaps a third of the some-500 trained men they could muster in 1938. Still they held together throughout the war, infiltrating the British army camps in Northern Ireland, carrying out raids for arms, causing trouble in jails and internment camps by protests and strikes to secure treatment as political prisoners, and using mobile radio transmitters to broadcast news of their successes. Between themselves and Mr. de Valera they saved the northern Irish from being conscripted during the war. When the British Parliament introduced conscription in April 1939, de Valera had commented in the Dail that it would be "an act of aggression against the Irish people" if it was extended to Northern Ireland. Two years later, Churchill again talked about the subject but raised such a storm of protest that he decided it would cost more than it would be worth.

Even before the war had ended in 1945, the IRA in Northern Ireland had gone so far underground that the authorities felt it held few further dangers for them. As one measure of their confidence, they had gradually released the suspects interned in 1939. From a high of 302 persons in 1940, the number declined to a mere 12 in 1944, and they were all let go shortly after the hostilities ended. It seemed at that time that the war experience had done much to solidify the division of the island. The neutral south had been forced in on itself to a greater extent than ever before, while the north identified with Britain in a war that brought great deprivation to the people and destruction of their cities by bombardment from the air, an experience shared by Belfast with Britain's major cities. The south, it now seemed, was going and would continue to go its own way, seeking the welfare of the people under its jurisdiction and forgetting all others. An action of the Dail in 1949 appeared to confirm that analysis. The previous year de Valera's Fianna Fail had been eased out of power after 16 years by a coalition of the right and the left against a party which had come to occupy the middle of the Irish political and social spectrum. The price demanded and received by the left was the formal proclamation—in 1949—of a republic for the area controlled since 1922 by the Free State and known as "Ireland" since the constitution of 1937. That was the same year in which Britain agreed to the retention of Commonwealth membership by India in spite of the fact that it declared itself a republic. In the case of Ireland, however, the British decision was to regard the introduction of the word *republic* as ending the relationship, which was also the intention of the Dublin Dail. The separation was unusually cordial, the two countries passing legislation to give to each other's citizens practically all the rights enjoyed within their territories by their own citizens, including total freedom of movement between the countries. At the urging of the Belfast regime, however, the British Parliament made a commitment not to change the border without the consent of the Stormont Parliament, and not to intervene in Northern Ireland's internal affairs except to control a breakdown of law and order. The first commitment had no legal value because one of the clearest conventions of Britain's unwritten constitution is that Parliament cannot bind itself. The second merely formalized what had been unbroken practice since 1922. The action, nevertheless, caused grave offense to the people of the Republic of Ireland and to the minority community in Northern Ireland. It was seen as an open encouragement to the partisan Orange-dominated government to continue its discrimination forever with Britain's assurance that it would neither interfere itself nor allow the neighboring Republic to do so.

For the IRA in both parts of Ireland these events were a godsend. Just a year earlier, their general headquarters had estimated that fully active membership in the whole of Ireland was down to 200, with some hundreds more on the fringe.⁵ The fact that so-called Republicans on the left would join with the hated Cosgrave party (now headed by John Costello) in accepting a 26-county republic meant that this remnant alone was left to vindicate the historical Irish claim to one indivisible 32-county republic. The parallel handwashing of the British was seen by the minority in the north as a warning that henceforth they could only count on physical force, their own physical force, to protect and vindicate their rights. The result was a rapid rise in membership of the IRA both north and south and the formation of a number of other groups, some political and others paramilitary. In 1954 the northern government banned the tricolor which had emerged as the Sinn Fein emblem during the War of Independence that followed the Easter Rising of 1916 and had since been the official flag of the Irish Free State, of the Republic of Ireland, and of the IRA. One of the new groups, calling itself Saor Uladh (Free Ulster), established an open political organization in 1953, and also a secret military arm. Another in 1954 raided the Armagh military barracks and got away with a quantity of arms, the project which had ended so ingloriously for Tom Barry and his Cork commandos several years earlier. The growing expertise of the IRA and their fellow freedom fighters was again demonstrated the following year when a 21-year-old trainee teacher, with gray-green eyes and a ready smile, led 12 men into the depot of the Royal Electrical and Mechanical Engineers at Arborfield, Berkshire, England, and emerged with five tons of arms. (Rory Brady, as he was then known, later used the Irish form of his name, Ruairi O Bradaigh.)

O Bradaigh was a different kind of IRA man, a college graduate always open to new ways of doing things. From friends in the Irish army he had learned a technique which he put to good use at Arborfield. Having surprised and overcome the two guards on duty in the early morning, the one cooking sausages and the other writing poetry, he woke the other 16 soldiers a few at a time, and lined them up against the wall in their vests, their genitals exposed, their feet some way out, their legs spread, leaning by their fingertips. No violence was used. It was not necessary for his purposes. All he wanted was to keep his captives conscious of the vulnerability of their most sensitive organs, putting possible thoughts of resistance or call for help out of their minds.[6] This technique, which—with horrible refinements—would be used against hundreds of IRA members and suspects in Belfast interrogation centers before many years more had passed, is part of a process for handling and interrogating prisoners now being studied and practiced all over the world.[7] O Bradaigh, a native of Longford, Ireland, was only one of many up-and-coming IRA members gaining military experience in England at that time. Two other arms raiders, John Stephenson and Cathal Goulding, had picked up a load of arms by stealth at an armory in Essex a short time earlier, then had the misfortune of being stopped by a police constable who noticed a van so overloaded that the tires were flat. The haul included 8 Bren guns, 10 Stens, a mortar, an antitank gun, and 99 rifles, but nobody was alert to repel attackers, and the single constable was able to haul the two raiders before a court where they each got eight years.

While justice was thereby served, it is less clear that the general weal was advanced. Both men followed an old IRA tradition by spending their incarceration in the study of Irish and meditation on subversion. English-born Stephenson, formerly a corporal in the British air force and later a railroad worker, not only learned to speak Irish fluently and changed his name to Sean Mac Stiofain, but emerged as a bitter man, totally and irrevocably committed to force. A vegetarian who neither smokes nor drinks, he has been the chief inspirer and stimulator of recent campaigns of IRA bombing and shooting in Northern Ireland. Goulding, a Dubliner, a house painter by trade and a friend of Brendan Behan, was affected differently. With minimal formal education—he left school at 13—he specialized in political science. He continued to believe in the IRA but sought to move it in new directions, having come to see the colonial relationship of Northern Ireland as the root of its malaise, the distortions maintained by means of the economic links between the ruling Unionists and the holders of power in London. He interprets the religious issue as a device to split the exploited Unionist worker from his natural ally, the even more shamefully exploited Catholic worker, and he believes the cure would follow quickly if a single nonsectarian system of education were introduced. A sensitive man, Goulding feels that the fossilized physical-force doctrine preached by Mac Stiofain is destructive of the young men, who are taught to regard the fight as an end in itself. His analysis and critique extend to the government and society of the Republic of Ireland, which he regards as a textbook version of neocolonialism. He is, in consequence, much more feared by the Irish politicians and clergy than the simple gunmen who leave their thinking to others.

Although O Braidaigh is a thoughtful and cultured man with a well-developed social conscience, he continued for some time in the traditional direction after the Arborfield raid. With Mac Stiofain and Goulding in jail, he quickly rose to Chief of Staff and was in command of the campaign initiated in December 1956. A statement then issued said that northern units of the IRA had attacked key British installations, thus starting "a decisive stage" of resistance to British rule in occupied Ireland. The statement warned against bigotry and sectarianism, "twin enemies of Irish republicanism," and urged the RUC and B-Specials to stand aside or join in the fight against tyranny. The campaign opened with a spectacular assault in which 150 men blew up targets in 10 areas along the border in a single night. The targets included two barracks, a courthouse, and a BBC transmitter. After this success, the IRA proceeded to organize centers in Derry, Armagh, Newry, and other predominantly Catholic cities and towns. They assumed that the local population would welcome them, provide recruits to ferry supplies from the south, engage in sabotage, and conduct ambushes. In this, they were gravely mistaken. While the Catholic community was not prepared to hand the IRA organizers over to the Belfast authorities, neither was it prepared to engage in a new round of warfare. As would soon become evident in different ways, the Catholics of Northern Ireland had come to a collective conclusion. If they were ever to secure their rights as citizens, it would have to be by new roads. And the securing of their rights as citizens would henceforth take precedence over the old dream of a united Ireland. They had not thrown the dream away, but they definitely had reversed priorities.

When the Dublin government joined that of Belfast in internment of IRA leaders, it was quickly apparent that the "decisive stage" proclaimed by the IRA was in reverse. Gestures continued here and there. Damage to property was considerable, but at the end of five years, the casualty figures hardly added up to a war, a total of two IRA men killed in action and seven others killed accidentally—mostly by the premature explosion of homemade bombs—with six deaths and thirty-two wounded on the other side. O Bradaigh finally made a public admission of failure, in a document which gives a significant explanation of the reasons for that failure. "The decision to end the Resistance Campaign has been taken in view of the general situation. Foremost among the factors motivating this course of action has been the attitude of the general public whose minds have been deliberately distracted from the supreme issue facing the Irish people— the unity and freedom of Ireland." [8]

O Bradaigh was correct in his conclusion that the attitude of the Catholic community in Northern Ireland was a decisive factor in the failure of the IRA campaign. Unfortunately, the Orange majority failed to understand the change in mentality that had occurred; or if it did, it was no more prepared to accept the minority as law-abiding citizens with equal rights than it had been to accept its previous demands to dismantle the state. As has been described above, when the minority started on the new road of nonviolent assertion of its rights to equal treatment in the allocation of jobs and houses during the 1960s, the response was as violent as that earlier evoked by the IRA who had come with guns. The failure or refusal to distinguish between these two challenges would ultimately lead to a repudiation by London of its satellite regime in Belfast. But that decisive happening was preceded by a further set of maneuvers, one of the results of which was to raise from the grave the corpse—long presumed dead—of the IRA.

13

Challenge of Civil Rights

*The maintenance of law and order in a democracy depends
quite as much upon support for the law and respect for
the law by the population at large as it does upon the actions
of the police.*

—TERENCE O'NEILL, Prime Minister of
Northern Ireland, in 1969 [1]

*Catholic enclaves are . . . now almost entirely isolated by
waste land in a kind of cordon sanitaire.*

—A 1972 Quaker study [2]

One of the many tantalizing "ifs" of Irish history is how
the society of Northern Ireland and the political life of both
parts of Ireland would have evolved if the Stormont government had read correctly the meaning of the civil rights movement as it developed from its beginnings as a demand for an
end to discrimination in housing at Dungannon, County
Tyrone, in 1964. As we saw in Chapter 4, the minority community was for the first time solidly committed to a nonviolent approach to change that involved recognition of the
legitimacy of the regime and committed the minority to coop-

erate with the regime across a broad social and economic spectrum. The movement was predominantly Roman Catholic in composition, which was inevitable, since the discriminations it was fighting were felt directly by Catholics. But it was nonsectarian not only in declared intent but in leadership and membership. It had the support and cooperation of the Northern Ireland Labor party and the Irish Congress of Trades Unions. The organizations of students and graduates of Queen's University, Belfast, who played a big part in its activities, were totally integrated religiously and culturally. The London-based National Conference of Civil Liberties helped to bring into being the coordinating body known as the Northern Ireland Civil Rights Association (NICRA), a body long chaired by veteran Communist Betty Sinclair. In the words of Lord Cameron, the Scottish judge appointed by the Stormont government under pressure from London in 1969 to inquire into the sources of violence in Northern Ireland, it had "a ballast of moderate and earnest men and women."

NICRA's official platform was modest: one-man-one-vote in local elections; the removal of gerrymandered boundaries; laws against discrimination by local government, and the provision of machinery to deal with complaints; repeal of the Special Powers Act; and disbanding of the B-Specials. And it went about the promotion of that platform in a reasoned and reasonable way. "We were impressed by the number of well-educated and responsible people who were or are in . . . the Civil Rights movement," Lord Cameron reported, "and by the depth and extent of the investigations they have made . . . to produce evidence to vouch their grievances and support their claims for remedy." [3]

The refusal of the regime in Northern Ireland to take the civil rights movement at its word was doubly bizarre because the movement had the solid support of the British Labor government which was in power from 1964 to 1970. Shortly before he took office as Prime Minister, Harold Wilson wrote in September 1964 to the Campaign for Social Justice, the

Dungannon organization which started the movement: "I agree with you as to the importance of the issues with which your campaign is concerned, and can assure you that a Labor government would do everything in its power to see that the infringements of justice to which you are so rightly drawing attention are effectively dealt with." [4] During his period in office, Wilson kept up unrelenting pressure on Stormont to change its way, and he did persuade it to make several positive changes in laws and procedures. But implementation of these changes never went beyond the token level. Stormont preferred to treat Wilson's pressures as part of the political maneuvering of the party in power against its opponents, relying on the commitment made by the Westminster Parliament in 1949 not to intervene in the internal affairs of Northern Ireland except to control "a breakdown of law and order."

Basic to the Stormont position was its insistence that the civil rights movement was only a front for the IRA. In fact, the movement was a mortal threat to what remained of the IRA, immediately provoking a deep ideological conflict for the IRA and creating the conditions for the formal split that would soon follow. The orthodox IRA attitude had always been that neither the Dublin nor the Stormont regime enjoyed any lawful authority and that it was in consequence the duty of all Irishmen to refuse to cooperate with any of their organs or institutions. This principle was carried to the point of refusing to recognize the courts when arrested on any charge, an intransigent stand that often brought heavy penalties when mere technicalities were at issue. The civil rights movement was starting from the basis of the legitimacy of the Stormont regime. It was saying to the IRA's constituents that they should get their feet on the ground and demand the rights that were theirs as loyal British subjects.

The challenge posed by the civil rights movement did not take the IRA entirely by surprise. Since the dismal failure of the campaign of violence in Northern Ireland between 1956 and 1961, some of its leaders were seeking a new way.

Chief among them was Brendan Behan's friend, Cathal Goulding, who had meditated and studied for eight years in an English jail for his part in the 1953 raid on an armory at Felsted, Essex. A sensitive man, he was shocked on his release at the damage being done to his young associates by the fossilized thinking within the IRA, which presented the fight as an end in itself. As Chief of Staff of the IRA from 1962, he saw that it was in the last throes of dissolution. "In August 1967," he subsequently told a newsman, "we called a meeting of local leadership throughout the country to assess the strength of the movement. We discovered that we had no movement." [5] Goulding's study had led him to apply the Marxist analysis to the Northern Ireland situation and to conclude that the colonial relationship to Britain was at the root of Ulster's malaise. The religious issue he saw as a weapon to split the Protestant worker from his natural ally, and he believed that only education conducted on a nonsectarian basis and within an atmosphere of nonviolence could destroy this issue.

Goulding attended the secret meeting which in August 1966 brought NICRA into existence, six months before it was announced publicly in Belfast. He was enthusiastic, as was Roy Johnston, a computer analyst and a Marxist who was then the IRA's chief theoretician. The IRA from that time onward gave all the help it could to the civil rights movement, but never controlled it. "We have investigated this matter with particular care," Lord Cameron later reported. "While there is evidence that members of the IRA are active in the organization, there is no sign that they are in any sense dominant or in a position to control or direct policy of the Civil Rights Association." The men of the IRA who served as stewards during demonstrations, Cameron further noted, were "efficient and exercised a high degree of discipline. There is no evidence . . . that such members either incited to riot or took part in acts of violence." [6]

The Cameron Commission Report dealt with the situation at the beginning of 1969. By the time the report was issued in

September of that year, many things had changed, including the role of the IRA. In April, Terence O'Neill had resigned as Prime Minister under pressure from extremists in the Unionist party who condemned as capitulation to the state's enemies his tentative efforts to redress some of the grievances formulated by the civil rights movement. The summer season of Orange marches brought violent outbreaks of civil strife, first in Derry and then in Belfast. Tension had built up in anticipation of the July 12 Orange parades. Riots raged in Lurgan, where Catholics put up barricades to protect themselves from attacks by the police. In Dungiven (County Derry) and in the city of Derry the parades of the Orangemen were followed by two days of rioting during which shops were wrecked and 60 people hospitalized. On July 12, Ian Paisley told an Orange assembly at Castlereagh, near Belfast, that they were engaged "in the great battle of biblical Protestantism against popery." A similar assembly at Moneymore, County Derry, the same day, was told by Major James D. Chichester-Clark, cousin of Captain Terence O'Neill and his successor as Prime Minister, that the Irish Republicans were murderers. For Chichester-Clark and his listeners the term "Republicans" encompassed all their enemies—the civil rights movement, the IRA, and the government and people of the neighboring Republic of Ireland. Tension rose further the following day when a man injured during the rioting at Dungiven—clubbed by the police, according to four witnesses—died of his wounds, and when on July 17 Samuel Devenney also died. Devenney was the man who had been beaten up with his family in the Bogside in April, as described earlier. In early August, the riots spread to Belfast. When an Orange mob from the Shankill was blocked by the police in an assault on high-rise apartments occupied by Catholics, they turned on the police. Soon a three-way battle developed in which Molotov cocktails, stones, bottles, and chunks of plate glass from broken store windows were thrown. During the weekend Catholic families were driven from their homes in predominantly Protestant neighborhoods, and attacks were begun on Catholics in the mixed areas which had grown up during the long peace since the last round of major pogroms in 1935. Catholic leaders urged a ban on further Orange marches, particularly on the Apprentice Boys' parade in Derry on August 12. The London authorities tried to persuade Chichester-Clark to accede, but he told them a ban could not be enforced and would cause more trouble than could result from the march. London bowed to his judgment, to the horror of the recently appointed Commander-in-Chief of British forces in Northern Ireland, Lieutenant-General Sir Ian Freeland. His total force was 2500 men, half of them allocated to guard public utilities since the attacks on power and water supplies earlier in the year, attacks which the Orange extremists were believed to have carried out in the hope that the IRA would be blamed. But Freeland had no voice in the decision. At this time, he was merely on an alert to respond to calls for help from the police, much as the governor of an American state might alert the National Guard in an anticipated emergency.

By this time, however, there was another ragged thin line of defense for the threatened Catholic ghettos, a line as yet scarcely visible and of doubtful strength. In their desperation the people were welcoming back the IRA whom they had rejected a decade earlier and asking them to perform the task for which they alone had the training and expertise, the protection of the ghettos from the police and Orange mobs.

The early 1960s had seen a radical change in sentiment and direction within the IRA under Goulding's leadership, especially in the Republic. The failure to secure popular support in any part of Ireland for the campaign of violence during the previous years in Northern Ireland created the need to reevaluate methods and goals. Goulding concentrated on economic and social programs to improve the conditions of the small farmers and the rural and urban workers, programs for development of cooperatives, for better housing, for an end to emigration. The ideals encouraged for 20 years by Peadar O'Donnell suddenly became popular. Republican clubs dedicated to the establishment of a socialist republic for the whole of Ireland were formed at Queen's College, Belfast, and the membership included students from both Catholic and Protestant cultural backgrounds. The clubs also were formed in Trinity College, Dublin, citadel for hundreds of years of the Protestant ascendency, and in the modern— and culturally Catholic—University College, Dublin.

As the appeal of the new direction grew, so did pressures to obtain the political power needed to put the theories involved into practice. For the old IRA the dilemma was obvious. Political action must be directed to penetrate the seats of power, the parliaments in Dublin and Belfast which for them constituted usurping bodies. De Valera had split the movement when he agreed to recognize the Dublin Parliament (Dail) as *de facto* holder of political power in Ireland and in due course he had carried his defection farther by proclaiming it also the *de jure* power. Other splits had come later over the same issue, the most important being the defection led by Sean MacBride in the 1940s. The moral basis for the claim of the IRA to use physical force again, if the situation tactically should so warrant, was being undermined.

The new direction, nevertheless, continued. Sinn Fein, as the open political organization claiming a historic continuity with the movement which had revived Irish nationalism in the early part of the century, came once again into the foreground. For the government of Northern Ireland, the decision to give priority to politics represented some progress. One of its recurrent complaints against the Nationalist minority was that a large number of its members had never accepted the existence of the state. Now at last, the Nationalists were drifting in this direction. And even if they came all the way, the most they could hope for was to unite a minority in constitutional opposition. No short- or middle-term threat to the majority of the Unionist party would result.

For the government of the Republic, however, the development was more immediately threatening. None knew better than Fianna Fail, the party of de Valera, how deep-rooted was the emotional tie of Irishmen to Sinn Fein and the IRA. If to this allegiance was added a policy of social reform in favor of the workers and lower middle classes, the balance of political power could easily be upset.

The violent response of the Northern Ireland regime, both through its police and the Orange mobs, to the nonviolent struggle of the civil rights movement suggested to some Fianna Fail leaders a way to block this development. If the IRA were encouraged to concentrate on protecting the civil righters in the north, they would forget their programs for social reform in the Republic. The proposal was attractive to several members of the Dublin cabinet whose origins lay close to the border and who were deeply involved emotionally in happenings that directly affected their families and personal friends. Although much uncertainty still exists as regards the details of the proposals, it is agreed that spokesmen for this group approached members of the IRA in Northern Ireland shortly after the January 1969 attacks at Burntollet Bridge near Derry city. They promised support for a project to reactivate and reequip IRA units for the defense of the Catholic population in Northern Ireland, the principal condition being that the Northern Ireland IRA would establish its own command independent of Dublin. The reason for insisting on an independent command might simply have been that the Dublin high command, led by Goulding, was publicly committed to nonviolence and had recognized the Northern Ireland regime by backing Bernadette Devlin's candidacy for Parliament among other acts. But there was an additional benefit for Fianna Fail in the arrangement: it would transfer to the sidelines the social movement led by Goulding by building up once more the physical-force men whose threat was to Stormont rather than to Dublin.

As the intensity of the pogroms in Northern Ireland increased, the Dublin Dail voted considerable sums to be spent through the Red Cross and other organizations for the victims, some part of which was apparently siphoned off for arms to be smuggled to the IRA in Northern Ireland. All

these efforts combined to increase pressures within the IRA
for a showdown between the supporters of peaceable agitation for social reform in all of Ireland and the supporters of
the old-style physical force. At an IRA convention in Dublin
in December 1969, a substantial majority of the delegates
voted *de facto* recognition of the Dublin and Belfast governments, and also of the London government which retained
overriding authority in Northern Ireland. The dissenters
withdrew to form what they called the Provisional Army
Council. "We declare our allegiance to the 32-county republic proclaimed at Easter 1916, established by the first Dail
Eireann in 1919, overthrown by force of arms in 1922 and
suppressed to this day by the existing British-imposed six-
county and 26-county partition states." Having criticized the
failure of their opponents to maintain the basic military role
of the organization, and in particular to provide the maximum
defense possible for the people of Belfast, they called "on
the Irish people at home and in exile for increased support
toward defending our people in the North and the eventual
achievement of the full political, social, economic, and cultural freedom of Ireland." [7] The appeal to the exiles was
quickly spread in the United States by special envoys who
were successful in rallying to the Provisionals the vast majority of the faithful.

Since that time, there have been two IRAs, known respectively as the Officials and the Provisionals, each with its
parallel political body calling itself Sinn Fein and usually
distinguished by the addition to the title of the name of the
Dublin street where they have their respective headquarters,
Kevin Street for the Sinn Fein organization which supports
the Provisionals and Gardiner Street for that of the Officials.

At the time of the split, the entire IRA strength in Belfast
was an estimated 150 men, about half of them fully active in
the organization.[8] Most stayed with the Officials, including
the company quartermasters who held whatever small supplies of arms were on hand. But the dynamics of the situation
favored the Provisionals who had defined their immediate

task as the defense of the beleaguered Nationalists. That by itself assured them of a regular supply of recruits, there being no man, woman, or child in the Catholic community who was not ready to use every available means to defend its territory. That is a basic fact of the conflict. Both communities regard Northern Ireland as their homeland and deserving of all sacrifice to protect.

The first arms and ammunition were taken in a raid on a Belfast gunsmith which netted 15 rifles and 1 pistol. The raid was made by some professional thieves who had decided the Provisionals would pay them a good price for the loot. But the Provisionals were short of money too, and they simply seized the stolen goods "in the name of the Republic." Shortly afterward, the Officials in three counties across the border in the Republic switched allegiance and sent the Belfast Provisionals 30 Thompson submachine guns, 27 rifles, and some pistols. Some of the money voted by the Dublin government for relief may also have reached them, but probably not more than a few thousand dollars. Sympathizers in Ireland, north and south, and in England have since continued to provide aid. The main source of funds and equipment seems, however, to have been the United States where many in the Irish community retain an inherited bitterness toward Britain and remain committed to a policy of physical force to complete the freeing of the homeland. American-Irish support for the Provisionals was further ensured when the Officials, who had previously tempered their language to minimize internal friction, took a more aggressively Marxist stand.[9]

The traditional function of the IRA in Belfast was not, however, changed by these events. Catholics in Belfast form only a quarter of the population. They are isolated from the main areas of Catholic strength in Derry and the border counties of Tyrone and Fermanagh by solidly hostile territory. In addition to the main ghetto of the Falls area, Belfast contains several smaller ghettos, of which the most exposed is the Short Strand–Mountpottinger crescent where

6000 Catholics are hemmed in by 60,000 Protestants and cut off by the river from retreat or reinforcement. Belfast's Catholics are thus hostages for the good behavior of the Catholic community of Derry and elsewhere, and the role of the IRA in Belfast was traditionally the defensive one of protecting against mob attack and retaliating when attacked. The IRA had exercised this role shortly before the split, in September 1969, when an IRA man had used a machine gun stolen from the British army to repel an Orange mob attacking an isolated block of Catholic-occupied apartments optimistically called Unity Walk. The Provisionals again exercised it in January 1970 when they planted a bomb close to an army billet after an alleged act of army misbehavior. The bomb blew a hole in the wall but caused no injury to the men inside. Apart from these two incidents, the Provisionals restricted themselves to building up their defensive strength and cementing their relations with the Catholic community up to the summer of 1970. By that time, events had ripened to a point where they could and did assume a more aggressive and central role.

The previous July and August the British government had practically come to the end of its patience with its subordinate government in Northern Ireland. Although it had not yet openly abandoned the long-standing convention not to interfere, it had been calling Prime Minister Chichester-Clark to London and telling him what to do and what not to do. It had—as mentioned above—wanted to stop the Orange parades, then reluctantly withdrew its veto when faced with two familiar Stormont arguments. The minister in charge of internal security said that the police had neither the resources nor the resolution to prevent the marches. And Chichester-Clark added that he would be ousted from office in favor of an extremist if anyone interfered with the marches. So London, after many meetings of a cabinet committee created to deal with the Northern Ireland crisis, backed down.

The August 12 parade of the Apprentice Boys in Derry provoked the worst riots of recent years. Anticipating trouble, the Bogsiders had formed a defense association. They built barricades, prepared petrol bombs, and formed patrols to maintain round-the-clock protection. Field hospitals were set up. Walkie-talkies provided internal communications. Two powerful radio transmitters were used to maintain contact with the outside. Even a fire brigade was created. "Free Derry," which was to prove a divisive symbol for long to come, had been born.

The experiences of the Bogside over the previous year, coupled with the broader failure of the Northern Ireland police forces to perform their duty impartially, were good reasons for these decisions. But the response was also foreseeable. The Apprentice Boys followed their age-old custom, parading on the walls overlooking the Bogside, singing ribald anti-Catholic songs, jeering at the people below, and offering the ultimate insult of throwing down pennies, the gesture of the rich and powerful to the beggarman at his gate. The Bogside youth, proud in its newfound strength, responded with sticks and stones. Soon the city was an inferno, with stores and factories ablaze.

The police attempted to penetrate the Bogside, as in principle they were perfectly entitled to do, for no government can tolerate an enclave in which its writ does not run. For two and a half days the battle raged. When batons and riot shields proved no match for the petrol bombs hurled from the roofs of the high-rise apartments, the police tried CS tear gas, the first time it was used anywhere in the United Kingdom of Great Britain and Northern Ireland.[10] The Bogsiders were ready for the CS, wet handkerchiefs to serve as masks, Vaseline for irritated eyes, and wet blankets to throw over the canisters as they hit the ground. As the RUC were gradually worn down by exhaustion, they called out the B-Specials to help them. But the only effect of this was to increase confusion and conflict in the city. The Bogside continued to repel all attackers.

Inevitably, the riots spread from town to town across Northern Ireland. In Dungiven, Catholics threatened the police barracks and burned down the courthouse and the Orange Hall. In Armagh, B-Specials used submachine guns and rifles, killing one man with a high-velocity bullet and wounding two others. On August 13, the Prime Minister of the Republic of Ireland said in a radio-television broadcast that the Stormont government had lost control, and that London and Dublin should meet to discuss the future of Northern Ireland. He set up field hospitals near the border, mobilized the diminutive army of the Republic, and called on the United Nations to send a peace-keeping force.[11]

On August 14, British troops were committed to police duty in Northern Ireland for the first time since the 1920s. Three hundred men were moved from a nearby naval base into the heart of Derry. The RUC withdrew from the barricades around the Bogside, and the military quickly arranged a truce with those inside, a truce which guaranteed that the RUC could enter only with the permission of the people of the Bogside.

Derry was quiet for the moment, but worse would quickly follow elsewhere. On August 13, in response to appeals from the Bogside for diversionary action, youths in Belfast had attacked two police barracks with petrol bombs and other improvised missiles. It was the start of extensive rioting. The following day, the B-Specials in Belfast were mobilized, and they began immediately to patrol Catholic districts, shooting wildly and burning down homes. Eight people lost their lives that night, one a fifteen-year-old boy who was helping a family to flee the terror, another a nine-year-old shot in his bed. Orange mobs drove hundreds of Catholics from their homes and set the buildings on fire. The terror was heightened by the appearance on the streets of armored cars, each equipped with a machine gun with a range of over two miles and which fired high-velocity bullets in bursts, a sophisticated weapon of war but one totally unsuited to riot control in city streets.[12] To protect themselves against the RUC armored cars and the B-Specials, the Catholics on the Falls Road followed the example of the Bogside, erecting barricades and manufacturing petrol bombs.

To the immense relief of the Catholics, London sent a contingent of troops to Belfast on August 15 and shortly afterward set up a barricade of metal and barbed wire to prevent irruptions from the Shankill into the Falls area or vice versa. James Callaghan, the man ultimately responsible, as Britain's Home Secretary, for the administration of Northern Ireland, visited Belfast in late August. He toured the riot districts, and imposed revolutionary reforms on Stormont. He said he wanted religious discrimination outlawed, a board of community relations established with equal representation of Protestants and Catholics, and a government minister responsible for community harmony. He said the RUC must be reformed and the B-Specials disbanded. Local government would have to be completely reorganized to give fair representation to all shades of opinion, and housing would become the responsibility of a single impartial authority. Before he left, he persuaded the Stormont authorities to join him in a public statement. Every citizen of Northern Ireland, it said, is entitled to equality of opportunity in public employment, protection against incitement to religious hatred, fair allocation of housing, effective machinery to investigate charges against public bodies, and proper representation on all elected bodies. To ensure that the words would not be forgotten when he went back to London, Callaghan installed Oliver Wright, with the title of United Kingdom Representative, in Stormont as watchdog. He was a high civil servant from London.

Both Wright and the British troops came to Northern Ireland anxious to do the best job in their power. But, like all other Englishmen who ever tried to deal with Ireland as friend or enemy, they were hopelessly handicapped by their ignorance. Wright, a career officer in the foreign service, had most recently been London's emissary in Rhodesia, and he quickly diagnosed the Northern Ireland mess in Rhodesian terms as "a settler problem plus a tribal problem." For an Englishman, impartiality between settlers and tribesmen is difficult.

The soldiers were even worse served. The army's information services had never anticipated the possibility that troops would be deployed in a conflict situation in Northern Ireland, and they had to pull together quickly a briefing manual to let the soldiers know what to anticipate. Even for this job their own resources were apparently inadequate, forcing them to appeal to the Belfast authorities for guidance. That is the only conclusion to be reasonably drawn from the document which emerged, the contents of which included the crudely forged oath all members of Sinn Fein were supposed to take.[13] That the army authorities could be tricked by such a blatant swindle is an indication of the prejudices with which they started out, prejudices inevitably transferred to the soldiers and ensuring a partisan approach to their peacekeeping job. To drive the point home, the booklet's map showing the division of the population into Catholic and Protestant ghettos included Wright's analysis in its caption. It was titled "Our Tribal Map." What is perhaps most shocking about this incident is that the Labor government then in power was positively anxious to be fair to the Catholic community. It was simply trapped by centuries of prejudice.

Even if it had been better informed about the two groups it was trying to keep apart, the army could hardly have maintained an objectively neutral presence for any length of time. Soldiers are not trained as diplomats. The power they have is excessive for the purposes here needed. In addition, success in maintaining order automatically favors the established order, and this was precisely the issue. By keeping Northern Ireland cool, the army was easing the pressures on Stormont to implement the reforms dictated by London. For a time, the Catholics waited patiently. They were particularly encouraged when London forced Stormont to accept a sweeping reorganization of the police. Sir Arthur Young, head of the police force of the city of London, was named head of a disarmed RUC, answerable to a new police authority on which the minority community would be represented. The B-Specials were to be disbanded. For the Orangemen this action was very serious, since the B-Specials were completely under their orders and the RUC also had consistently sided with them in community conflicts. The very same evening that Young arrived in Belfast, the Orangemen organized an attack on a block of apartments occupied by Catholics to express their disgust, only to be halted on the road by a cordon of the police on whose behalf they were demonstrating. The ensuing encounter brought to public attention a hitherto understressed aspect of the conflict in Northern Ireland. According to army estimates, the rioters fired more than a thousand rounds from weapons which included a machine gun and several submachine guns. Although at this time the Catholic community had practically no weapons, the revival of the IRA being still in the future, the Protestant community was well armed and equipped. In addition to 100,000 weapons, in large part shotguns and hand pistols, for which the owners had permits, there was an unknown but substantial quantity of illegally held weapons of heavier caliber and more sophisticated deadliness. It had long been the practice of the police authorities to give permits for defensive weapons freely to "loyalists" while denying them to members of the minority community. While Brian Faulkner was Prime Minister between March 1971 and March 1972, 33,000 additional permits were issued.[14]

In response to the use of firearms by the mob, the army was called to the support of the police. It held its fire for an hour and a half, during which time 22 soldiers were injured. Then the army returned the fire, killing two men and wounding many more. The army riot squads then moved up to disperse the mob, beating many of its members mercilessly in the process. The Catholics were understandably encouraged and reassured as they saw what they regarded as equal justice finally being meted out to their opponents. But the real lesson of the encounter was very different. It demonstrated the unsuitability of troops for dealing with civil disturbance, a lesson that would soon become apparent to the Catholics also.

Through the final months of 1969 and the first months of 1970, things seemed to improve. Sir Arthur Young disarmed the RUC and disbanded the B-Specials. The army made a series of informal deals with the leaders of both communities that kept the mobs off the streets. When Oliver Wright, the United Kingdom Representative, ended his tour of duty in March 1970, his message to the press was: "Cheer up. Things are better than you think." But he was deluding himself. The critical six months had been largely wasted. Executive power still rested in Stormont, and Stormont was as totally controlled by intransigent Orangemen as ever. They had found ways to circumvent or neutralize every reform. The army had removed some of the heavier armaments of the RUC, "enough to equip a division" from a single armory, in the words of an army officer. But the RUC gradually found ways to rearm, first with shotguns, later with pistols and bigger automatic weapons. The demobilized B-Specials were allowed to retain their weapons by forming "gun clubs," and they quickly reassembled as a territorial Ulster Defence Regiment. The inquest in December 1969 on Samuel Devenney, who had died of a heart attack in July after being beaten by police in the Bogside in April, caused many Catholics to doubt Young's sincerity. Although no challenge to the evidence of police brutality was offered at the inquest, Young was unable to identify and punish the six or eight policemen involved. Detectives imported from Scotland Yard were defeated by what Young called "a conspiracy of silence" among the police in Derry. If Young is serious, the Catholics argued, he has to get rid of this force and start afresh. But for that he did not have the authority. And so the impasse continued.

So also did the conviction within the Catholic community that, for the foreseeable future, it would need its own protective forces. While the army was around, relative calm might be assured. But with calm the army would leave and then where would they be? The consequence was the re-emergence of the IRA, as described above. It was during these same months of relative calm and hope in Northern Ireland that the IRA, both in the north and south, was going through the convulsions which led to the split into Officials and Provisionals in December 1969. The overwhelming majority of Catholics in Northern Ireland were as opposed to the tactics of the gunmen then as they had shown themselves to be ten years earlier. Their situation as a beleaguered minority made them even more conservative and less interested in the socialism of the Officials than their fellow Catholics in the south. But both Provisionals and Officials were assured not only of survival but support and growth for as long as the Catholic community felt in need of their protection from actual or potential Orange mobs.

Here is the dilemma with which the people of Northern Ireland have lived in one form or another since the state was created as a separate political unit, a dilemma still unresolved. To resolve it, the structures of discrimination must be replaced by structures which will not only be non-discriminatory but which will appear as such to the Catholic community and which will rest on a power base that will ensure the permanence of these structures.

An indication of the lack of interest of the Catholic community in Northern Ireland in the policies and programs of the IRA as such is provided by its indiscriminate support of both branches since the split. All the Catholics wanted was their own defense force, and either group of the IRA would provide that. Indeed, during the subsequent years the split in Northern Ireland has never prevented the two groups from cooperating in the function that justifies their existence for the people, namely, defense from mob attack. As a rule, either one group or the other assumes responsibility for the defense of a particular ghetto, the choice being dictated by the accident of the allegiance of the IRA nucleus in that particular area.

Tensions began to rise again in Belfast as the summer of

1970 approached. Summer in Northern Ireland brings not only wild flowers in the hedgerows and swallows but the Orange processions. But in 1970, the game had acquired for the Catholics a new significance. Here they saw focused in the most precise way the whole issue of their civil rights. They did not mind that the Orangemen celebrated their traditional rites in their own areas. But they were no longer prepared to accept without protest the flaunting of Orange supremacy expressed by parading in Catholic territory.

Preparations for the events of July and August begin early. As Belfast grew in the years following World War II, the pattern of religious segregation had been maintained in the new housing clusters—in Belfast called "estates"—on the western edge of the city. Even the pattern of domination had been symbolically retained, with two Protestant estates (Highfield and New Barnsley) on a hill overlooking the Catholic Ballymurphy in the hollow. As a sociological profile of Ballymurphy made by Queen's University a few years ago established, it had moved to the suburbs all the characteristics of the older Catholic ghettos. They included high unemployment (20 percent at that time, subsequently higher), juvenile delinquency, high rates of crime, and venereal disease. The average family had eight members and subsisted on $50 a week. All that held it together was a common sense of victimization by an oppressive system, a sense which expressed itself in an aggressive commitment to the ideals and symbols of Irish nationalism.

Like Catholics elsewhere in Northern Ireland, those of Ballymurphy had lost their patience by 1970. They were angered when the Junior Orangemen of Highfield and New Barnsley announced a rally for Easter Tuesday, April 1, on the way to which they would march along Springfield Road where it overhangs Ballymurphy. The marchers went through without incident in the morning, but angry crowds were waiting for them as they returned in the evening. A small army detachment tried to keep the two groups apart. Twenty-five of the soldiers were injured by stones and bottles thrown by some 400 Catholic schoolboys and teen-agers. The rioting resumed the following evening, and 600 troops supported by armored cars moved into Ballymurphy. Met by a shower of stones and bottles, they smothered the area in CS gas. That ended the rioting, but it had a further, inescapable effect. It convinced the Ballymurphy people that the army was their enemy. Henceforth, they felt that the IRA was the only force on which they could depend. IRA men had in fact been involved in the clash, but their role had been to try to stop the rioters. As one of them explained later, "Our full-time active strength then was no more than thirty. The last thing we wanted was a confrontation with the British army or the Protestants." [15]

Following this experience, the English heads of the army and of the police in Northern Ireland conducted a long discussion with their political chiefs in Stormont and in London over the advisability of banning all marches and parades for the summer. They were convinced that marches would bring major conflict, and their superiors in London agreed. But London was mainly concerned at this time with preparations for a general election to be held on June 18, an election which would unexpectedly bring the Conservatives back to power and thus complicate events in Northern Ireland. So the viewpoint of Stormont's Prime Minister, Chichester-Clark, was allowed to prevail. Just as he had done the year before, he said his followers would destroy him if the marches were banned. The army and police heads acquiesced the more readily because they did not believe they had the manpower to prevent the illegal marches which Chichester-Clark said were the only alternatives to legal ones.

The marches went on, and so did the rioting. By this time, the IRA had made some progress in getting arms and in recruiting and training men.[16] Whenever trouble started, they were quickly on the scene. An attack with petrol bombs by a Belfast mob on a Catholic church at the entrance to the Short Strand enclave down by the river ran into such organized opposition that two of the attackers were killed on the spot and two more died of their wounds. Widespread rioting in that one June weekend caused six deaths and property damage exceeding a million dollars. The newly elected Conservative government in London, still in the process of organization, found itself with its first crisis on its hands. It felt the need to demonstrate the superiority of its policies and methods over those of the ousted Laborites. As a first step, it sent the new Home Secretary to Belfast to see things for himself.

14

The End of Stormont

*There is no alternative to the invincible combination of the
Orange Order and the Unionist Party. . . . The Unionist Party
relies upon the Orange Order and likewise we in the Order
trust the party. That vital faith must never be jeopardized by
either partner.*

> —BRIAN FAULKNER, Prime Minister of
> Northern Ireland before direct rule [1]

*If there is one thing I have learned, it is that the English can-
not run Ireland.*

> —ROY JENKINS, British cabinet minister, in 1969 [2]

Reginald Maudling, on whom now rested the responsibility for maintaining or restoring order in Northern Ireland, had been deputy leader of the Conservatives for five
years. A colleague had recently described him as "the best
brain in the Tory party." Perhaps he was, but he was also a
typical Englishman in his total ignorance of Ireland, and he
was determined to keep it that way. "For God's sake, bring
me a large Scotch," he exploded as he boarded his plane at
the end of his one-day visit. "What a bloody awful country." [3]

But the mere fact of a change of government in London was in itself a major alteration of the Northern Ireland balance. Labor had consistently over the years criticized the conduct of affairs by Stormont. Its traditions were anti-imperialist and supportive of the underdog. (Its constituency also included several millions of Irish by birth or descent living in Great Britain.) The Conservatives formed a single party with the northern Unionists. Their sympathies were clearly with the "settlers" against the "tribesmen."

While Maudling was in Belfast, the Joint Security Committee responsible for army and police policy made a decision which illustrates the change of climate. The trouble over the previous weekend, it decided, resulted from the failure of the army to use sufficient force. Now it would have to be tougher. The next day, another of the new Conservative appointees arrived from London, the junior Minister of Defense. He approved the decision to restore the image of the military by having the troops take a tougher posture. Twenty-four hours later, the entire Falls ghetto was full of soldiers, thanks to the escalation of the get-tough policy in what started as a search for arms in a single house, a search triggered by information secured in raids on several IRA houses in London. A crowd gathered. A military vehicle maneuvering to withdraw crushed a man. Escape routes for the soldiers were blocked by angry crowds. Reinforcements were called in. They in turn found themselves under siege and called for more reinforcements. By this time, the Falls people were convinced that a full-scale invasion was in progress, and they replied with petrol bombs and with homemade explosives known, from their active ingredient, as nail bombs. A few grenades were also thrown, injuring five soldiers. The army withdrew to regroup, then—in line with the new policy—came back to establish its authority, thereby playing into the hands of the IRA. For the people of the Falls, the army was now as clearly the enemy as was the police. The only friend left was the IRA, now finally free to pursue its own policies without fear of repudiation by the people. A hostage situation had been created.

The invading troops were met by some IRA fire and returned it vigorously, though apparently without casualties on either side. The decisive weapon was CS gas. The troops quickly deluged the area, some of the canisters crashing through roofs to fill the houses with smoke. A curfew was then proclaimed, restricting 20,000 people to their homes for 35 hours while the soldiers conducted a house-to-house search for arms. The haul was not impressive, 28 rifles, 2 carbines, 52 pistols, 24 shotguns, 100 petrol bombs, 20 pounds of gelignite, 20,000 rounds of assorted ammunition. The price included four dead, one killed by an army vehicle, the others shot for violating the curfew. But the bigger price was the same as that paid earlier in Ballymurphy, the alienation of the people.

The army authorities now made an imaginative effort to set the record straight and recover their standing with the Catholic community. They urged the Joint Security Committee to call in legally held arms. These numbered about a hundred thousand, all owned by Unionists. Most were shotguns, but there were 32,000 rifles, pistols, and heavier weapons, including the modern military weapons retained by the B-Specials when they were disbanded.[4] The politicians and police representatives on the Security Committee rejected the recommendation of the military. The weapons remained where they were, a continuing element of threat and instability. In such circumstances, Callaghan would probably have imposed London's will on Stormont, but Maudling refused to interfere. In other areas of reform, the processes set in motion by Callaghan similarly slowed down or were reversed.

Meanwhile, Chichester-Clark came under mounting pressures from the extremists in his own party. The new situation created by the Conservative victory should be used, they urged, to reassert the "democratic will" of the majority and put the minority back where it belonged. In particular, they wanted the army to get tougher with the IRA, it being clear to everyone by now that the IRA had emerged as a significant factor. Army officers and IRA spokesmen were in

constant touch in the Falls area, in Ballymurphy, and elsewhere, both sides recognizing that this was the simplest way
to keep the disturbances at a minimum. But when a Provisional leader boasted publicly in January 1971 that the IRA
was enforcing law and order in certain areas of Belfast,
areas in which the police were not welcome, there was an
understandable outcry from the Orange extremists. The disclosure started a series of events which led first to the breaking off of contacts between the army and the IRA and then
to an IRA offensive against the army.

This represented a totally new situation. While for nearly
a year the army had been under frequent assaults from
youths armed with stones and petrol bombs, not a single
soldier had been killed. Now, however, the Provisionals decided that the time had come to shoot to kill. Their first victim was a 20-year-old soldier shot on the night of February 6,
1971. Four of his companions were wounded, one critically;
and in a separate encounter the same night, three more
soldiers were wounded. The next day Prime Minister
Chichester-Clark announced on television that "Northern
Ireland is at war with the Irish Republican Army Provisionals." [5] For the following seven weeks his response to
each new incident was an appeal to London to send more
troops and to adopt more repressive measures. He finally increased his demands to include such measures as block
searchers, a total curfew in Catholic areas, activation of the
Ulster Defence Regiment (the former B-Specials), and
"punitive expeditions" into Catholic areas as reprisals for
ambushes. When London refused to give him all he asked,
he resigned as Prime Minister in late March. Chichester-
Clark had been in office for just under two years and had
enacted into law more reforms than all his predecessors
combined. But his contribution was superficial. The more
significant symbols of his rule were the "peace line" separating Belfast's Catholics and Protestants, and the increase
in British troops in Northern Ireland from under 3000 to
10,000. The power structures were untouched, however,

ensuring that the laws remained a dead letter, and the circumstances of his departure ensured that this situation would continue.

Brian Faulkner, voted party leader by an overwhelming majority of the Unionist members of the Stormont Parliament, an election which automatically made him Prime Minister, had an established reputation as a hard-liner. He had consistently fought the civil rights movement, denying the need to reform local government or to change the practices under which houses and jobs were allocated. Political commentator Andrew Boyd, himself a Protestant from Northern Ireland but a liberal in outlook, said he had searched extensively but had failed to discover that "Faulkner had ever said a kindly word about anyone." He could, said Boyd, "hardly be regarded as fit to be a Prime Minister, even of so miserable a place as Northern Ireland." [6]

Faulkner's major success—a short-term one—was to persuade London that the reforms promised in 1969, in what had come to be known as the Downing Street Declaration, had in fact been implemented. The growth of IRA terrorism demonstrated that the enemies of Northern Ireland would not be satisfied by reform, he insisted, leaving no alternative but to step up military pressure, a policy with which the Provisionals were only too happy to cooperate. Even as additional troops poured in from England and Orange extremists openly organized vigilante armies, the Provisionals never faltered in their confidence that they would emerge victorious from a showdown. The Unionists, according to their rationale, were deeply divided because they lacked a mystique, a distinctive national sense, and all that held them together was the material advantage provided by the regime. Since the Unionists owned all the wealth, they alone would suffer the ravages of a civil war, and when they saw their property being destroyed, they would quickly seek an accommodation. In addition, they lacked the organization and the experience in guerrilla warfare which the IRA had built up for over more than half a century. The Provisionals were further convinced that an increase in oppressive measures by the government would solidify the support of the Catholic community, "whose minds had been deliberately distracted from the supreme issue," as they had said in explaining the failure of their last major attack on the Northern Ireland regime in 1962.

For the first four months of the Faulkner regime, the Provisionals set off an average of two explosions a day, their campaign reaching a crescendo in July to coincide with the Orange marches. In one period of 12 hours, 20 explosions wrecked stores, banks, and saloons. Pressure on the army was simultaneously maintained, with 4 soldiers killed and 29 wounded.

Even before he had become prime minister, Faulkner had formulated a concrete plan to deal with the terrorists. As a member of Chichester-Clark's cabinet, he had urged at each meeting the reactivation of the section of the Special Powers Act which authorized internment of suspects. He had always been voted down because the army and police chiefs insisted that internment would create more problems than it would solve. As soon as he took office, he set the machinery for internment in motion, ordering lists of suspects to be drawn up and camps prepared for holding them. The July violence enabled him to overcome London's hesitation, and August 9 was fixed as the day for the first sweep.

Home Secretary Reginald Maulding, in a speech in the House of Commons, assured British and world opinion that internment represented no change in the objectives sought by his government.

There has been no attempt to move away from the reform program. . . . Succeeding Northern Ireland governments have faithfully carried out their part of the declaration. The police force is civilianized and is operating entirely within the recommendations of the Hunt Report. A police authority has been established and steps are in train to set up a public prosecutor. A parliamentary commissioner for administration has been appointed and he has already carried out a great deal of work. There is a commissioner for complaints in local authorities and public authorities. Fair representation at elections to parliamentary and local government is accepted, and universal adult suffrage—already applied to Stormont—has been accepted for local government. Measures have been taken to ensure equality of opportunity in employment. There is an antidiscrimination clause in government contracts. A points scheme was introduced for housing allocation. There was the appointment of a minister of community relations. These and other measures carried out have faithfully enacted the Spirit of the Downing Street Declaration.[7]

The Maudling speech was a summary of the claims made in a White Paper issued that same month by Stormont Prime Minister Brian Faulkner, claims immediately challenged by a group of Catholics who had earlier served the Stormont regime on government boards and committees. The B-Specials, they said,

did not disappear; they merely laid aside their uniforms and rearmed with the consent of Stormont . . . the police were officially rearmed, with the approval of Westminster. . . . The police in Derry . . . had covered up the policemen who were responsible for a cowardly and murderous attack on a man and his family of young children. . . . Neither Chichester-Clark nor Faulkner had done anything to correct the discrimination and abuses in employment that were the fruits of fifty years of Unionist government.

The Incitement to Hatred Act, they added, was shown to be "ineffective" when tested in the courts. The rules under which the ombudsman (commissioner for complaints) was put to work prevented him from having any impact on the imbalance in Northern Ireland's society.

"It would probably be closer to the truth," wrote political commentator Henry Kelly,

to say that real reform, reform that would have any significance, was never tried in Northern Ireland. . . . When Stormont was examined, it was found that it couldn't reform itself and continue in existence.

. . . Out of the many incidents involving death, injury or loss of property over the last three years [to 1972] for which either the police or the B-Specials were clearly responsible, whether by outright killing as in the Rooney case, or by negligence as in the case of standing-by while Protestant mobs attacked Catholic property, no police officer or B-Special has ever appeared in court to answer a charge. . . . Catholics have no more chance of employment after reform than they had before. . . . The Community Relations Commission . . . has failed also to be a significant force for reform in Northern society at any level. . . . The Prevention of Incitement to Religious Hatred Act . . . is a piece of legislative nonsense which is no more a reform than would an Act to Outlaw Sin by Thought. . . . Reform in fact was a failure.[8]

Far from taking action to ensure equal opportunity in employment, as he informed London, Faulkner was trying to maintain the existing discriminations. In 1971, he committed a fifth of his entire industrial aid budget to propping up an ailing company which employs five Catholics in a work force of nine hundred, Sirocco Engineering (owned by a South African investment group) which has a factory in the heart of the Catholic ghetto of Seaforde Street–Short Strand, in Belfast. In May 1971, the government loaned it half a million dollars without insisting on any change in hiring practices, and in December guaranteed a bank loan of a further three quarters of a million, all on the recommendation of "an advisory committee of Belfast businessmen." The following May, the Central Citizens' Defence Committee charged that "the minority ghettos in Belfast, particularly the Falls, Ballymurphy and Andersonstown, are completely starved of factories and jobs, despite millions being poured into other areas."[9]

Faulkner's assurances to the faithful back home were similarly quite different from what he was putting out for British consumption. Now that his hands were untied by London's new Conservative government, he promised a quick return to normality as it had always been understood in Northern Ireland. "There has been too much confusion of po-

litical initiatives with military objectives," he said at a political meeting shortly after Maudling's statement.

For while it is to be hoped that, in the future, when the present
wave of terrorism has been put down, political progress will help
ensure that terrorism does not again take root in our community, in
the short term no political initiative will mollify the gunman in the
slightest degree. There is only one way to deal with the IRA at
present, and that is to defeat them militarily by inflicting such losses
on them that they will come to the conclusion that they are not
going to shake the will of this community or to overthrow the government.[10]

Even after internment had been decided upon, the army
wanted to round up only about 150 key people without
whom, it was believed, the IRA would not be able to operate.
But Faulkner himself had the final say, and he insisted on a
list containing 500 names. It included men who had been interned previously and were therefore ruled to be subver-
sives, and even some politicians who might make a fuss
when internment was announced. Most prominent of these
was Michael Farrell, a lecturer at Queen's University, head
of a socialist movement called People's Democracy, and a
civil rights veteran. In a closely coordinated army police
operation, 342 people were arrested the first day. But the IRA
structures were not even dented. The Provisionals had
known in advance and warned their men to go "on the run."
If a man was seized in his own home, they said, his family
would not be entitled to aid while he was held. "Our command structure remains intact," they boasted at an underground press conference four days later.

The reaction of the Catholic community, against which
all the internments had been directed, exceeded the worst
fears of the authorities. They had expected trouble but believed they could contain it until it quickly wore itself out.
That might indeed have happened, were it not for the stories
of torture that began to trickle from the internment camps
within a few days. At first they seemed incredible, but

gradually a mountain of incontrovertible evidence was assembled. Some of the reports dealt with the behavior of policemen and soldiers toward men they arrested. Desmond O'Hagan, a lecturer at a teachers' training college, had a bag placed over his head. His hands were handcuffed behind his back. Then he was tied by a rope to a vehicle and dragged along the street. Soldiers urinated on prisoners lying trussed in a truck. When prisoners arrived in a camp, they were made to run barefoot over broken glass, beaten by soldiers, and harried by Alsatian dogs. All of this might simply represent the unauthorized action of perverted individuals. But soon a far more sinister story came to light. Highly sophisticated torture techniques were being used in the interrogation of the suspects.

These techniques are described in detail, with a wealth of supporting statements including those of doctors who subsequently examined the victims, in a booklet published by the Campaign for Social Justice in Northern Ireland, the Dungannon-based organization which had pioneered in civil rights in 1963. The accuracy of its reports have been confirmed by Amnesty International, the British National Council for Civil Liberties, and other outside investigators. According to an official statement made in the House of Commons in November 1971, formal authorization for these procedures had been given by Brian Faulkner, the Prime Minister of Northern Ireland, with the knowledge and concurrence of the British government.

Among the incidents reported in the booklet is one involving 12 men arrested on August 9 and removed two days later, "their heads covered by a cloth hood, two layers in thickness," to a military barracks. There, they

were tortured by being spread-eagled against the wall, heads hooded, barefoot, clad only in army overalls. Their bodies were kept at an angle of maximum strain, resting only on their fingertips shaped like a right angle. No food, no drink, and no sleep contributed to their disorientation. The air was filled with the sound of compressed air escaping, which literally drove them out of their minds. Other simulated sounds were "a death service," hymns, an execution order, protest moans, sounds of a firing squad and a mob singing.

The prisoners were kicked on all parts of the body, including the sensitive genital area. They were "drummed behind the ears" as many as 200 to 300 times to upset their balance. They were lifted up, spun around and dropped on the ground. Many other kinds of physical brutality were tried. During the fifth and sixth days, they were interrogated many times by members of the Special Branch [detectives] of the Royal Ulster Constabulary. When they refused to give the necessary information, they were sent back into the torture room for more ill-treatment.

The ill-treatment itself was carried out by Englishmen. They did not speak with North of Ireland accents. To the prisoners it sounded like Cockney, certainly British, and—in one case—a Scottish accent. They were in fact members of the Twenty-second Special Air Service Regiment, who had been infiltrated into other regiments of the British army. The S.A.S. are an elite commando group who specialize in counter-insurgency tactics. They have a high intelligence quotient, are superbly fit and are reputed to be able to survive for months in deserts. They are a secret group and are the subject of a "D notice" to newspapers in Britain.[11] In Cyprus they were known to have aggravated the local strife by blowing up waterworks and carrying out illegal actions. Morality does not seem to concern them very much. Books about the S.A.S. include *Legacy of Strife*, by Charles Foley [Penguin], and a Fontana book called *Inverted Dagger*.

One of the twelve men tortured at the Palace Military Barracks by these British commandos recalls how these men with British voices lifted him upon their shoulders spinning him around and throwing him to the ground. He was dressed only in the army overalls, his hands were bound by handcuffs, and the thick hood covered his head. Then for one dramatic moment, the bag fell off and he saw his torturers—a group of very fit young men dressed in immaculate white jeans and brown shoes, naked from the waist up. The bag was clapped on again and the torture continued. The detainee whose blindfold slipped, and who reported the incident personally to one of us, is a highly respected member of the County Tyrone community, Mr. Patrick McClean. . . . Mr. McClean's occupation of remedial teacher is not one whose members are noted for wild fabrications or irresponsible behavior.[12]

Another commonly reported experience was the "helicopter treatment." Men were hooded so that they could not see where they were, then flown in a helicopter until they had formed the impression that they were at a great altitude, at which point they would be thrown out at a height that actually was only a few feet from the ground. "I was brought out and a rope was tied around me under the armpits," one man said. "This was attached to a helicopter and the helicopter suddenly rose, taking me with it, hanging underneath it. I don't know how high it went up. I was finding it difficult to breathe. Then the helicopter came down again, and when I was about fifteen feet or so above the ground, I was suddenly dropped to the ground." [13]

The principal objective of these tortures is to disorient the victim on the assumption that he will then provide information he otherwise would not divulge. Experts differ as to the quality of the information so obtained, but this has not stopped the armed forces of many countries from using these methods. According to the *Sunday Times* of London, one of England's most reputable newspapers, "the 'disorientation' technique of interrogation is among the most secret areas of the British armed services' training techniques. Using Russian brainwash techniques, it was refined for British service by an RAF wing-commander, who committed suicide later. It is taught to select military personnel at the Joint Services Interrogation Centre, whose location is an official secret." [14]

At the core of the system is the "hooding" of the victim. Dr. Rona Field, of Clark University in Worcester, Massachusetts, one of a group studying the long-term effects of hooding in Northern Ireland and elsewhere, says it causes a severe deprivation of oxygen, rapidly producing disorientation and hallucinations. Excessive deprivation is believed to cause irreversible neurological damage to the brain. The British first experimented with the technique in the 1930s, according to Dr. Field's research. They passed it to the Pentagon where it was further refined. The refined method was then fed back to Britain when its troops participated in the

Korean War. Such interrogation practices are apparently now almost universal. Highly verified documentation from Brazil and Uruguay, two countries whose armed forces are guided by United States mentors, show a pattern of their use on political suspects.[15]

Under pressure from the communications media, the British government named the Compton Committee to investigate the charges that prisoners were being tortured. However, it was limited to examining only the men interned on the first day, August 9. It was to meet in private and had no power to subpoena either witnesses or documents. Witnesses did not have to testify under oath, and they could not be cross-examined. The internees decided it was a whitewash and all but one boycotted it. In consequence, it heard (apart from this one witness) only newspaper reports and the story of the army and police. All these circumstances make its conclusions the more remarkable. It found that the main charges concerning the treatment of 11 men were indeed true and did constitute ill treatment. The testimony revealed that the spread-eagled posture was imposed at the wall, to which one man was subjected for over 43 hours, that men were subjected to hooding, continuous and monotonous noise, together with deprivation of sleep and of food and water. While this constitutes ill treatment, the committee added, it does not constitute brutality, because "we consider that brutality is an inhuman or savage form of cruelty, and that cruelty implies a disposition to inflict suffering, coupled with indifference to, or pleasure in, the victim's pain." [16]

Such fine semantic distinctions were lost not only on the internees but on the entire Catholic community. Its views were set out in a statement issued in November 1971 and signed by 425 Roman Catholic priests, 80 percent of all priests working in Northern Ireland.

We, the undersigned priests, are convinced that brutality, physical and mental torture and psychological pressures have been inflicted on men arrested under the Special Powers Act on the ninth of

August and subsequently. We believe that these barbarities are still being inflicted on innocent people—convicted of no crime—at the Palace Military Barracks, Holywood, under the protection of law by the Special Branch of the RUC. We base our conviction on substantial medical evidence, on the testimony of priests who saw the injuries, and on the statements of men whose truthfulness is already known to us through our pastoral work. . . . We therefore demand that brutality and torture by the forces of the law be stopped immediately. . . . We want an immediate end to imprisonment without trial which is immoral and unjust.[17]

The British army authorities offered as justification for the interrogation techniques described before the Compton Committee the fact that they were used only on persons "believed to possess information of a kind which it was operationally necessary to obtain as rapidly as possible in the interest of saving lives," and the Compton Report included this explanation without comment. A spokesman for the London government gave assurances in general terms that the rights of suspects would be carefully protected, and the publicity would seem to have had some impact. The overwhelming weight of evidence, nevertheless, indicated that the basic interrogation procedures were retained. This is supported by depositions taken during the following year by the Association for Legal Justice, as well as by evidence collected by the *Sunday Times* which reported in May 1972 that "something is still wrong with the army and police methods of interrogation in Northern Ireland," and that there was "a wealth of testimony of physical brutality." [18]

Far from crippling the IRA, as Faulkner had promised, internment immediately escalated the violence. During the previous four months, there had been eight killings, four soldiers and four civilians. For the following four months, the figure was 114, 30 soldiers, 11 policemen, and 73 civilians. Many of the dead were demonstrably innocent people, caught in crossfire or in bomb blasts. Some were army explosives experts killed while attempting to defuse bombs placed in stolen automobiles. Soon the army introduced the practice of blowing up any automobile left unattended in a built-up area. Banks and post offices were robbed. Hotels became a primary target for bombers and their business declined disastrously. Stores and saloons closed early. By the end of the year, the number of arrests under the Special Powers Act exceeded 1500. Although Orange extremists escalated their attacks on the Catholic ghettos in direct proportion to the IRA bombings, not a single one of them was interned by the Faulkner government, a discrimination which inevitably polarized the moderates on the Catholic side.

Polarization was further intensified by an incident in Derry in late January 1972. Civil rights demonstrators, marching in defiance of a ban, were fired on by British paratroopers, and 13 of them were killed. Army spokesmen claimed that marchers had first fired on the troops, but the overwhelming weight of evidence at a subsequent official inquiry contradicted this claim. One paratrooper officer admitted under oath at the inquiry that he had lied when, immediately after the shooting, he stated on television that he had seen a demonstrator fire a gun. It was conclusively established that none of those killed had been armed.

Even before "Bloody Sunday," as the Derry incident immediately came to be called, it was obvious that internment had not achieved its intended aims and would not achieve them. Symptomatic of the political collapse was the action of the Social Democratic and Labor Party (SDLP). The SDLP had been formed in 1970 by the six members of the Stormont Parliament who between them constituted the parliamentary opposition. The only thing they really had in common was that all of them represented constituencies with a Catholic majority. They had been elected under four different labels, as Republican Labor, Northern Ireland Labor, Nationalist, and Independent, and they had difficulty in finding any name that would represent the divergency of their attitudes and interests. An interesting point about the name they did choose is that it omits "republican." They wanted to reflect exactly the position of the civil rights movement, which they correctly read as that of the people who had elected them. They were consequently willing to leave aside the constitutional issue and function as a "loyal opposition" within the political structures then existing in Northern Ireland. Their claim to be not only loyal but nonsectarian was strengthened by the fact that one member, Ivan Lee Cooper, was a Protestant, a Protestant elected by the votes of Catholics in the predominantly Catholic constituency of Mid-Londonderry.

SDLP's life as a loyal opposition was brief. There was a moment of hope in June 1971 when Faulkner offered the opposition an active role in his administration by allowing it to choose the chairmen of two important committees. But within a month, the cooperation had ceased. The SDLP said it would withdraw from Parliament and set up "an alternative parliament" if the administration failed to hold an independent public inquiry into the deaths of two civilians shot by the army in circumstances that had greatly aroused the people whom the SDLP represented. The demand was rejected, and the Assembly of the Northern Ireland People duly met at Dungiven in County Derry. The gesture recalled the meeting in Dublin in 1919 of the Irish members of the Westminster Parliament and their reaffirmation of the Republic proclaimed by the leaders of the Easter Rising of 1916. But there were major differences. The Dublin group had the backing of more than three-quarters of the people of Ireland, and they offered a viable alternative to the existing order. Those at Dungiven spoke for only a third of the people of Northern Ireland and offered nothing more than a vigorous condemnation of the existing lack of order. But they did spell out more clearly than ever before that the Stormont Parliament left the community represented by the SDLP without any voice in the conduct of public affairs.

By the end of 1971 it had become clear to the British government, as to most observers, that the Faulkner policy of military repression was not defeating the IRA or restoring peace to Northern Ireland. Edward Heath, the British Prime Minister, was fully occupied with the negotiations for Britain's entry into the European Economic Community (the Common Market), but Bloody Sunday shocked him into realizing that action was urgent. He assumed direct responsibility for dealing with Faulkner and summoned him to London half a dozen times over the following months, telling him face to face that the long-standing rumors of British plans to sideline the Stormont regime and resume direct control of Northern Ireland were indeed well founded.

The growth of these rumors produced a response which both helped and threatened Faulkner. Ulster Vanguard was founded as a modern version of the "Orange Card" with which Lord Randolph Churchill had in 1886 wrecked Gladstone's Home Rule plans. Described by its founders as "an umbrella for traditional loyalist groups," it brought under a single policy committee the Loyalist Association of Workers, the Ulster Special Constabulary Association, the Grand Orange Lodge of Ireland, the Apprentice Boys of Derry, the Black Institution (an inner circle of Orangemen), the Young Unionist Council, and the Ulster Defence Association. Its central council included four Grand Masters of the Orange Order. What this body did was to bring into the open the potential military strength of the right-wing extremists who previously had operated without any overall coordination. Its meetings quickly assumed a militarist form that was reminiscent of the fascist rallies in Germany, Italy, and other countries in the years preceding World War II. William Craig, a former Stormont Minister of Home Affairs who headed Vanguard, told the people at these rallies that any moves to change the constitution of Northern Ireland would bring "a holocaust such as few of us could contain." Although he made it clear that he was opposed to direct rule from London, his main concern was to prevent any understanding with the Republic of Ireland. Week by week his speeches became more inflammatory. Vanguard, he said, would "make no accommodation with the enemies of this country." It would "deal with the republican community throughout the province." It would "build up dossiers on men and women who are the enemies of this country, because one day, if the politicians failed, it would be its job to liquidate the enemy." That last threat was spoken to a cheering crowd of 70,000 supporters in Belfast on March 18. Many of them were in some form of military attire, some imitating the Provisionals by wearing combat jackets, black sunglasses, and berets.

"Would this mean killing all Catholics in Belfast?" Craig was asked by a television interviewer. "It might not go as far as that," he replied, "but it could go as far as killing. It could be similar to the situation in the 1920s where Roman Catholics identified in Republican rebellion could find themselves unwelcome in their places of work and under pressure to leave their homes." [19] Everyone knew what he meant. The memory of the pogroms which followed the creation of Northern Ireland are fresh in all minds. Only the Provisionals were not unhappy about these developments. They felt that Craig was doing a general service by his formulation of the issues. But the British government, like most observers, saw that civil war was only a step away. On March 24 it suspended the Stormont Parliament and regime for a year, during which time Northern Ireland was to be ruled directly from London through a Secretary of State advised by a commission.

15

Direct Rule and After

I would in principle prefer to be ruled by a Protestant Irishman rather than an Englishman. That is what Irish nationalism is about.
    —EDDIE MCATEER, leader of the Northern Ireland
    Nationalist party [1]

It is a difficult country to hold though easy to overrun.
    —EDMUND CURTIS, historian [2]

Stormont's suspension produced a sigh of relief around the world, a world whose digestion had suffered over the previous several years, as television news brought to it each mealtime the latest atrocity from Northern Ireland. In an unusual show of solidarity, China joined with the United States in approval. So did the European Common Market and the government of the Republic of Ireland.

Within Northern Ireland, the response was more nuanced. The ordinary people who had been caught in the middle were grateful at the prospect of at least a temporary relaxation of tension. The promised backlash of the Orange extremists failed to materialize, but some 200,000 workers and shopkeepers joined in a two-day strike called by Vanguard. They closed industry, cut power supplies, and stopped public transport. A march on Stormont by 25,000 Vanguard members was defused by Faulkner who addressed them from a balcony, provoking a bitter controversy between Faulkner and Vanguard leader Craig. The end result was to demonstrate publicly how deep were the divisions within the Unionists.

London's plan placed full authority for the administration of Northern Ireland in a member of its own cabinet, who would be advised by "a body of persons fully representative of opinion in Northern Ireland." The announcement promised that "those internees whose release is no longer thought likely to involve an unacceptable risk to security" would be freed, and it defined the purpose of the temporary takeover as being "to find a means of ensuring for the minority as well as the majority community an active, permanent and guaranteed role in the life and public affairs of the province."

The leaders of SDLP, the opposition party which had withdrawn from Stormont the previous June and set up its separate rump assembly, decided to accept the London proposals and undertook to work with the new administrator. They asked the IRA to cease hostilities, but agreed that the civil resistance campaign should continue as long as internment did. The civil resistance campaign had been developed by the civil rights movement in pursuit of its objectives. The principal form the campaign took was the withholding of rents, taxes, and other payments to public authorities, a loss of revenue which had seriously embarrassed the government.

The Official IRA condemned direct rule. Any Irish government, it said, is better than a British one. Irish history had no episode so disastrous from every angle as the period of direct rule by London from 1800 to 1920. It was a viewpoint with which most Irishmen basically agreed, even if many were resigned to the apparently inevitable.

The leader of the Northern Ireland Nationalist party,

Eddie McAteer, shared the sentiments of the Officials. "This is a day of sadness. I find no joy in being ruled from the remote insensitive smokerooms of Westminster. Faced with the choice, I would in principle prefer to be ruled by a Protestant Irishman rather than an Englishman. That is what Irish nationalism is about. . . . The root problem is to bind together the two communities. Perhaps, we will now at last find common ground as equal people without sectional power—brothers against the government." [3]

The Northern Ireland Civil Rights Association (NICRA) said that direct rule had, in itself, changed nothing.

The 1971 decision to introduce internment, under the Special Powers Act, was specifically sanctioned by the Tory government at Westminster; and every act of one-sided repression in the last days of Unionist party rule was carried out by the British arm under London's, not Belfast's, ultimate control. . . . The suspension . . . does not, of itself, dismantle the Orange-Unionist system which, by polarizing the community here, has resulted in the denial of everyone's democratic freedoms. Specifically, the manner in which the act was carried out means that every antidemocratic "law" on Stormont's statute book is still operative. . . . The essence of NICRA's program is a demand that, having now suspended the Stormont assembly, Westminster should suspend its legislation too and concede to the long-suffering people of Northern Ireland, for so long as the area remains a part of the United Kingdom, their right to enjoy equal standards of democracy with their fellow taxpayers in London, Glasgow and Cardiff.[4]

In spite of such reservations, these groups were all willing to give William Whitelaw, the British plenipotentiary, a chance to prove himself. Not so, however, the Provisionals. "We are sticking to our three points for peace," said Sean Mac Stiophain, Chief of Staff of the Provisionals, "total amnesty for all, whether tried or untried, withdrawal of the British troops from the streets of Northern Ireland, and the suspension of Stormont." [5] The terror campaign of bombings and shootings was continued. Seven soldiers and 12 civilians were killed in the first three weeks of direct rule.

Whitelaw was too practiced a politician to reveal any disappointment he might have felt at the intransigence of the Provisionals. He had made his reputation as a master of conciliation while leader of the House of Commons, and he set out in Belfast to maintain that reputation. A highly decorated officer in the Scots Guards during World War II and a crack golfer, Whitelaw at 53 retained enormous energy, and he also had a capacity for getting on with people. He quickly identified the dilemma of the Catholic community, which neither approved of the methods nor shared the aims of the Provisionals, yet needed their protection against its neighbors. He worked hard to assure them that his proposed conference of all parties and groups in Northern Ireland would readjust power structures to ensure the protection they needed. The women, in particular, were tired of the years of conflict and of the emotional distortions suffered by their children. Groups of women formed in Belfast and Derry to pressure the Provisionals. People for Peace in Derry's Bogside circulated a petition urging an immediate cease-fire and said they had collected 4000 signatures. Whitelaw nursed such initiatives. A complicated series of secret negotiations with leaders of the SDLP and of the Provisionals was culminated in an announcement by the Provisionals on June 26 that they would suspend offensive operations at midnight the following Monday "provided that a public reciprocal response" was forthcoming from the British. Within a few hours, Whitelaw announced with satisfaction in the House of Commons that "Her Majesty's forces will obviously reciprocate."

The news produced euphoria in Britain, in the Republic of Ireland, and in the Catholic community in Northern Ireland. Admiration for Whitelaw was unbounded. In a mere two months he had persuaded all parties to the conflict that the conference table was preferable to the gun, or so it seemed. Many details were still to be settled. Each of the parties was ready to talk only to Whitelaw himself, not yet to each other. But Whitelaw's confidence was contagious.

The most skeptical began to believe he could pull it off. He might even be able to hold the elections for the reformed local councils within six months, as he had promised.

The euphoria was short-lived. Although the massive Orange backlash anticipated when Stormont was suspended had then failed to materialize, the Unionists saw more clearly each day that Whitelaw was moving along a road that would mean the end of their monopoly of power. It had long been an article of Orange faith that military force had been decisive in its favor at critical moments in history, that the Ulster Volunteers organized and armed in 1913 had saved them from being included in a Catholic-dominated Ireland, that the RUC and B-Specials had smashed the IRA each time they made trouble, most recently in 1962, and that the only reason they now had problems was because London had disbanded the B-Specials and tied the hands of the police. On the basis of this analysis, as politically superficial as that of the IRA about itself, the Orange extremists decided to bring back the glories of 1912. An unofficial paramilitary organization emerged as the main statewide expression of this viewpoint, the Ulster Defence Association (UDA), for a time a member of Vanguard. Before the introduction of direct rule and subsequently, it engaged in a war of threats against the IRA, threats often reinforced by open violence against Catholic enclaves. In the UDA view, all Catholics shared in the IRA rebellion, protecting the gunmen and preventing the police and army from patrolling the No-Go areas. Whitelaw agreed in principle that the No-Go areas should be patrolled, but he opposed a military invasion. "It would," he said early in May, "make Bloody Sunday look like a children's teaparty." [6] Besides, the basic problem was not the military defeat of an identifiable enemy. None of the Belfast enclaves was ever for any length of time physically barred to the army. Patrols could come and go, so long as they did not interfere with the community's life. Barricades were mainly intended to prevent hit-and-run attacks by terrorists, a reasonable arrangement as long as the army could not guarantee safety from them. So what Whitelaw sought was a negotiated end to No-Go areas as part of a larger settlement.

When announcing direct rule, British Prime Minister Heath had promised periodic plebiscites, the first "as soon as practicable in the near future," to allow the people to make known their views on the desirability of uniting with the Republic of Ireland. A referendum or plebiscite, he reasoned, would reassure the Unionists that London would not force them against their will to join the Republic. If Whitelaw had been able to hold the first such referendum quickly, it would undoubtedly have eased Protestant anxieties and lessened support for the UDA. Heath, however, refused absolutely to introduce the required legislation in the Westminster Parliament, and that for a reason totally unrelated to events in Ireland. He was under strong pressures at home for a referendum on joining the European Economic Community. He did not want it because he was afraid he would lose. But the only reason he could give was that a referendum is alien to the British system which locates all power in Parliament. As long as the EEC issue remained unresolved, accordingly, it would have been politically devastating to sponsor a referendum on another issue in part of the United Kingdom. So once again, Britain's concerns of state in making a decision on the Irish issue took precedence.

Even before the Whitelaw–IRA truce, the UDA had decided to erect its own barricades around major Protestant strongholds. Its purpose was to force Whitelaw to end the Catholic No-Go areas. Its justification was that Protestants had to be protected against IRA gunmen operating from their officially tolerated shelters. The UDA barricades were originally planned only for weekends. After the truce was announced, however, they were made permanent. Whitelaw had maintained constant communication with the UDA leaders, but had failed to convince them that his concessions to win a truce had not been excessive. Actually, the UDA seemed to regard any recognition of the IRA as already an excessive concession. Many of their members thought the truce was a fraud, useful only to the hard-pressed Provisionals as an opportunity to regroup and replenish supplies. One UDA spokesman, Dave Fogel, later admitted that they did not want the truce to last. "It's probably fair to say," he told the press, "that a majority of members of the UDA Council felt—I did myself—that the quicker the truce broke, the better." [7]

The UDA barricades would not have brought about the breaking of the truce were it not for one important detail. The leaders decided to use the barricades in the same way that Orangemen used their marches, namely to "take in" new territory. Instead of locating them at the edge of completely Protestant areas, they moved them forward to embrace cross streets in which the population was mixed. Behind the barricades roved gangs of youths, known as Tartan Gangs from scarves or patches proclaiming their Scottish ancestry, who warned Catholic residents that they had to get out before the deadline of the July 12 celebrations—a mere week away.

The first major confrontation came at the junction of Springfield Road and Woodvale Avenue. Immediately to the north of Springfield was a small salient in which 65 Catholic families lived in streets—including Springfield—with an equal or greater number of Protestant families. The district was more middle class than the adjoining Falls and Shankill areas, to the south and north, respectively. Most of the people were buying their homes and had an average equity of $5000, a major investment in relation to Belfast living levels. The Tartan Gangs and the masked UDA men had been active for some time in this area, and by the beginning of July 1972, eight of the Catholic families had fled from their homes, bricking up the doors and windows to prevent the UDA from moving in Protestant families. Those who were left had formed a neighborhood defense association in close liaison with the IRA based on the nearby Falls. Nightly patrols sought to discourage incursions by gangs of Tartans and UDA firing bursts from automatic weapons and throwing petrol bombs through windows of the homes of Catholics.

Consternation seized these remaining Catholics when the UDA erected barricades on Woodvale Avenue at its junction with Springfield Road. With other barricades already in position, this isolated them in enemy territory. Their fears were heightened by the fact that during the previous weeks, ever since the UDA had emerged as a major factor in the many-sided confrontation, the level of violence had risen sharply, people being killed at random for no apparent reason other than as a warning to opponents. For example, a bomb had exploded outside a bar in a Catholic district, in circumstances which permitted each side to accuse the other of planting it. Sixty-three persons were hospitalized, some with severed limbs, and it started a chain reaction which caused eight deaths, including that of a 13-year-old girl and a 15-year-old boy, as well as sundry injuries to persons and damage to property in later bombing incidents. The truce had ended attacks on the army but it had not affected the pattern of communal violence. There were 16 unsolved murders in Belfast alone in the 10 or 12 days following its declaration. Most of the victims were Catholics, and the Catholic community saw these murders as the expression of UDA terrorist policy.

Whitelaw was quickly notified by intermediaries with the IRA that the barricades on Woodvale Avenue jeopardized the truce. Complicated negotiations produced what promised to be a satisfactory compromise. The army would erect its own barricades on Springfield Avenue as a guarantee to the Protestants north of that road that they would be safe from terrorist attacks from the Falls. The UDA would move their barricades back some five or six blocks, leaving the contested salient as a no-man's-land to be patrolled both by the army and by the UDA. The leaders of the Catholic neighborhood defense association soon became convinced, however, that army officers on the spot had instructions from higher up to keep their patrols at a token level, leaving effective control to the UDA. They concluded that Whitelaw had an understanding with the UDA which conflicted with his assurances to them. They were further incensed by the refusal of the army authorities to recognize as threats a series of activities in which the UDA patrols engaged. Because of these UDA activities, the defense association had decided that it could not guarantee the safety of its people, who consequently were arranging to abandon their homes. But unless these people could later establish in court that they had fled under threats or intimidation, they would get no compensation, and all of them had their life savings invested in their homes. They recalled bitterly the distinction made the previous year by the Compton Commission when it ruled that interrogation methods with arrested suspects involved ill treatment but not brutality. The dictionary, they said, was being used once again, this time to defraud them of their life savings.

Recognizing that his entire program of reconciliation could be destroyed by such a detail as the confrontation on Woodvale Avenue, Whitelaw speeded up his timetable and received seven leaders of the Provisionals for a secret discussion in London. The meeting did little more than confirm how far apart the two sides remained. The Provisionals wanted the future of Ireland to be determined by "the whole people of Ireland acting and voting as a unit." Whitelaw had constantly reaffirmed the long-standing British position, confirmed by Parliament in 1949, that no change in the territorial identity of Northern Ireland would occur without approval of the majority of the citizens of that state.[8] The Provisionals also wanted the immediate end of internment, and a total withdrawal of the British from all of Ireland by the end of 1974. Whitelaw raised no objection to the principle of British withdrawal, a principle which London had for some time already accepted, but he insisted that events alone would determine the timetable. Concerning internment, he pleaded that he was phasing it out as quickly as was possible without creating an angry backlash from the Unionists. That had always been his contention, although many in the Catholic community had become convinced that he was using the internees as bargaining counters, releasing a few of them each time he had secured some concession from the IRA or the SDLP.

The only agreement reached was to meet again a week later. But even before they had parted, another trivial clash in Belfast was getting out of hand. Lenadoon Avenue in Belfast's western suburbs is like Woodvale Avenue in that it runs between a Catholic and a Protestant enclave and has residents belonging to both factions. Some days earlier, an ad hoc group of local Catholics called the Lenadoon Housing Committee and asked the British lieutenant-colonel in charge of the neighborhood to allow Catholic refugees from other areas to move into 16 empty houses on Lenadoon Avenue. He suggested they should check with the Northern Ireland Housing Executive, a body given exclusive authority the previous year for all of the building and allocation of public housing throughout Northern Ireland. With the approval of the Housing Executive, the first of a number of Catholic families moved in, and within hours gangs of Protestant protestors, including UDA men, rushed from other parts of Belfast, gathered on the street, and were shouting abuse at the newcomers. Negotiations were carried out in the street for several days between the army, men from Whitelaw's office, the UDA, and the Provisionals. Finally, the IRA decided to break the deadlock by sending in another of the Catholic families. Furniture was loaded on a truck and a large crowd formed behind. As the truck approached its destination, the army rammed it with an armored car. The crowd grew angry, causing the army to fire rubber bullets, then to use water cannon and CS gas. By evening both sides were firing real bullets and the Provisional leadership announced that the truce was over.

More important even than the ending of the truce, always precarious and at no time suspending the random killings by terrorists, was the fact that it was ended leaving the

Provisionals as the protectors of the civil rights of the Catholic community. In what the Catholics saw as two clear cases of basic justice, Woodvale Avenue and Lenadoon Road, Whitelaw and the army had allowed the UDA to impose its will. Simultaneously, the Provisionals damaged Whitelaw's image by revealing that he had conducted secret negotiations with them. Although the negotiations had achieved nothing, the Protestant extremists were outraged that Whitelaw would sit down with "murderers."

The renewed Provisional bombing campaign built up to a crescendo two weeks later when in little more than an hour one sunny afternoon, 22 bombs exploded in Belfast, most of them in stolen cars. Two of the explosions in crowded city streets took 11 lives, 2 of the dead being soldiers, and injured 130 others, quickly meriting for the carnage the name of "Bloody Friday." Even many IRA sympathizers were shocked by the callous disregard for innocent life, and Whitelaw took advantage of the mood to invade the Catholic No-Go areas. To his surprise and relief, the massive forces led by tanks met no resistance. Soon the barricades of both IRA and UDA were swept away, although the change was more symbolic than real. The army could send armored vehicles through the streets, but little attempt was made to smoke out the gunmen from their safe havens.

Whitelaw now returned to his cherished idea of a conference of all interested parties, that is to say, all but the two wings of the IRA. The SDLP would represent the moderates in the Catholic community, and it was agreed off-the-record that it could and would through its own lines of communication bring to the meeting the views of both IRA wings and that of the Republic of Ireland. Ian Paisley and William Craig would speak for Orange extremists, and there would be no difficulty in getting spokesmen for the Unionist politicians who had previously monopolized power in Stormont. But even this modest plan was ruined before it could be put into effect, for the UDA had, not unreasonably, interpreted the ending of "No-Go" as a major victory for itself, and it quickly ran into conflict with the army when it sought to expand its victory by free-lance attacks on suspected IRA men and sympathizers. Paisley and Craig dropped out. Then the SDLP, anxious to show the Catholic community that it could do more than the IRA for it, said internment would have to end before the conference started. Whitelaw had by now released 724 men, and those inside—including 30 new detentions— were down to 241. But Whitelaw would not yield on them, claiming that the Orange backlash would be excessive. So the SDLP stayed away, as did two other small parties which had joined them in demanding an end to internment, the Nationalist party and Republican Labor. The only people who finally turned up at the meeting in September were a delegation from the Unionist party headed by suspended Prime Minister Brian Faulkner, and representatives of two small groups speaking for viewpoints close to those of Faulkner. They had nothing to say that was not already well known, and the absence of opposing views prevented any further sharpening of the issues.

Six months of direct rule had now passed with little to show for all of Whitelaw's efforts. He bravely struggled forward. In October he announced that local government elections would be held in two months, as a step in the implementation of London's promise to give the minority community "an active, permanent and guaranteed role in the life and public affairs" of Northern Ireland. This meant ungerrymandered constituencies and voting by proportional representation. The Orange extremists would have no part of such a sellout. They said that proportional representation was un-British, and they promised to use all necessary force to keep people from voting. To give teeth to their words, they started a wave of rioting in the wholly Protestant territory of East Belfast, a wave that soon swept across the river and extended all the way across the state to Derry. The riots were directed mainly against the British army at first, but soon Catholics also were included. In one Catholic church in East Belfast the statues were smashed with sledgehammers, and another was set on fire. UDA leader Craig said publicly in London that "we are prepared to come out and shoot to kill." Far from repudiating him, the Ulster Loyalist Council of which Craig is chairman, said he was "giving voice to the feelings of most loyalists." The council is spokesman for the major extremist groups, including Vanguard.

Once again Whitelaw had to accept public defeat and cancel the elections. But he now saw clearly that normality would involve more than simply defeating the IRA. Means must be found to isolate the extremists on the other side also. As long as they retained the mass support they now obviously enjoyed, his political task was hopeless. As a result he made a subtle but significant change in the pressures, less on the Provisionals and more on the UDA. The Provisionals for their part cooperated with Whitelaw by reducing the level of their attacks and avoiding spectaculars along the lines of "Bloody Friday."

The pressure on the Orange extremists was further increased when a series of moves was made against the IRA by the government of the Republic. Dublin had played an ambiguous role for many reasons. At first, some had hoped that intensification of strife in the north would encourage Britain to pull out, and that reunification of the country would follow automatically. Even after it had become clear that a British withdrawal would bring only a civil war, many in the south agreed with the Catholic community in the north that it needed the IRA for self-defense. One aspect of Whitelaw's strategy was to persuade Dublin that the freedom of speech and movement allowed the IRA in the Republic was aggravating the north's agony. It increased his difficulty in dealing with Orange extremists for whom the Republic was a safe sanctuary and also a source of arms and supplies for the IRA gunmen. The growing estrangement between the British army and the Orange extremists helped to improve Whitelaw's public image in the Republic and to encourage the Dublin government to limit access to the communications media for IRA spokesmen, and finally to set up special courts to put identified members of the IRA behind bars. It was Whitelaw's greatest success to date, yet only a minor one.

The Orange extremists refused to be placated. On the contrary, they took seriously the advice given them by UDA leader Craig "to come out and shoot to kill." In December, Whitelaw announced a task force of military and police charged with tracking down the murderers who since the beginning of the year had killed 106 people, leaving some of the victims mutilated and with evidence of having been tortured before killing, some also boobytrapped with explosives. All but 13 were found in Belfast, and 77 of the victims were Catholics. The first year of direct rule was in fact far worse than anything that had preceded it, a total of 473 violent deaths as compared with 208 the previous year and 38 the year before that. More than a hundred of those killed in 1972 were British soldiers.[9]

On the first anniversary of direct rule in March 1973, London admitted its failure to achieve the declared objectives by extending direct rule for a further year. The British also issued a White Paper setting out plans for restoring political normalcy in Northern Ireland, and promised that these plans would be implemented before the end of the second year of direct rule. This promise or threat seemed based less on any objective evaluation of the prospects of resolving the issues than on a sense of need to cut the Gordian knot if it could not be untied. The dominant characteristic of the White Paper was that it left almost everything to be worked out at some future time, a measure of the low level of the confidence of its drafters in its workability. One of the few specifics was that Northern Ireland would remain "a separate territory" within the United Kingdom, and would remain part of the United Kingdom for "as long as that is the wish of a majority of its people."

The first significant step toward implementation of the new plans was the election in June 1973 of a 78-member assembly. Election was by proportional representation, and in order to exclude any possibility of gerrymandering in the cre-

ation of constituencies, the electoral unit was that already
fixed for elections in Northern Ireland to the British Parliament. Since twelve members are elected to Westminster by
the "first past the post" system, the number of units was
twelve, but since the actual number of voters varies from unit
to unit, some of them elected as few as five members to the
assembly, while others elected as many as eight. With proportional representation by the single transferable vote, this
meant that a minority of one-fifth in the smallest constituency
and of one-eighth in the biggest could elect one assembly-
man for that constituency, and bigger groups would be similarly represented according to their size. The legislation of
the British Parliament creating this assembly did not give it
any legislative or other power. It was authorized to function
merely as an advisory body to the Secretary of State for
Northern Ireland, who would be a member of the United
Kingdom cabinet, the post held since March 1972 by William
Whitelaw. The idea was that it would function as government
under tutelage, with its every decision subject to the veto of
the Secretary of State. Only after it worked out a system of
sharing power with the minority or minorities would London
began to transfer legislative and executive authority to it; and
when it showed its ability and willingness to exercise such
authority fairly, the process would be gradually extended.
London, however, made it clear that it did not intend to
allow Northern Ireland to return to its previous level of self-
government. Its executive would not under any circumstances be again authorized to appoint certain higher judges
and magistrates, or be responsible for the conduct of public
prosecutions, elections, the franchise, and "exceptional measure in the law and order field to cope with emergency situations." And "certain other matters, notably in the 'law and
order' field, will be reserved to the British government."

Each of these limitations and restrictions reflected a
judgment by the British government on the previous behavior of the Northern Ireland regime, and acceptance of the discrimination charges made by the civil rights movement. The

group which formerly monopolized legislative and executive power would henceforth have to share it. The sharing would have to be not only formal but substantive according to the judgment of the London-named Secretary of State, the permanent overseer and arbiter. Concretely, Stormont would no longer be able to gerrymander, to restrict the franchise, to manipulate the law courts. The Special Powers Act, the basis for internment without trial and other restrictions on human rights and the most specific source of the discriminations resented by the minority, would be repealed; but only after the British Parliament enacted "emergency legislation for the more effective combatting of terrorism." The assembly would be debarred from passing legislation of a discriminatory nature. It would also be debarred from legislating to require an oath or declaration as a qualification for office or employment where that was not required in comparable circumstances in the rest of the United Kingdom. Where such oaths or declarations were now required, they would be eliminated. This would mean that citizens formerly excluded from public life because of their commitment to union of Northern Ireland with the Republic of Ireland would be able to pursue their objectives by lawful means.

Discriminatory executive action by central and local government and other public bodies was also specifically banned under the new British proposals, a measure designed to ensure (among other things) nondiscriminatory allocation of public housing. A charter of human rights incorporating safeguards and protections for the individual was promised. Complaints against the police would be handled by a body "with an independent element," its rules to conform to those shortly to be introduced in Great Britain. The British Parliament would also enact legislation to deal with job discrimination in the private sector. Or, as the White Paper summed it up, citizens were given absolute guarantees of "effective protection against any arbitrary or discriminatory use of power to all, whatever their religion or political beliefs."

Reflecting a frequently repeated statement of the British government that normality in Northern Ireland must have an

"Irish dimension," the White Paper said that London "favors and is prepared to facilitate the establishment of institutional arrangements for consultation and cooperation between Northern Ireland and the Republic of Ireland." London would shortly invite representatives of both parts of Ireland to a conference with a three-point agenda: acceptance of the present status of Northern Ireland, together with the possibility of subsequent change of that status by the majority in Northern Ireland; effective consultation and cooperation in Ireland for the benefit of both north and south; and concerted governmental and community action against terrorist organizations.

Basic to the success of the plan was the proposed assembly. It was stipulated that its first task would be to agree on a series of committees drawn from its own membership, the committees "to reflect the balance of parties," and the chairmen of the committees to form the executive collectively and be the political heads of the departments. This would follow the British system of government in which the executive is chosen by and answers directly to the legislature. When the Secretary of State was satisfied that the executive chosen by the assembly was in fact a reflection and expression not just of the majority but of the various parties in the assembly according to the strength of each, and that it was functioning properly as an expression of the variety of interests it represented, he would start the devolution to it of the powers which in his opinion and that of his government in London it was capable of exercising fairly. But for that devolution, the law insisted, the executive could "no longer be based upon any single party, if that party draws its support and its elected representation virtually entirely from only one section of a divided community." What that politically unique formula meant was that the British government was determined not to allow the Unionists in Northern Ireland to regain the monopoly of legislative and executive power which they enjoyed from the creation of the state up to the suspension of Stormont.

An analysis of the voting in previous elections in Northern Ireland had suggested to some observers the possibility that the "nationalist" groups opposed to the Unionist monopoly of power might now be able to join with various labor elements in a coalition that would command a majority in the assembly. Local elections for urban and rural councils held in early June 1973 did in fact establish the existence of a substantial "moderate" vote, though far less than a majority. The SDLP, the representative of the civil rights movement and of other "nationalist" groups willing to work within the constitutional framework of the Northern Ireland state, secured a total of 82 of the 526 council seats. The Alliance party, which seeks to unite the moderates of the Catholic and Protestant communities, won 63. But the official Unionists, the traditional power holders, had 210, and dissident Unionist extremists opposed to any compromise had an additional 81. The prospects for a moderate center were further dashed four weeks later by the elections for the assembly itself. The hardliners led by Ian Paisley and William Craig emerged as the biggest bloc with 27 seats, followed by Brian Faulkner's official Unionists with 23, SDLP with 19, Alliance with 8, and the nonsectarian Northern Ireland Labor party with 1. The poor showing of the Alliance and of Labor is particularly significant. While the Catholic community is prepared to cooperate in a Northern Ireland regime which will give it a share of power and civil equality—something that was not always true—the Protestants are still determined to retain their position of privilege. The extent of the Catholic shift is further stressed by the failure of the Official wing of the IRA to elect a single candidate, and by the parallel failure of the ballot-spoiling Provisional IRA to get more than 2 percent of the electors to register their protest.

The opening meeting of the assembly in July 1973 showed that the basic realities of Northern Ireland politics were little changed. On the basis of surveys made five years earlier, when Northern Ireland was far less polarized than it has since become, Richard Rose argues convincingly in his excellently documented study of party allegiances that the multiparty system in Northern Ireland operates "within the framework of a dichotomous division" for and against the survival of the state as a separate administration. Coalitions or shifting of party allegiance is possible only on whichever side of the divide the voters or their representatives are located.[10] The assembly immediately proceeded to demonstrate the accuracy of his statement. The official Unionists and the Paisley-Craig bloc offered candidates for the post of chairman, and the Alliance party supported the official Unionists, thereby electing their choice, when SDLP and Labor abstained.

That, however, was the only business transacted. When the chairman read a "directive" from the Secretary of State that he (the chairman) should name a committee to recommend rules of procedure, the Paisley-Craig bloc challenged the validity of such a directive. Within minutes, with shouts, jeers, and exchange of insults the session was adjourned without even arranging for a further meeting. The Paisley-Craig members then held their own rump session, at which they reaffirmed their opposition to any formula for sharing power with the Catholics or developing closer relations with the Republic of Ireland, and pledged to make the assembly unworkable.

In December 1973, after long and tortuous negotiations, London won agreement on a coalition executive in which the Unionists headed by Brian Faulkner have 6 representatives, the SDLP 4, and the Alliance party 1. The new executive then met with Liam Cosgrave, Prime Minister of the Republic of Ireland, and agreed to set up a Council of Ireland. The council will consist of 7 members of the Republic's government and 7 of the Northern Ireland executive. It will have its own secretariat and will be helped by a consultative body comprising 30 members of the Parliament of the Republic and 30 of the Northern Ireland Assembly. Progress was, nevertheless, more apparent than real. The Northern Ireland executive can function without conflict because it has no decisions to make, London retaining control over all substantive matters. Similarly, the functions of the Council of Ireland were postponed for later formulation.

But even such nebulous approaches to compromise were more than the extremists on both sides were ready to tolerate. All through 1973, while the British pursued their search for an escape, violence continued on the streets, and in the factories, supermarkets, hotels, and stores of Northern Ireland. By late summer a campaign of letter bombs and other incendiary devices spread to London's stores and to the British Embassy in Washington. The news of the agreement on the membership of the executive brought an upsurge of killings, and violence again flared with the announcement of the Council of Ireland. All of this built up to a very negative prognosis for the new Stormont assembly and for the British plan to which it is central. And while that plan remains frustrated, London can hardly escape from its entrapment in direct rule of a resistant population. The record of failure of direct English rule in Ireland over 750 years gives scant reason for confidence now.

16

Conclusions

The future administration of Northern Ireland must be seen to be completely even-handed both in law and in fact.
  —London government policy statement, October 1972 [1]

We are too small to be apart or for the border to be there for all time.
  —LORD CRAIGAVON, first Prime Minister
  of Northern Ireland [2]

Each reader must draw his own conclusions from the facts set out in the preceding narrative. The process of assembling and correlating them forced me to modify previously held views and to bring into clearer focus the magnitude of the issues that separate the protagonists. But it also strengthened my belief that those issues are not insoluble. In consequence, I reject Richard Rose's conclusion [3] that the world is inescapably saddled with this conflict for the foreseeable future. Alternative possibilities exist.

First of all, I see no possibility of a solution by force. It is quite true that force maintained the Northern Ireland state in the terms dictated by the majority community for 50 years, at

times with the use of naked violence and always by means of
institutionalized violence. But if one thing is clear as a result
of the civil rights movement of the 1960s and the subsequent
developments, a return to that system is excluded. The only
way in which it could be revived would be by a unilateral
declaration of independence (UDI) on the Rhodesian model.
While that seems unlikely, it cannot be ruled out absolutely.
But instead of being a solution, it would only exacerbate the
problem.

UDI would present Britain with most unattractive alternatives. With the present commitment of large numbers of
British troops to maintain internal order in Northern Ireland,
it would be embarrassing simply to withdraw. But to stay and
put down the massive revolt which the Orange extremists
could mount would not only be costly and enormously un-
popular at home, it would still leave the political problem
unsettled and would in addition create an emotional climate
far more resistant to any reasonable settlement than the
present one.

If the British withdrew, the Orange extremists could almost certainly impose a precarious domination on the minority community. But no final solution is imaginable. Attempts
at expulsion of significant numbers of the disaffected would
undoubtedly produce a military response from the neighboring Republic, probably official or at least officially
encouraged, as well as a massive support for the potential
victims from sympathizers in Britain and the United
States. Rather than the overthrow of the Orange regime, the
result would most likely be a military stalemate leading to a
guerrilla war of indefinite duration with horrendous impact
on the economy and society of all parts of Ireland.

The prospect of a resolution by an Orange military victory is remote, but a military victory of the other side is even
more remote. The Orange nightmare envisages a mass uprising of the Catholics of Ireland to annihilate all Protestants, a
situation in which they would be outnumbered three to one
and further handicapped because the enemy would be simul-

taneously outside and within. That nightmare neglects two significant factors. The military potential of the Republic is nominal. Any attempt to mobilize it for the envisaged purposes would be met by overwhelmingly superior assistance from Britain. More importantly, the experience of the past 50 years has demonstrated conclusively that the will to impose such a solution is absent both in the Republic and in the Catholic community in Northern Ireland. Nothing has been clearer than the repeated failure of the IRA to win popular backing for an offensive war. Their support is dependent on the belief of Northern Ireland Catholics that they need it to protect them from annihilation in their ghettos. I shall later submit a suggestion of how to resolve that issue, but first I should set out other conclusions I have reached.

Both communities have equal rights to live in Northern Ireland, and to hold and reverence their respective traditions. Equal rights means precisely that. Neither has the right to lord it over the other or to use its rights in such a way as to derogate from those of the other. These principles, when stated so baldly, may seem so elementary as scarcely to be worth formulating. Yet I think it should by now be clear that people on both sides do not accept them or at least violate them in practice. Many Catholics still see their Protestant neighbors as usurpers, occupying land and wealth which by right belongs to them. I sympathize with this feeling, but such an attitude does not make political sense. There comes a time when a title acquired by conquest becomes irreversible. And if three centuries is not enough, what is? Were the titles of those dispossessed in the seventeenth century any stronger than those of today's descendants of the seventeenth-century usurpers? If some disagree with this reasoning, then I suggest that elementary political sense still demands that they waive the moral right they think they have, not only legally but emotionally. They will never enforce it, and while they hold it, they harm themselves more than anyone else.

To recognize that the Catholics have equal rights in-

volves a much more radical change on the part of the Protestant community. If one thing is clear to me from my study of
the record of 50 years, it is that the Protestant community as a
power structure bears the major responsibility for continuing
injustices. I recognize many qualifications are in order and
many extenuating circumstances exist. But I think it essential
to reject the rather common assumption that both sides are
equally blameworthy, as well as the other assumption—
frequent among well-meaning outsiders—that reconciliation
is possible without first eliminating the unjust structures. In
an earlier chapter I mentioned one point that influenced me
strongly in reaching this conclusion. While both communities live in equal fear of each other, the level of hatred I en-
countered on the Protestant side was much higher than that
on the Catholic. That hatred I can interpret only as a defensive mechanism to "justify" policies recognized at a deeper
level to be unjust. I know too many of the Protestants involved to think that all are individually guilty. Many would
welcome an end to injustice and some work openly to that
end. But the structures that dominate the life of Northern Ireland respond to the stand of the overwhelming majority of
the state's Protestants and only of them. These are the structures that must go, together with the mentality that made
them.

Here the key element, expressed by some, assumed by
others, is the notion of a Protestant "establishment." This expression has deep roots in Irish history, and like many other
disturbing elements in that history, it came from England. Its
origins are found in the series of laws passed by the Westminster Parliament as part of the process of transferring the
crown from James II to William and Mary in 1689 and the
concomitant assertion by Parliament of its own sovereignty to
which even kings are subject. These laws created two levels
of citizenship, one for members of the Established Church,
one for all others. The historic effect of these laws in Ireland
has already been reviewed. Here it suffices to note that the
legal effects were canceled throughout both Great Britain

and Ireland early in the nineteenth century, and that the economic disabilities gradually disappeared in Great Britain and in most of Ireland in the course of that century. But the dominant Protestant community in Northern Ireland retained the spirit of those laws and incorporated it into the structures by which the state and society have functioned since 1920. The only change has been that the division has shifted, leaving Roman Catholics alone in the second-class category, while all Reformed faiths cluster together under the umbrella of the Orange Order in first class.

How deep-rooted this attitude is was made evident when Terence O'Neill attempted to meet some of the more obvious complaints of the civil rights movement. As it became clear that he contemplated the possibility that even some Catholics were entitled to be treated as equal citizens, his support was steadily eroded by the more intransigent members of his party who were committed to retaining the by now traditional discriminations. When London's pressures rose to the point where the will and ability of the Unionist party to resist came into question, still more extreme groupings quickly found a popular backing. Loyalty to the Crown was explicitly defined as subject to the provisions of the Protestant "establishment" of 1689. Or, as Rev. Ian Paisley put it, "I am loyal to the Queen and throne of Britain, being Protestant in the terms of the Revolution Settlement." To which Rev. Martin Smyth, Grand Master of the Belfast Orange Lodge, added: "We love the Union, but we love our Protestant heritage more." [4] The meaning was further clarified in the constitution of the Ulster Constitution Defence Committee and Ulster Protestant Volunteers, a Paisley-sponsored paramilitary organization formed in 1969. Its preamble directs Protestants to confine themselves to "lawful methods . . . as long as the United Kingdom maintains a Protestant monarchy and the terms of the Revolution settlement"; but when this settlement is threatened, a member must pledge "his first loyalty to the Society." [5]

Such an arrangement is in open violation of the Government of Ireland Act enacted by the Westminster Parliament in 1920, which created the state and defines its legal powers. And that brings me to another of my basic conclusions. It is that we can make no progress until it is recognized by all concerned—including the London government—that Great Britain continues to be part of the problem and consequently cannot provide the solution.

This proposition must also be qualified in various ways. The source of the problem in its most generic terms is the effort conducted over 700 years, first by England, then by Great Britain, to dominate Ireland militarily and absorb it culturally and economically. The specific source was the introduction of settlers and the subjection of the natives to them. That created a classical colonial situation, a supply of cheap labor for the settlers within an inherently unstable political situation which ensured continued dependence of the settlers on the colonizing country.

When, in the aftermath of World War I, Britain decided that the price of holding Ireland was too high, its disengagement was on the basis of its own continuing advantage. It may be said that such is the normal and reasonable way for a big power—or for any country—to behave. I don't dispute that. But I want the fact to be fed into the equation. And I also want to stress that the solution chosen was not a statesmanlike one and consequently not good ultimately for Britain itself. It was, in the words of Arnold Toynbee, an Englishman never known to be partial to anything Irish, a "social disaster," and "a confession of political bankruptcy." [6] Toynbee was referring directly to the decision to split the country in two in order to maintain a bridgehead in part of it. Even worse was the location of the line of partition, designed to retain the largest area and the largest number of unwilling people capable of being stategically secured, a decision that further guaranteed a continuance of social and political disequilibrium with corresponding assurance of dependence on the colonizing power. Britain has paid dearly for that decision and may yet pay far more dearly.

With hindsight, an Irishman might regret that the Sinn Fein effort was so successful. If colonial status had been endured until after World War II, Ireland would presumably have shared the freedom secured by India and the African colonies and most likely would have emerged as a single independent state. On the other hand, the independence movements in those other states might never have become successful without the Irish example. The British probably have reason for blaming Ireland for the breakdown of their world empire, as I believe they in fact do in their deep subconscious. If only Irish youngsters had agreed to become "happy English children," perhaps Hindus and Ibos and Hottentots would have followed.[7]

The congenital British assumption that the Irish are inherently inferior has prevented agreement as equals at any time. When the Act of Union created the United Kingdom of Great Britain and Ireland in 1800, Ireland had one-third of the entire population of the United Kingdom but was "granted" only 15 percent of the seats in Westminster's House of Commons. England, with 53 percent of the population, cornered 74 percent of the seats. Scotland and Wales didn't come out very well either, but they had been longer in the Union and were already depopulated. During the following century, England's automatic majority enabled it to tax Ireland at twice the rate it taxed the rest of the United Kingdom, in relation to ability to pay.[8] During the 1840s it amended the laws governing the bankruptcy of local authorities to make sure that other local authorities within Ireland would shoulder the entire burden imposed on those of their associates bankrupted by the Great Famine's demand for emergency feeding. No English money should go to thwart the natural laws of economics by keeping starving Irishmen alive. In 1921, after six months of negotiating in London, Lloyd George gave the Irish delegates the choice of signing his proposals the same day he submitted them, without time to consult principals in Dublin, or face immediate renewal of war to the death. And to come up to

1972, Mr. Whitelaw used the Special Powers Act in Northern
Ireland to hold hundreds of Catholics without trial, but not a
single Orangeman, during his first nine months in office, at a
time when all indicators pointed to at least two cold-blooded
murders by the heavily armed Orange UDA to one by the
much smaller and less well-equipped IRA.

What I am trying to say is that Britain is hopelessly mistaken when it assumes that it can perform the function of
honest broker. I recognize that it no longer has the economic
or strategic reasons which made it feel the need in 1920 for a
bridgehead in Ireland. I recognize that it is all too conscious
that Northern Ireland is an economic liability and a political
embarrassment and in consequence wants nothing more than
to get out gracefully. The pressure of public opinion is growing, the opinion polls showing that a majority of the British
want their soldiers withdrawn from Northern Ireland. Indeed, my recurrent nightmare is that London will dump the
mess and walk out. That was obviously what Hugh Frazer, a
Conservative member of Parliament, had in mind when he
criticized the 1973 White Paper for its implication that British involvement would continue for the foreseeable future.
"How long," he asked, "before we soldier out—not on? How
long before we disengage? How long before we decolo-
nize?" [9]

I see, at the same time, a positive element in the Frazer
comment. It seems to recognize that Britain is trapped in history no less than Ireland, saddled with the same ghosts of co-
lonialism, incapable of placing "settler" and "native" in the
same balance. If so, it opens the possibility that Britain may
be coming to recognize belatedly that it can free itself only
by disqualifying itself as judge and jury and seeking outside
arbitration. I shall return to this possibility. But as yet, there
are few indications that Britain's decision makers are approaching such terms. Most of them can no more be bothered
with the facts today than they were in the past, as witness the
record of the London administration over the past three or
four years and the guidance given the troops when sent in as

peace-keepers. William Whitelaw promised for a moment to
be a variation from the millenial pattern. But only for a moment.[10]

What is particularly disturbing is the revelation that the
Whitelaw administration is unwilling to deal effectively with
issues which are officially presented to it. In June 1973, the
enterprise of some newsmen uncovered the report prepared
for and suppressed by the Community Relations Commission, an official body whose reason for existence is to stamp
out discrimination. The report showed that 60,000 people
had been driven from their homes between August 1969 and
February 1973. This, it suggested, was the largest fixed population movement anywhere in western Europe since World
War II. And it placed the blame squarely on the Housing Executive and other government bodies. The effect of this
disclosure was to cause many to question the sincerity of
Whitelaw's commitment to equal justice. That judgment was
strengthened the following month when a prominent social
scientist revealed in a British magazine the existence of another suppressed report, this one on the religious composition of the Northern Ireland civil service. Of 477 civil
servants in the top grades, 95 percent are Protestants, an imbalance all the more serious today because the elimination of
elected bodies has left administrative power in the civil
service. Although many precedents exist in Britain for dealing with such problems, the Whitelaw administration preferred to pretend that it didn't exist or was irrelevant.[11]

I do not impugn Britain's goodwill, of which no doubt
there is plenty. But I think I have established two capital
points. Its emotions are so involved in this mess of its making
that centuries of national psychoanalysis in depth would be
needed to unravel them. Even if this were done, the other
parties would still have to be convinced. Northern Ireland's
Catholics would need a similar reverse psychoanalysis. And
the Protestants also have problems. "We don't like the English," says Jim Best, a leading Orangeman in the United
States, a native of Belfast. "They look down on us as on all

the Irish." Reverend Martin Smyth, Presbyterian minister and Grand Master of the Belfast Orange Lodge, agrees. "Northern Ireland Presbyterians have a strand of dislike for the English, because we have seen Englishmen betray their trust time and again." Besides, he adds, giving the lie both to Whitelaw and to Prime Minister Heath, "the Northern Irishman is a Celt." Reverend Canon Charles Gray-Stack of the Church of Ireland (Anglican communion) puts it more graphically. "You can always trust the English for one thing. Sooner or later, they will let their friends down." All of which was summed up earlier by Sir Edward Carson, the man most responsible for bringing Northern Ireland into existence. "What a fool I was! I was only a puppet, and so was Ulster, and so was Ireland, in the political game." [12]

This reasoning forces me to conclude that the 1973 White Paper described in the previous chapter is not the solution. Its ultimate assumption is that individual goodwill can prove stronger than entrenched power structures, an assumption contrary to all past experience. The internal logic of the situation will force either a return to the former power monopoly enjoyed by Stormont or development of permanent direct rule from London, and neither alternative will bring peace. The best that can be hoped is a breathing space of reduced tension while different groups jockey for position within the modified framework. Even a temporary cessation of violence is not guaranteed.

If permanent incorporation into Britain, a return to Stormont and UDI are all ruled out, the only surviving alternative would seem to be a reunification of Ireland. Geography, economics, and race are not the only pointers in that direction. While those immediately involved see the conflicting interpretations of history and symbols of group identification from a distance, the underlying similarities in moral principles and other cultural elements are more apparent. Many countries of Europe, including Britain, have fused communities with equal or greater elements of conflict into a national harmony. The process should be easier in today's world climate of pluralism.

The Republic does start with one advantage, a tradition of nonsectarianism, a tradition in which individual Protestants are enshrined in the pantheon of its patriots and cultural leaders, Wolfe Tone, John Mitchel, William Butler Yeats, and Douglas Hyde. Unfortunately, that is not enough. In its 50 years of self-government it has built a society in which the million Protestants of Northern Ireland do not fit and to which they could not adjust themselves. It may not be as abhorrent as it seems to the wearer of Orange glasses peering at it across the border, but the image he receives is based on solid facts. Ireland can no more be united on the Dublin premises than on those of Stormont.

It is not easy to put one's finger on what makes the Republic so repulsive to northerners. Rather than one big obvious thing, it is an integrated system. It is in large part a question of attitudes, each a molehill but cumulatively a mountain. The Orange rejection of a "Green" Ireland is primarily emotional, but that does not automatically make it unreasonable. The symbols each side values are emotional symbols, the flags, the days of glory and of shame. The problem is that each has its own set. There is no common memory of victories and defeats. For one, "1916" means the Easter Rising; for the other, the Battle of the Somme.

It ought to be relatively easy for the Republic to eliminate the laws which are positively offensive to the Orangemen. It eliminated one by constitutional amendment in 1972, the "special position" recognized to the Roman Catholic church. Contraceptives would not be significantly more available or more destructive of public morals without the present laws than they are with them; and censorship has similarly ceased to have a significant impact on social attitudes. But the Republic has built up a mystique which makes it as important to flaunt these empty symbols in the faces of northern Protestants as it is for the Orangemen to "take in" a "Fenian street" in their July 12 celebration of the "Glorious" Boyne.

Some claim or pretend that they retain the admittedly anachronous laws for use as bargaining counters at some future round-table conferences. Others are more intransigent. The head of the Roman Catholic church in Ireland (in both parts of it!), Cardinal William Conway, asserted in 1972 that even in a pluralistic society, the majority is entitled to prevent the minority from doing things their conscience allows, if this is necessary to prevent change or damage to "the kind of society we have." Specifically as regards divorce, he said he was confident that a vast majority would reject a change in the existing constitutional prohibition, if the issue went to a referendum.

Here we have a circular argument typical of rationalization in the Republic. On issues of faith and morals, the Cardinal counts on the people to accept and implement his judgment. They will vote to deny divorce to fellow citizens whose conscience authorizes—and in some circumstances urges—them to divorce, because that is what the Cardinal tells them is their duty. The mentality behind all this is what the Orangeman abhors, and reasonably abhors. That is what he means by "Rome Rule," and he will have none of it. He does not want to be part of such an Ireland, above all as a minority.

Irish politicians, like politicians everywhere, know what they must do to survive. Regardless of party affiliation, they spout the same rhetoric about the determination of their constituents to reject change, to live in a Victorian backwater, though they are members of the European Economic Community. Even a Protestant like Erskine Childers, educated in an English "public" (that is, private) school, has the spiel down pat. "I don't think it is the churches that impose our laws in regard to public morality," Childers said in 1972, the year before he was elected President of the Republic.

The people who compose the flocks of these churches wish for no change. If anyone tells me that in order to achieve reunification we should have a total secularization of society, then I'd just like everyone to think again. Apart from political crime in the north [Northern Ireland], we have the lowest crime rate in Europe, the lowest illegitimacy rate, the lowest venereal disease rate. We are the happiest country in Europe to live in, in times of peace, one of the principal reasons being the influence of the churches. If anybody wants me to exchange for our kind of ways of life the ways of life of any of the supersecular states, I have no wish to do so, nor do I believe the majority of the Northern Ireland Protestants wish to either.[13]

Mr. Childer's last comment is undoubtedly accurate, if not in the sense in which he intended it. As I said above, the key element in the structure of the Stormont state was the notion of a Protestant "establishment" in the terms of the seventeenth-century Williamite Settlement. The key element in the Republic, though expressed less aggressively because of its almost universal acceptance, is a mirror-image Catholic "establishment," a theocracy in the spirit of the Council of Trent, a concept of law as designed to implement ultimate moral purposes. Its persistence is a measure of the failure of Pope John and the Second Vatican Council to make any effective impact on the Catholic church in Ireland. While it remains, it constitutes an absolute block to reunification of the country.

Closely allied to this socioreligious obscurantism is the economic conservatism of the Republic. It is not simply that its productivity is lower than that of Britain and even than that of Northern Ireland, an inevitable consequence of previous centuries of exploitation and decapitalization. It is that the benefits of that productivity, such as it is, are excessively concentrated among a small group of industrialists, businessmen, and capitalists. Some attempt was made to spread the wealth at one time, especially during the first period of Fianna Fail in power, in the 1930s, but all that has been forgotten since World War II. "By the time of the Whitaker Report [1958] on *Economic Development,* it was government policy to put greater emphasis on 'productive' purposes rather than housing and social investments," writes James J. Lamb, of the Center for the Study of Development and Social Change. "With the 1966 Anglo-Irish Trade Agreement the

Republic had moved well down the capitalistic path and toward economic dependence on England. And the gap between rich and poor steadily mounted." [14]

The only study of the rich-poor gap in the Republic I have been able to discover was published in 1972 by Patrick M. Lyons, professor of economics at Trinity College, Dublin.[15] He calculates total personal wealth in the Republic for 1966 at about $5 billion, equal to two and a half times that year's national income. Real property, land, houses, business premises, and the like formed 30.3 percent of the total, with a further 35 percent in Irish stocks and shares, 21 percent in foreign stocks and shares, 17.3 percent in cash, and 14.5 percent in insurance policies. Nearly two-thirds of the adult population owned no wealth, while 5 percent owned about 70 percent of all wealth, an inequality greater than in Great Britain or the United States.

To avoid getting lost in a subject that calls for an entire book, I shall limit myself to one quotation which expresses perfectly my own conclusions. "It is significant that a nation born in revolution should so soon lose so much of its social vitality," Dr. Stephen McGonagle, president of the Irish Congress of Trades Unions, said in 1972.

The Irish community is still struggling with basic concepts of free opportunity in education, adequate housing, a meaningful social welfare code, and a philosophy which can produce a really worthwhile set of policies for eliminating poverty. It is only now talking the language used by the Fabians in Britain in the 1880s, as though daring to break into the dangerous, unexplored territory of social reform a quarter century after the welfare state arrived, weary and late, in Britain. . . . Today it is floundering around, afraid to grasp the nettle of a simple community schools system, because we cannot get rid of our inhibitions regarding the so-called rights of chosen enclaves of our people to an elitist education, whether provided in a secular institution or in a polished convent establishment which has never admitted the rough accents of the daughters and sons of the poor. Many towns and cities are structured to keep the rich and the poor apart, the one clinging to life, the other ostentatiously wealthy.[16]

James Lamb (quoted two paragraphs above) came to the study of Ireland, as I did, from many years of involvement with the problems of development in Latin America. We were both immediately struck by the extraordinary similarities of the economy and society of those former Spanish colonies and this former British colony. Both are subjected to the same neocolonial influences exercised by the same multinational companies. Some 2500 foreign corporations dominate the "growth sector" of Ireland, north and south, according to Lamb. While foreign capital pours in, acquiring control of enterprises previously owned by Irishmen and progressively dictating the decisions of government, 21 percent of accumulated personal wealth is invested abroad. The economy remains incapable of providing employment to all the citizens, and concentration of capital in technologically sophisticated activities with low labor content makes the worker ever more marginal.[17]

The big difference between Ireland and Latin America is that in Ireland no influential voice has questioned the wisdom of handing over the economy to the multinational companies which in the past 20 years have taken out of the poor countries of the world almost three times as much as they invested in them, while simultaneously increasing threefold the value of their holdings in those countries. The extent of the penetration in the Republic of Ireland may be gauged by the figures for new and expanded investment for 1972. The United States put in $164 million, and Britain, $96 million. Smaller amounts came from Japan and several European countries. Yet Irish capitalists contributed only $125 million, and that meant that some three-quarters of the economic growth was on the account of and for the benefit of the multinationals. Their greater access to technology and credit means in Ireland, as in other poor countries, that nationals are unable to compete with them, a situation now further aggravated by Ireland's accession to the European Economic Community.[18]

Only the Official IRA, the ones who have decided that violence will not end partition, are concerned about this trend and offer alternatives, but they are refused a hearing as "Marxists." The Irish church is still trapped in the corner into which Pope Leo XIII painted it when he condemned the socialists, Communists, and other nihilists for refusing to obey all constituted authority, for advocating collective property, and for proclaiming the absolute equality of all men. The church in Latin America, following Vatican Council II and Pope Paul's encyclical on world development (*Populorum progressio*) no longer fears the Marxist analysis. The hemisphere's bishops as a body in 1968 officially repudiated the oppressing power of the institutionalized violence which grinds down the poor in Latin America and Ireland alike, the neocolonialism of the national oligarchies, and the external neocolonialism of the international monopolies and the international imperialism of money.[19] Its thinkers have developed the theology of liberation which calls on man to assume conscious responsibility for his own destiny, a theology that is affecting Catholic thought significantly in many parts of the world, but not in Ireland.[20]

It is not my purpose to offer a blueprint of the social reforms needed in the Republic. The only point I want to make is that unification of Ireland is impossible as long as the Republic retains its cryptotheocracy. Latin America is introduced here simply as an example of a society with similar experiences and backgrounds which has come to see the distortions which follow from a legitimation of injustice by the Church and is taking corrective action. It is suggested that a similar evolution in Ireland would produce a society free of the elements which the northern Protestant finds abhorrent. I do not want to exaggerate. The Catholic church in Latin America has not been transformed overnight. But significant sections of it, including an encouraging number of bishops, have formally and to a large extent emotionally divested themselves of privilege and inherited wealth. They have committed themselves to a mission of justice for the most needy, joining on a level of equality with similarly minded Protestants, Jews, and nonbelievers to implement programs defending human rights and promoting human dignity. In this alliance, they are open to repudiate what is bad in capitalism and to support what is good in socialism. Ideological taboos are excluded.

Change of this kind in the Republic will take time, though not necessarily a great deal of time, once people are persuaded of its necessity. Northern Ireland, too, requires time to find a permanent solution to its problems. But Northern Ireland has one problem that cannot wait. The killing of people and destruction of property must stop. The communities have to find a way to live side by side until they are able to live together. It seems to me that world public opinion, and especially opinion in the United States which has so often in the past exercised and is still capable of exercising a decisive influence on decision making in Ireland, is not sufficiently aware of its power at this critical point. If the Irish organizations and sympathizers in the United States were to place a much higher priority on the ending of violence as not only useless but self-escalating, much could be accomplished. Few now seem to give it such priority, except for some small groups of Catholic and Protestant clergy, and their efforts have been discounted by some as an attempt to promote personal reconciliation as a substitute for the elimination of unjust structures. I think it should be clear from this book that the structures are the problem, not the people of either community. But the structures cannot realistically be changed without the agreement of the majority community, and that will never be won at gunpoint.

One who has made this vital point eloquently and persuasively is Irish politician and historian Conor Cruise O'Brien. His white-hot concern for a quick end to violence comes across as the dominant theme in his recent book *States of Ireland*,[21] in many other writings, and in public addresses. It will be clear from this book that I also share his rejection of the assumption of much of Irish nationalistic thought that Britain can and must be made to end partition by handing over Northern Ireland to the Republic. I think I stress Britain's continuing complicity in partition more than he does, but I accept his major point. Northern Protestants cannot and should not be coerced. And I further share his criticism of the churches, Catholic and Protestant alike, for "encouraging, exalting, and extending the kind of trivial-sectarian self-righteousness which forms a culture in which violence so easily multiplies." [22]

I have already stated my belief, I think quite clearly, that both Britain and the Republic of Ireland lack the objectivity and the acceptability by both Northern Ireland communities to perform the required peace-keeping function successfully. If that is so, we have to look elsewhere for help. The principle of outside intervention under UN auspices is no longer novel. The Republic of Ireland has already urged this approach. Britain has hitherto resisted, but the continued failure of its own initiatives must make it more amenable to new approaches. The actual choice of a country to provide administrators and troops would be important. It should be a small country without territorial or other world ambitions. Switzerland would be ideal. It is not tied to any power bloc, and it has a record of centuries of friendly coexistence of Protestants and Catholics who once battled more bitterly than do the two communities in Northern Ireland. Its army traditions give equal honor to the Swiss soldiers who protected John Calvin and those who protected Pope Pius IX. In an area half the size of Ireland it holds together in enviable amity 6.3 million citizens, 53 percent Protestant, 45 percent Roman Catholic, speaking four languages. To do this it had to fragment the country into 22 highly decentralized cantons. Ireland would probably require no more than 5 or 6.

It is, however, none of my intention to present a blueprint for the future. What I have sought to establish is that the related problems of violence in Northern Ireland and the division of the island into two antagonistic states can be resolved only by the introduction of new factors. I can see the multimillion Irish community in America playing a critical role here. In recent times it has made itself felt mainly by such irrelevancies as annual parades to honor St. Patrick and the selection of "Pat Nixons" as Irishwomen of the Year. But its past contributions to the survival of the concept of Irish nationalism was decisive in bringing Ireland to its present level of autonomy. As we have seen, it was particularly important in restoring hope and self-respect in the second half of the nineteenth century, after the trauma of the Great Famine, and again in the struggle in the early twentieth century that led to the Anglo-Irish Treaty of 1921. It was historically inevitable that the concern of the Irish in America in those times should have been expressed in large part in enmity to England. Britain's changed role and objectives require a major change in that respect. Today, it is more in need of encouragement than of threats. But it has a role to play in the solution, and the United States has even more leverage now than on earlier occasions to influence it to play that role generously. By concentrating on that task, the Irish in America could again be decisive in completing the liberation of all of Ireland, north and south.

Notes

Introduction

1 Richard Rose, *Governing Without Consensus* (London: Faber, 1971), p. 74.
2 Roger M. Williams gives the figure of 13.3 million in *World* magazine, April 24, 1973, p. 28. This is an extrapolation from the 1960 census. The 1970 census, however, had a specific question on national origins, in response to which 16,325,000 Americans claimed Irish ancestry.
3 See in particular Chapter 2.
4 Quotation from *Tricontinental*, in *The New York Times*, Dec. 1, 1971; Liam de Paor's statement, in *Irish Times*, April 4, 1973; IRA's international connections, in New York *Times* news service story in *Irish Times*, July 15, 1972.
5 For changes introduced by Westminster in 1973, including restoration of proportional representation, see pp. 57–58. Each constituency elects five, six, seven or eight members, and each voter indicates a series of preferences on his ballot. The effect is to enable a minority of only one-fifth of the voters (one-sixth or one-seventh or one-eighth) to elect one representative, and bigger groups will be similary represented according to size. Two previous elections to Stormont were held under proportional representation, in May 1921 and in April 1925. Parties supporting the Union elected 40 members on both occasions, and the Nationalists and other antipartitionists elected 12. Abolition of proportional representation did not change that proportion significantly in later elections. The slight success of antipartitionists in those early elections is attributed in part to the disturbed political conditions which prevented full mobilization of

their strength, in part to the decision of many antipartitionists to boycott the elections as an expression of their refusal to recognize the state. The regime's reasons for abolishing proportional representation will be found on p. 58.

6 *Fortnight* magazine, Belfast, July 1972, p. 4.

7 Figures for the percentages of each denomination are from official censuses. The most recent figures on religious affiliation available are those for 1961. A discussion and analysis of the fertility rates will be found in "Religion and Demographic Behaviour in Ireland," by Brendan M. Walsh (Dublin: Economic and Social Research Institute, Paper No. 55, May 1970). Percentages of Catholic children in primary schools through 1957 are in M. W. Heslinga's, *The Irish Border as a Cultural Divide* (Assen: Van Gorcum, 1971), p. 64, with the *Ulster Yearbooks* cited as source. The 1968 figure of 51 percent was given in that year by Terence O'Neill, then Prime Minister of Northern Ireland. *The Plain Truth* (Castlefields, Dungannon: Campaign for Social Justice, 1972), p. 2. Because job opportunities in Britain have declined since 1961, in part through higher unemployment there, in part because of English resentment to killing of British soldiers in Northern Ireland, the proportion of Catholics in the population of Northern Ireland may be somewhat higher now than it was in 1961. But even if all emigration from Northern Ireland ceased and the present disparity in the fertility of the two communities remained constant (two conditions most unlikely to be fulfilled), the minority would still be a minority well into the next century.

8 Richard Rose, *Governing Without Consensus*, p. 261. "The average Irish Catholic will claim his nationality is Irish and be done with it; the average Protestant will claim he's British, but all the same, his hatred for the Englishman is almost greater than the Catholic's. For the Ulster Protestant feels he is an inferior English citizen. . . . But if it came to a conflict between being British and being an Ulster Protestant, every last one of them would forsake their British heritage. They would miss the Queen, but there is nothing else they would miss." Bernadette Devlin, *The Price of My Soul* (New York: Knopf, 1969), p. 165.

9 Douglas Gageby, "Northern Ireland," in *Conor Cruise O'Brien Introduces Ireland*, Owen Dudley Edwards ed. (New York: McGraw-Hill, 1969), pp. 179 and 197.

10 My coverage of the Council as a newsman resulted in a book, *What Happened at Rome?* (New York: Holt, Rinehart and Winston, 1966), and in paperback by Doubleday-Echo (1967).

Chapter 1

1 The information about Alfie Hannaway comes from the author's on-the-spot investigations and his interviews with Mr. Hannaway and several of his friends and neighbors.

2 Information about Mrs. Meehan and Mrs. McKeever from the author's interviews with them.

3 "The use of the term 'cages' to describe the internment compounds originated with the prison officials themselves. Each compound is completely wire enclosed as would be a laboratory cage. Crowding reached the proportional level at which laboratory rats would eat each other." Rona M. Fields, "Ulster: a Psychological Experiment?" *New Humanist*, March 1973, p. 448.

4 *The Guardian*, London, Jan. 13, 1973.

5 Detention of two men in February 1973 caused the UDA and allied groups to call a one-day general strike. It was marked by rioting, burning, and shooting in which three men died. No further detentions of members of this group were reported. See *Sunday Times*, London, March 18, 1973.

6 The first of many unofficial paramilitary organizations of Unionist extremists was the Ulster Volunteer Force established in January 1913 to fight—if necessary—the inclusion of Ulster in a self-governing Ireland. It was banned by Terence O'Neill, Stormont Prime Minister, in 1966 as "a sordid conspiracy of criminals." It emerged again in November 1968 as the Ulster Protestant Volunteers, a vigilante group opposing the civil rights movement. In January 1972, Martin Smyth and William Craig formed Ulster Vanguard as an umbrella organization. The Ulster Guard was added soon after and served as an umbrella military organization paralleling Vanguard's own role in the political area. The cornerstone of Vanguard was the Loyalist Association of Workers, a powerful group led by Billy Hull representing dockers, truck drivers, and municipal employees. Hull's group also had a paramilitary section. Other paramilitary groups have developed under the Vanguard umbrella, including the Orange Volunteers and the Ulster Defence Association. While all these groups are equally opposed to any diminution of the Orange monopoly of power in Northern Ireland, they constantly change their formal relations to each other under the pressure of day-to-day politics.

7 Even the animals feel the strain. Aidene Duff of the Ulster Society for the Prevention of Cruelty to Animals reports that "cats can usually fend for themselves (when people leave), but a lot of

dogs are in a nervous state—they bark and cry and get very frightened."

8 This does not mean that Fenianism lacked all importance. It was very influential in the United States in the nineteenth century and even later, holding together a hard core of men bitterly anti-English and dedicated to freeing Ireland by every means available. Sir William Harcourt, British Home Secretary in the 1880s, understood the significance of this departure. "In former Irish rebellions the Irish were in Ireland. We could reach their forces, cut off their reserves in men and money, and then to subjugate them was comparatively easy. Now there is an Irish nation in the United States, equally hostile, with plenty of money, absolutely beyond our reach and yet within ten days' sail of our shores." Quoted by Conor Cruise O'Brien, *States of Ireland* (New York: Pantheon Books, 1972), p. 45. Karl Marx had earlier made a similar comment. "With the accumulation of rents in Ireland, the accumulation of the Irish in America keeps pace. The Irishman, banned by the sheep and the ox, reappears on the other side of the ocean as a Fenian, and face to face with the old queen of the sea rises, threatening and more threatening, the young, giant Republic." *Capital*, Great Books, Vol. 50 (Chicago: Encyclopaedia Britannica, 1952), p. 353. For the impact of the Fenians under their alternative name of Irish Republican Brotherhood or Irish Revolutionary Brotherhood (the original meaning of IRB is disputed) on the separatist movement of the early twentieth century, see p. 159.

9 This flag, which since the introduction of direct rule in 1972 has been displayed far more prominently in the Orange ghettos than the Union Jack, illustrates the ambivalence of allegiance. The cross of St. George, and the crown, point to the British heritage. The red hand is the emblem of the O'Neills, the native rulers of much of Ulster who held out against the English longer than any other Gaelic chieftains.

10 *The Plain Truth* (Castlefields, Dungannon: Campaign for Social Justice, 1972), p. 4. For Ireland's religious demography since 1861, see Paper No. 55 of the Economic and Social Research Institute, by Brendan M. Walsh (Dublin, May 1970).

11 Personal communication to the author, as is all the material attributed to him in this book.

12 Personal communication to the author.

13 Extract from a signed letter in the *Irish Times*, July 24, 1970, drawn to the author's attention by Mr. McCaughey himself.

14 Lord O'Neill, *The Autobiography of Terence O'Neill* (London: Rupert Hart-Davis, 1972.)

15 For a more detailed discussion of Orangeism, see pp. 127–128.
16 This and the following quotation are from Douglas Gageby, "Northern Ireland," in *Conor Cruise O'Brien Introduces Ireland,* Owen Dudley Edwards ed. (New York: McGraw-Hill, 1969), pp. 181–182.

Chapter 2

1 Richard Rose, *Governing Without Consensus* (London: Faber, 1971), p. 534.
2 "Papish" is regarded as more disparaging than the dictionary "papist." "Taig" or "Teague" comes from a common Irish peasant name, Tadhg, anglicized Terence. Its use may be influenced by the English dialectic "tyke" or "tike," meaning a contemptible person, which the etymologists trace through Middle English to the Icelandic word for a bitch. The origin of Fenian was explained at pp. 26–27.
3 Protestants usually think of themselves, according to a 1968 opinion survey, as primarily British (39 percent), Ulstermen (32 percent), or Irish (20 percent), three descriptions which are not for them mutually exclusive. For Catholics the percentages are 15, 5 and 76. See Richard Rose, *Governing Without Consensus,* p. 208.
4 Although Alcuin was a Yorkshireman by birth, his incorporation by the "myth" can be justified. His teacher was Coelchu of Clonmacnois, and he was deeply indebted for his culture to other Irish associates. See Helen Waddell, *Medieval Latin Lyrics* (London: Constable, 1933), p. 310. Derry's official name has been Londonderry since a Company of Adventurers from London was entrusted by the Crown in the early seventeenth century with the task of settling this region. Its inhabitants of all kinds and conditions call it Derry. Londonderry seldom appears except in a context stressing Orange determination to keep control of a city that is three-quarters Roman Catholic.
5 *Hibernoires hibernicis ipsis* in the medieval Latin of the chronicler, an ecclesiastic whose personal integrity was questioned by many of his contemporaries, as was his objectivity as a historian by many in later centuries. He visited Ireland in 1184.
6 Conor Cruise O'Brien, *States of Ireland* (New York: Pantheon Books, 1972), p. 59.
7 A more sophisticated version of the myth sees the arrival of the settlers from Scotland as a return to ancestral homes. "The Ulster Scot, as his description implies, was originally a Northern Irishman who went to Scotland to civilize it and make it Chris-

tian, . . . and then, having civilized the Scots, returned to their own country to recivilize it, after it had fallen into the unthrifty guard of the 'native Irish.' " St. John Ervine, *Craigavon: Ulsterman* (London: Allen and Unwin, 1949), p. 5. Ervine says the reason the Ulster Scot's description implies this is that the Scots were the Celtic tribe long domiciled in the north of Ireland who about the fifth century A.D. occupied the territory since called Scotland after them. Although this version has historic roots, it is not stressed at the popular level.

8 For a fuller discussion of the term and its origins, see p. 26.

9 Richard Rose has included in *Governing Without Consensus* the results of a survey analyzing religious attitudes in Northern Ireland in depth. On p. 256 he writes: "The pattern of dislikes shows greater Protestant antipathy toward the Catholic church than Catholics show toward Protestant churches."

10 The heroicity of the Apprentice Boys is a historical fact. The importance of the Battle of the Boyne, fought on July 1, old-style calendar, is greatly exaggerated by the tradition. William's decisive victory came a year and eleven days later, July 12 old-style, at Aughrim near Galway.

11 As a member of the Anglican Communion, the Church of Ireland is more correctly called Reformed or Anglo-Catholic than Protestant. In Ireland, nevertheless, both its members and others commonly use the word Protestant, a usage here followed for convenience.

12 See p. 128.

13 See pp. 222 ff.

14 See p. 230.

15 Bernadette Devlin, *The Price of My Soul* (New York: Knopf, 1969), p. 3.

16 Richard Rose downplays the role of segregated education on maintaining the conflicting myths, but for once his reasoning seems to be less than convincing. What is significant is that his survey shows 69 percent of Roman Catholics in Northern Ireland in favor of integrated education. See Richard Rose, *Governing Without Consensus*, p. 335. Protestants generally criticize the separate schools as "one of the main reasons for the deep divisions in Northern Ireland," to quote D.P. Barritt and A. Booth in *Orange and Green: A Quaker Study of Community Relations* (Brigflatts, Sedbergh, Yorkshire: Northern Friends' Peace Board, 1972), p. 31. This raises the question if vested interests on both sides rather than the wishes of the people concerned perpetuate the segregation of education along lines of religion.

17 Not "ourselves alone," as frequently stated. Pronounced *shin fayne*.

18 "The last stage in the long-drawn-out process of the obliteration of a distinctive Far Western Christian culture in Ireland has been the establishment of the Irish Free State. . . . Among the Irish themselves, this happy event has been widely regarded as a great act of restoration—a liberation of the Irish genius from the shackles placed upon it by the successive acts of foreign aggression which have followed one another since the seventh century. This is surely an amiable illusion; for, when the nature of modern nationalism is analyzed, it proves, like Zionism, to be really a radical form of 'Assimilationism.' . . . The captivation of the Irish by nationalism, like the captivation of the Jews by Zionism, signifies the final renunciation of a great but tragic past in the hope of securing in exchange a more modest but perhaps less uncomfortable future. . . . Thus the establishment of the Irish Free State . . . signifies that the romance of Ancient Ireland has at last come to an end, and that Modern Ireland has made up her mind, in our generation, to find her level as a willing inmate in our workaday Western World." Arnold J. Toynbee, *A Study of History* (Oxford University Press: New York, Vol. II, Annex 3; first published in 1934), p. 425. Toynbee noted that civil servants and school teachers were already then rebelling against the "non-utilitarian accomplishment" of effective knowledge of Irish. Relaxation of the rules on this point by the coalition government which took office in Dublin in 1973 suggest they have finally won out. If so, we can mark the final death pangs of a civilization which was destroyed ecclesiastically in the twelfth century, politically and in literature in the seventeenth, and linguistically in the nineteenth.
19 See p. 219.
20 Quotes from Liam de Paor's, *Divided Ulster* (Harmondsworth, Middlesex: Penguin Books, 1970), p. 78 and 80.
21 Text in *Ulster*, by the Sunday Times Insight Team (Harmondsworth; Middlesex: Penguin Books, 1972), p. 152. It has been reprinted, among others, by Ian Paisley's *Protestant Telegraph*. When the British rushed troops to Northern Ireland in August 1969 to deal with the threatened collapse of public order, the army's information service included this oath in a booklet issued to the troops to inform them of the kind of enemy they would face! See p. 236. Actually, members of the IRA have taken since 1925, not an oath but this promise: "I . . . promise that I will promote the objects of Oglaigh na h-Eireann to the best of my knowledge and ability, and that I will obey all orders and regulations issued to me by the Army Authorities and by my superior officers." Previously, there was a conventional oath of allegiance to Dail Eireann as the Parliament of the Irish Republic.

See J. Bowyer Bell, *The Secret Army* (London: Sphere Books, 1972), p. 89. Ernie O'Malley, a top IRA leader from 1919 to 1921, says that even then a man might affirm instead of taking an oath: "I do solemnly swear or affirm that I do not and shall not yield a voluntary support to any pretended government . . . , that to the best of my knowledge and ability I shall support and defend the Irish Republic. . . ." Ernie O'Malley, *Army Without Banners* (Boston: Houghton Mifflin, 1937), p. 128.

Chapter 3

1 Patrick O'Farrell, *Ireland's English Question* (New York: Schocken Books, 1971), p. 300.
2 Parliamentary Debates, N. I., Vol. XVI, Cols. 1091–95, April 24, 1934.
3 T. J. Campbell, *Fifty Years of Ulster* (Belfast: Irish News, 1941), p. 25.
4 In 1914, of 48 heads and deputy-heads of departments and branches of the British administration in Ireland, only 20 were Catholics, and 10 of the 28 Protestants were British. D. R. O'Connor Lysaght, *The Republic of Ireland* (Cork: Mercier Press, 1970), p. 43.
5 T. J. Campbell, *Fifty Years of Ulster*, p. 109.
6 London decided in 1973 to reintroduce proportional representation in Northern Ireland. See pp. 274–275, also footnote 4 to Introduction.
7 Sean Cronin, *Ireland Since the Treaty* (Dublin: Irish Freedom Press, 1971), p. 55.
8 Following the 1969 Downing Street Declaration, London forced Stormont to introduce universal suffrage in local elections. Further changes envisaged in the 1973 White Paper are described at p. 268.
9 *The Plain Truth* (Castlefields, Dungannon: Campaign for Social Justice, 1972), p. 20.
10 *Ibid.*, pp. 22–30.
11 Sean Cronin, *Ireland Since the Treaty*, p. 46.
12 *Ulster*, by the Sunday Times Insight Team (Harmondsworth, Middlesex: Penguin Books, 1972), p. 33.
13 Andrew Boyd, *Holy War in Belfast* (New York: Grove Press, 1972), p. 177.
14 T. J. Campbell, *Fifty Years of Ulster*, p. 114.
15 *Ibid.*, p. 116.
16 *Belfast Newsletter*, July 13, 1922.
17 Richard Rose, *Governing Without Consensus* (London: Faber, 1971), p. 229.

18 *Fermanagh Times*, July 13, 1933, and *Londonderry Sentinel*, March 20, 1934.
19 *The Plain Truth*, p. 34.
20 Andrew Boyd, *Holy War in Belfast*, p. 178.
21 *The Plain Truth*, p. 6.
22 Figures on gerrymandering from *The Plain Truth*. Most figures are for 1968 and are drawn from official sources. Statistics of religious affiliation are from the 1961 census, the latest available. Some improvements occurred after 1969, as a result of open intervention—for the first time since 1922—by London in the internal affairs of Northern Ireland. The situation before 1969 is presented, however, as indicative of the action of the Northern Ireland government when left to its own discretion.
23 Bishop William Philbin, of Down and Connor, the diocese in which Belfast is situated, identified the firm in an open letter as Sirocco Engineering. News reports in 1973 said the firm was then 100 percent Protestant in its personnel.
24 *Irish Times*, June 24, 1972. Other estimates in this paragraph supplied to author by local newsmen.
25 *The Plain Truth*, p. 15.
26 *Sunday Independent*, Dublin, Aug. 13, 1972.
27 *This Week*, Dublin, Sept. 24, 1971.

Chapter 4

1 Referring to American Civil War in a broadcast (1938) from Geneva to United States. The Earl of Longford and Thomas P. O'Neill, *Eamon de Valera* (Boston: Houghton Mifflin Co., 1971), p. 223.
2 Richard Eder in *The New York Times*, March 18, 1973, puts the Irish community in Britain, counting immigrants of first, second, and third generations, at about 4.5 million, the overwhelming majority Roman Catholic and one million Irish born. The largest concentration—some 800,000—is in London. The Irish-born hold the balance of political power in 25 parliamentary constituencies in which they form from 6.5 to 14.5 percent of the voters. See *This Week*, Dublin, April 6, 1972, p. 10.
3 *Ulster*, by the Sunday Times Insight Team (Harmondsworth, Middlesex: Penguin Books, 1972), p. 37.
4 *Ibid.*, p. 38. These statements were apparently made to stave off any mass influx of Catholics into the Unionist Party. In 1969, about a dozen Catholics were in fact members. See *The Plain Truth*, (Castelefields, Dungannon: Campaign for Social Justice, 1972), p. 1.

5 In 1961. See Andrew Boyd, *Holy War in Belfast* (New York: Grove Press, 1972), p. 192.
6 Dungannon in 1872 was the scene of the first National Convention of Irish Volunteers, a mainly Protestant organization which was largely responsible that same year for winning legislative independence for Ireland. This gain was negated by the Act of Union in 1800.
7 *The Plain Truth*, p. 29.
8 "Mr. Paisley came of Baptist stock and was educated at Ballymena Technical School and the Barry School of Evangelism in South Wales. He took degrees at the Pioneer Theological Seminary at Rockford in South Wales, and the Burton College and Seminary at Manitou Springs, Colorado. The Bob Jones University of South Carolina awarded him, in 1966, an Honorary Doctorate of Divinity. This is a fundamentalist Christian School with about 4000 students. It does not award science degrees, and is nondenominational, its divinity degrees not being recognized by any major denomination." D. P. Barritt and A. Booth, *Orange and Green: A Quaker Study of Community Relations* (Brigflatts, Sedbergh, Yorkshire: Northern Friends' Peace Board, 1972), p. 42.
9 A survey published in 1967 reported that 90 percent of the Cromac houses lacked an indoor toilet, a hand basin, a fixed bath or hot water. See Richard Rose, *Governing Without Consensus* (London: Faber, 1971), p. 294.
10 *Ulster*, p. 44.
11 Richard Rose, *Governing Without Consensus*, p. 100.
12 *Ibid.*, p. 101.
13 Bernadette Devlin, *The Price of My Soul* (New York: Knopf, 1969), p. 92.
14 *Ibid.*, p. 99.

Chapter 5

1 Lord O'Neill, *The Autobiography of Terence O'Neill* (London: Rupert Hart-Davis, 1972).
2 *The Review of Politics*, April 1972, p. 148.
3 *The Plain Truth* (Castlefields, Dungannon: Campaign for Social Justice, 1972), p. 2 of Cover.
4 *Ulster*, by the Sunday Times Insight Team (Harmondsworth, Middlesex: Penguin Books, 1972), p. 59.
5 *Ibid.*, p. 60.
6 Liam de Paor, *Divided Ulster* (Harmondsworth, Middlesex: Penguin Books, 1970), p. 188.

7 *Ibid.*, p. 189.
8 Bernadette Devlin, *The Price of My Soul* (New York: Knopf, 1969), p. 146.
9 Cameron Report, *Disturbances in Northern Ireland* (Belfast: HMSO, Cmd 532, 1969), par. 177.
10 Richard Rose, *Governing Without Consensus* (London: Faber, 1971), p. 105.
11 Liam de Paor, *Divided Ulster*, p. 191. The Monkees were a popular singing group.
12 *Ibid.*, p. 192.
13 *Ulster*, p. 75.
14 Richard Rose, *Governing Without Consensus*, p. 153. Further data about the Ulster Volunteers and related organizations will be found in Note 6 to Chapter 1.

Chapter 6

1 D. P. Barritt and A. Booth, *Orange and Green: A Quaker Study of Community Relations* (Brigflatts, Sedbergh, Yorkshire: Northern Friends Peace Board, 1972), p. 48.
2 The background and development of the constitution of 1937 are well reviewed in *Eamon de Valera*, by the Earl of Longford and Thomas P. O'Neill, (Boston: Houghton Mifflin Co., 1971).
3 Citizens of the Republic of Ireland are actually in the anomalous position of enjoying rights to enter and reside in Great Britain denied to nonwhite British citizens such as those of Indian and Pakistani ancestry expelled from Uganda in 1972.
4 "We repudiate the so-called Protestant spirit that deliberately sets out to suppress and intimidate, that allows and encourages ghettos within cities, and victimizes men and women because of their religious or political convictions. We have known no such ghettos in the South. No man has been prevented from voting in any election because of his position or belief. We have been fairly and honorably treated as first class citizens and have been happily integrated into the community. In contrast, 50 years of Unionist and Protestant government in Northern Ireland has produced the present holocaust." Rev. F. M. Johnston, Protestant Dean of Cork, 1969 (A sermon quoted in *Newsletter* of American Committee for Ulster Justice, New York, Dec. 1, 1972).
5 At meeting of Association of Irish Priests (Roman Catholic) at Ballymascanlon, Dundalk, June 24, 1972, at which author was present. Latest figures for the Republic are from the 1961 census.

6 T. J. Campbell, *Fifty Years of Ulster* (Belfast: Irish News, 1941), p. 75.

7 Arnold J. Toynbee, *A Study of History* (New York: Oxford University Press, 1962), II, p. 329.

8 The bitterness of the Irish monk vis-à-vis Rome emerges in a gloss written by an Irish hand and in the Irish language, on the margin of a ninth-century manuscript of the Epistles of St. Paul, the Codex Boernerianus in the Royal Library of Dresden. It is quoted by Arnold J. Toynbee, *A Study of History*, p. 333. "To go to Rome is great labor and little profit. Thou wilt not find the King thou goest to seek there unless thou bring him with thee. It is folly, frenzy, insanity, unreason—since thou goest out to meet certain death—that thou shouldest call down upon thee the wrath of the Son of Mary."

9 Kenneth Nicholls, *Gaelic and Gaelicised Ireland in the Middle Ages* (Dublin: Gill and Macmillan, 1972), p. 73. Nicholls also notes that the efforts of Rome after the Ango-Norman conquest to enforce clerical celibacy and end hereditary succession to church offices were only partially successful. On pp. 92–98 he gives examples of these practices continuing to the late sixteenth century.

10 Quoted by James Plunkett, *The Gems She Wore* (New York: Holt, Rinehart and Winston, 1973), p. 149. M. W. Heslinga, in *The Irish Border as a Cultural Divide* (Assen: Van Gorcum and Co., 1971), pp. 158–159, says that many of the Scottish immigrants "must have had distant Irish (i.e., Gaelic) ancestors," and that many of the native population "had also come fairly recently from Scotland." Ulster-born Irish historian Eoin MacNeill had earlier asserted in the Introduction to *Handbook of the Ulster Question* (Dublin: North-East Boundary Bureau, 1923), that the newcomers and the previous inhabitants were "identical in race."

11 Margaret MacCurtain, *Tudor and Stuart Ireland* (Dublin: Gill and Macmillan, 1972), p. 116.

12 "Efforts to outlaw polygamous practices among the Irish were put forward by Carew in 1611 and again at the 1634 Parliament. They were aimed at invalidating the Irish law of marriage which countenanced plurality of wives and conferred a certain legality on various types of extramarital unions, as well as allowing extensive pleadings for divorce. English law coincided with the enforcements of Tridentine ecclesiastical regulations." Margaret MacCurtain, *Tudor and Stuart Ireland*, p. 117.

Chapter 7

1 C. Desmond Greaves, *The Irish Crisis* (London: Lawrence & Wishart, 1972), p. 61.
2 Andrew Boyd, *Holy War in Belfast* (New York: Grove Press, 1969), p. 7.
3 See Liam de Paor, *Divided Ulster* (Harmondsworth, Middlesex: Penguin Books, 1970), p. 34.
4 Andrew Boyd, *Holy War in Belfast*, p. 8.
5 Richard Rose, *Governing Without Consensus* (London: Faber, 1971), p. 85. Andrew Boyd, *Holy War in Belfast*, p. 9.
6 T. J. Campbell, *Fifty Years of Ulster* (Belfast: Irish News, 1941), p. 17. Andrew Boyd, *Holy War in Belfast*, p. 9.
7 Andrew Boyd, *Holy War in Belfast*, p. 12.
8 Cecil Woodham-Smith, *The Great Hunger* (London: Hamish Hamilton, 1962), p. 412.
9 Andrew Boyd, *Holy War in Belfast*, p. 123.
10 T. J. Campbell, *Fifty Years of Ulster*, p. 52.

Chapter 8

1 In *General Introduction for My Work*, 1937; quoted by Conor Cruise O'Brien, *States of Ireland* (New York: Pantheon Books, 1972), p. 68.
2 The quotation is from the eighth-century Táin Bó Cuailnge. The youth Cú Chulainn, already renowned for his strength, cunning, and prowess, is in the presence of the king and seeks to be knighted immediately because he has heard this is a propitious day. "It is a good day, indeed," said Cathbad the druid. "It is clear that he who takes arms today will be famous and renowned, but he will be short-lived." "That is excellent," said Cú Chulainn. "I care not that I am only one day in the world, provided I am famous."
3 "The Rebel." Reprinted in *1000 Years of Irish Poetry*, Kathleen Hoagland, ed. (New York: Devin-Adair, 1949).
4 T. J. Campbell, *Fifty Years of Ulster* (Belfast: Irish News, 1941), p. 80.

Chapter 9

1 Rosita Sweetman, *On Our Knees* (London: Pan Books, 1972), p. 11.
2 Patrick O'Farrell, *Ireland's English Question* (New York: Schocken Books, 1971), p. 93.

3 Joseph Lee, *The Modernization of Irish Society 1848–1918* (Dublin: Gill and Macmillan, 1973), p. 54.
4 Irish-born members of the Union army during the Civil War, according to an official report issued in 1869, numbered 144,221. Many of them joined in order to gain experience which would fit them to return as a fighting force to free their own country. Leonard Patrick O'Connor Wibberley, *The Coming of the Green* (New York: Henry Holt, 1958), pp. 55 and 57.
5 Sean Cronin, *The McGarrity Papers* (Tralee: Anvil Books, 1972), p. 32.
6 The best analysis of this wedding of nationalism and religion is in Patrick O'Farrell, *Ireland's English Question*, p. 231 ff, source of quotations given here.
7 *Ibid.*, p. 274.
8 *Ibid.*, p. 287.
9 J. Bowyer Bell, *The Secret Army* (London: Sphere Books, 1972), p. 27.
10 See p. 54.
11 Estimates of men and equipment from J. Bowyer Bell, *The Secret Army*, p. 40.

Chapter 10

1 Bernadette Devlin, *The Price of My Soul* (New York: Knopf, 1969), p. 71.
2 Tom Barry, *Guerrilla Days in Ireland* (Tralee, Ireland: The Kerryman, 1955), pp. 189–190.
3 Father of the Erskine Childers mentioned at p. 38 is now President of the Republic of Ireland. Childers was a leading opponent of the Anglo-Irish Treaty, and he was deeply offended when Arthur Griffith, leader of the pro-Treaty faction called him "an interloper and an Englishman." Replying in the Dail, he said he was not an Englishman in any true sense of the word. He had become an Irish citizen. His mother was Irish and he had been brought up in Ireland from the age of 13 years. It was true that he went to an English public school and had become "thoroughly Britonized," and that he had fought in the Boer War. "I am sorry that I did so, but one cannot relive one's life. But—by a process of moral and intellectual conviction—I came away from Unionism finally to Republicanism." See Michael McInerney, *The Riddle of Erskine Childers* (Dublin: E. and T. O'Brien, 1971), p. 36.
4 J. Bowyer Bell, *The Secret Army* (London: Sphere Books, 1972), p. 71.

5 D. R. O'Conner Lysaght, *The Republic of Ireland* (Cork: Mercier Press, 1970), p. 64. The under-representation of farmers and workers continued later. A study of social composition of the political elite of the Free State and the Republic of Ireland for 50 years breaks down to 13 percent agricultural, 2 percent artisan, 6 percent skilled and unskilled labor and union official, 11 percent business and general merchant, 6 percent journalists and artists, 4 percent civil service, 5 percent managerial, and 53 percent professional. Al Cohen, *The Irish Political Elite* (Dublin: Gill and Macmillan, 1972), p. 35.

6 Patrick O'Farrell, *Ireland's English Question* (New York: Schocken Books, 1971), p. 296.

7 J. Bowyer Bell, *The Secret Army*, p. 113.

8 Patrick O'Farrell, *Ireland's English Question*, p. 285.

Chapter 11

1 Speech at Arbour Hill prison, Dublin. *Irish Press*, April 24, 1933.

2 Dail Eireann debates, lxiv, 1277, Dec. 11, 1936.

3 Leo McCabe, *Wolfe Tone and the United Irishmen. For or Against Christ?* London, 1937.

4 Brian Inglis, *The Story of Ireland* (London: Faber, 1960), p. 248.

5 Edward Cahill, S. J., *Ireland's Peril* (Dublin: An Rioghacht, 1930), p. 1.

6 The Earl of Longford and Thomas P. O'Neill, *Eamon de Valera* (Boston: Houghton Mifflin Co., 1971), p. 296.

7 British cabinet papers for 1939 dealing with Irish neutrality published on Jan. 1, 1970, are analyzed in Longford and O'Neill's *Eamon de Valera*, p. 352 ff. They show Sir John Maffey, British Representative in Dublin, as defending de Valera's stand in his dispatches to London, while Winston Churchill was the most critical member of the cabinet. "It would not be quite true, though close to the truth," the authors conclude, "to say that Winston Churchill urged the invasion of Ireland. He got as far as suggesting that 'we should take stock of the weapons of coercion.' If it had not been for Chamberlain, Eden and Maffey, Ireland might have been faced with a very nasty situation."

Chapter 12

1 Liam de Paor, *Divided Ulster* (Harmondsworth, Middlesex: Penguin Books, 1970), p. 114.

2 T. J. Campbell, *Fifty Years of Ulster* (Belfast: Irish News, 1941), p. 30.

3 *Ibid.*, p. 31.
4 *Ibid.*, pp. 31–32.
5 J. Bowyer Bell, *The Secret Army* (London: Sphere Books, 1972), p. 290.
6 *Ulster*, by Sunday Times Insight Team (Harmondsworth, Middlesex: Penguin Books, 1972), p. 12.
7 Rona M. Fields comments on studies in Australia, Japan, and Yugoslavia reported in the technical literature of psychology and psychopathology, in *New Humanist*, March 1973. For her own observations in Northern Ireland, see note 10 to Chapter 14.
8 J. Bowyer Bell, *The Secret Army*, p. 394.

Chapter 13

1 Statement made Jan. 5, 1969. Liam de Paor, *Divided Ulster* (Harmondsworth, Middlesex: Penguin Books, 1970), p. 192.
2 D. P. Barritt and A. Booth, *Orange and Green* (Brigflatts, Sedbergh, Yorkshire: Northern Friends' Peace Board, 1972), p. 65.
3 Cameron Report, *Disturbances in Northern Ireland* (Belfast: HMSO. Cmd. 532, 1969).
4 *The Plain Truth* (Castlefields, Dungannon: Campaign for Social Justice, 1972), on inside front cover.
5 *Ulster*, by Sunday Times Insight Team (Harmondsworth: Middlesex: Penguin Books, 1972), p. 26.
6 Cameron Report, *Disturbances in Northern Ireland.*
7 *Irish Times*, Dec. 29, 1969.
8 *Ulster*, p. 195.
9 *Ibid.*, pp. 195–196. For current attitudes to the IRA among Irish Americans, see Robert M. Williams, "American Aid: Lifeblood for the IRA," in *World* magazine, April 24, 1973. Col. Muammar el-Gaddafi, chairman of Libya's Revolutionary Command Council, said his government had financed the IRA. *The New York Times*, April 21, 1973.
10 By chance the British government had discovered a short time earlier that the RUC had stocks of CN for use in such circumstances. CN is a gas as defined and forbidden by the Geneva Convention. The British had persuaded the RUC to surrender the CN in return for supplies of CS which the British military authorities claim is "smoke." *Ulster*, p. 111. General Ordinance Equipment Corporation, of Pittsburgh, Pa., describes the CS it manufactures as "a non-lethal 'street-cleaner'" which causes "temporary tear-producing, burning and 'I-can't-breathe' sensations." Advertisement in *The Police Chief*, Nov. 1970.

11 The theoretical strength of the army of the Republic of Ireland is 13,000, including 1,200 officers; but the actual strength in 1972 was 10,000, plus 1,300 reserves. Local defense, a kind of national guard, had 18,000 men. The army's principal experience has been as a UN peace-keeping force, starting with 50 officers as observers in Lebanon in 1958, others subsequently in West New Guinea, India and Pakistan. It sent a total of 5,000 troops to the Congo and suffered casualties, 26 dead and 57 wounded or injured. Units have been stationed in Cyprus since 1964.

12 The revelation that the Northern Ireland police had armored cars caused a sensation. The government of the Republic of Ireland, whose police have never carried arms of any kind, regarded it a breach of a treaty it had signed with Britain. The cars, known as Shorlans, carried a Browning 0.30-inch medium machine gun. They had been secretly built in the Belfast shipyards in 1967. *Ulster*, p. 129.

13 For text of bogus oath, see p. 51.

14 *Irish Independent*, August 14, 1972.

15 *Ulster*, p. 204.

16 Many estimates of current IRA strength exist. Lord Chalfont notes that in Northern Ireland they are concentrated in Belfast and Derry, as "urban guerrillas," *The Ulster Debate* (London: Bodley Head, 1972), p. 59. The London *Economist*, July 22, 1972, put "the really active Provisional gunmen in Northern Ireland" at just over 200, with as many as 1,500 ready to fight (1,000 Provisionals and 500 Officials), backed by 1,500 auxiliaries. *This Week*, Dublin, May 4, 1972, said Martin McGuinness, the 21-year-old Provisional commander of "free Derry" had one battalion consisting of four companies with an estimated 250 men, a third of them being "full-time." Full-time men, it added, were paid $12.50 a week if single and $25 if married, regardless of rank. They also got free food and lodgings from sympathizers. McGuinness and his men were described as "strongly Catholic"; the Officials in Derry also being 95 percent Catholic (with two Protestant members) but "not so religious." Six officers of the Belfast Provisional battalion are Protestants, according to Geoffrey Coulter, a Protestant who was himself prominent in the "socialist" wing of the IRA in the 1930s. *Irish Times*, July 6, 1972. Colin Smith, London *Observer*, July 30, 1972, said McGuinness had then 70 young gunmen in the Derry Bogside to meet an anticipated army attack.

Chapter 14

1 Addressing Orange rally, July 12, 1958. Andrew Boyd, *Brian Faulkner and the Crisis of Ulster Unionism* (Tralee: Anvil Books, 1972), p. 25.

2 *Ulster*, by the Sunday Times Insight Team (Harmondsworth, Middlesex: Penguin Books, 1972), p. 105.

3 *Ibid*, p. 213. One of the best informed newsmen resident in Belfast, the representative of the Dublin *Irish Times*, has said of Maudling that he "can justly claim to know as little about Northern Ireland as any British politician before him or since." Henry Kelly, *How Stormont Fell* (Dublin: Gill and Macmillan, 1972), p. 10.

4 Institute for the Study of Conflict, *The Ulster Debate* (London: Bodley Head, 1972), p. 66.

5 *Ulster*, p. 245.

6 Andrew Boyd, *Brian Faulkner and the Crisis of Ulster Unionism*, p. 7.

7 *Ibid.*, p. 70.

8 Henry Kelly, *How Stormont Fell*, pp. 71–92. See also Andrew Boyd, *Brian Faulkner and the Crisis of Ulster Unionism*, p. 72.

9 *Sunday Times*, London, Aug. 6, 1972, for government aid to Sirocco; New York *Times*, May 25, 1972, for statement about minority ghettos.

10 Andrew Boyd, *Brian Faulkner and the Crisis of Ulster Unionism*, p. 70.

11 This is the normal method of administrative peacetime censorship in Britain. Publication of any matter covered by a "D notice" renders the publisher liable to prosecution under the Official Secrets laws.

12 *The Mailed Fist*, with foreword by Tony Smythe, secretary of the National Council for Civil Liberties, London (Castlefields, Dungannon: Campaign for Social Justice in Northern Ireland, 1971), p. 15. An appendix gives the text of the attested statements of Patrick McClean and other internees.

13 *Ibid.*, p. 14.

14 *Sunday Times*, London, Oct. 17, 1971.

15 See, for example, *Terror in Brazil*, a dossier. American Committee for Information on Brazil, New York, April 1970. See also Gary MacEoin, *Revolution Next Door: Latin America in the 1970s* (New York: Holt, Rinehart and Winston, 1971), p. 190. As regards Belfast, Dr. Fields says: "I have interviewed many detainees in Northern Ireland, and I know that what they have been subjected to has included the following. One barracks has

a section containing a series of cubicles which are all white, lined with perforated sound-proofed tiles. The men are put into these, in a selected uncomfortable position and made to stare at the walls for a long period of time. The only sound they may hear is if one of the other men in another cubicle moves out of position, when he may be beaten, so that there will be a scream or a shriek or something. There is no other interference with the process of wall-staring. The most common effect of these conditions, just as in the original laboratory experiments, is hallucinations, which may continue intermittently long after the actual 'experiment' has ended, if only in the form of night-mares. This is in addition to what most people know about, the hooding of detainees for long periods, or the simple blindfolding of them. Then there are the stress conditions, which have the ef-fect over a long period of reducing the independent individu-ality of the victim and increasing his suggestibility, either to make him more receptive to what you want him to hear, or to make him tell you what you want to know (which may not always be the truth, of course). Contrary to what you might ex-pect, these stress conditions, which are basically, as used in Northern Ireland, making a man lean at about forty-five degrees, standing on his toes with his legs wide apart and his fingertips against a wall, are not necessarily painful, since the victims soon become numb. Their main effect is to induce extreme fatigue and a lowering of the oxygen level in the blood, with the addi-tional effect of inducing a feeling of complete subservience." *New Humanist*, March 1973, p. 446. Dr. Field has elsewhere ex-pressed fears about the long-term impact of sensory deprivation. One 40-year-old man she interviewed was apparently senile, mentally and physically, a condition inconsistent with his health when he was interned. "This big burly man walks like he's 65," she said, "whimpers in the dark, is afraid of heights, and has an attention span so short that he cannot carry on a conversation." *This Week*, Dublin, Feb. 10, 1972. Psychiatry professor Robert Daly, formerly of the University of North Carolina, reported in July 1973 that his continuing study of 20 Northern Ireland vic-tims of "hooding" showed that almost all had suffered long-term mental injury, the commonest symptoms being "marked anxiety, fear and dread, as well as insomnia, nightmares and startle-responses." *The New York Times*, July 9, 1973.

16 *Ulster*, p. 293.
17 *The Mailed Fist*, p. 64.
18 *Sunday Times*, London, May 7, 1972, that is, after imposition of direct rule. An example of the masses of evidence accumulated

by the Association for Legal Justice, 25 Divis Street, Belfast, is a "report on the arrest, interrogation, torture, inhuman and degrading treatment of Gerard Donnelly (29), Gerard Bradley (20), and Edward Duffy (17)." It is dated April 20, 1972, and it describes their treatment after their arrest by British soldiers the previous April 20. According to Joseph O'Malley, editor of the Dublin newsmagazine *Profile*, the torture had decreased by early 1973 "because of closer medical scrutiny" and "presumably" because Britain had been cited before the European Court of Human Rights in Strasbourg. O'Malley added that the torture had been a response to "a post-internment desperation on the part of the British Army" when it realized that the information provided by the Northern Ireland police (RUC) was hopelessly out of date. The reason for that was that the RUC had been effectively excluded for years from the Catholic ghettos. The Holywood barracks, where much of the torture and ill-treatment took place, has been closed down.

The paramilitary organizations of both sides, the UDA and the IRA, were encouraged to imitate the interrogation methods of the British, though usually in a haphazard way that was often needlessly cruel and destructive of the victims. Both were partial to smashing a victim's knee cap with a bullet, a technique regarded as combining discipline and interrogation. Hooding was also extensively practiced by both. The IRA often beat suspects intensively and fired shots over the heads of blindfolded suspects, in simulated execution situations, alternating periods of punishment and of blandishment. Although the Republic of Ireland has at various times interned and imprisoned members of the IRA, no charges of ill-treatment of suspects have ever been made, nor has the government felt the need to call in the military to support the police, except to deal occasionally with potential riot situations.

The so-called motiveless murders—selection of a victim apparently at random as a warning to the other side—often included torture before killing. In one series of 37 such murders, 30 presented evidence of such tortures as burning with cigarettes, stabbing, beating, kicking, breaking bones, setting alight while still living. These motiveless murders reached a crescendo in 1972, with 33 in month of July, and 122 for the entire year.

19 Henry Kelly, *How Stormont Fell*, p. 125.

Chapter 15

1 Andrew Boyd, *Brian Faulkner and the Crisis of Ulster Unionism* (Tralee: Anvil Books, 1972), p. 114.

2 Edmund Curtis, *A History of Ireland* (London: Methuen, 1957), p. v.

3 Andrew Boyd, *Brian Faulkner,* p. 114.

4 *Direct Rule,* a pamphlet prepared by Robert W. Heatley on behalf of Belfast Regional Executive of Northern Ireland Civil Rights Association, printed by *Irish News,* Belfast, 1972, p. 3.

5 Andrew Boyd, *Brian Faulkner,* p. 112.

6 *Sunday Times,* March 11, 1973.

7 *Sunday Times,* March 11, 1973.

8 The Westminster Parliament guaranteed in 1949 that no change in the constitutional status of Northern Ireland would take place without approval of the Stormont Parliament. Recent statements of the British government speak of approval by a majority of the citizens of Northern Ireland, often indicating a referendum as the way to determine the issue.

9 *Sunday Times,* London, March 11 and March 18, 1973.

10 Richard Rose, *Governing Without Consensus* (London: Faber, 1971), pp. 218 ff.

Chapter 16

1 "The Future of Northern Ireland," a British government "Green Paper," text in *The Guardian* (London), Oct. 31, 1972.

2 Quoted by G. C. Duggan, *Northern Ireland, Success or Failure* (Dublin: Irish Times, 1950), p. 21.

3 Richard Rose, *Governing Without Consensus* (London: Faber, 1971), p. 21.

4 Paisley in *Belfast Telegraph,* Oct. 10, 1969; Smyth in *Irish Times,* July 13, 1972, a report of speech at July 12 Orange parade in Belfast.

5 Text as appendix in Cameron Report, *Disturbances in Northern Ireland* (Belfast: HMSO, Cmd. 532, 1969).

6 Arnold J. Toynbee, *A Study of History* (New York: Oxford University Press, 1962), IV, P. 293. The comment was published in 1939, but its context suggests that it was written much earlier.

7 When a national school system for Ireland was set up in the 1830s, the censors excluded textbooks containing such dangerous sentiments as Walter Scott's "Breathes there the man/With soul so dead,/That never to himself has said/This is my own, my native land?"; and "Freedom shrieked when Kosciusco fell," as well as Moore's Melodies and all other Irish airs; while leaving "I thank the goodness and the grace/Which on my birth has smiled/And made me in these Christian days/A happy English child."

8 C. Desmond Greaves, *Liam Mellows and the Irish Revolution* (London: Lawrence and Wishart, 1971), p. 9.

9 Frazer quoted by Anthony Lewis in *The New York Times,* March 24, 1973. For British opinion polls, see *The New York Times,* Sept. 27, 1972. Lord O'Neill of the Maine, Prime Minister of Northern Ireland as Terence O'Neill from 1963 to 1968, echoed the Frazer comment in June 1973. "If violence, murder and arson continue indefinitely, then I have no doubt whatever that the British people will get fed up with pouring men and money into an ungrateful province . . . . The future of Northern Ireland will not be settled in Belfast, Dublin or London, but rather in the British constituencies." London *Observer,* June 24, 1973.

10 "The vast Indian-Pakistan tragedy, together with similar cases in many other areas of the former British Empire, strongly suggest that the British are ill-qualified to resolve, fundamentally, colonial problems they have created. Their indefinite presence, beyond an important facilitating role combined with stringless economic reparations, can only help Northern Ireland in the same sense that America has helped the Vietnamese people." James Lamb, *Perspectives* No. 2 (1972), an occasional publication of the Center for the Study of Development and Social Change, Cambridge, Mass.

11 *Fortnight,* Belfast, June 8, 1973; and David Donnison, Director of the Centre for Environmental Studies, in *New Society,* London, July 5, 1973.

12 Carson statement in H. Montgomery Hyde, *Carson* (London: Heinemann, 1953), p. 465. The Best, Smyth, and Gray-Stack statements were personal communications to the author.

13 Personal communication to author. Conor Cruise O'Brien gives a unique insight into the mentality, the assumptions, and the language in which messages are flashed. "Quite recently in the Dail, the then Minister of Justice, Mr. Micheál O Móráin, in answering some questions about adoption law, used the cryptic phrase: 'There's a stone wall there.' He did not develop the allusion, and a foreign reader of the Dail Debates might well be puzzled by it. No one in the Dail was puzzled. The Minister's 'stone wall' was the veto of the Catholic Church." *States of Ireland* (New York: Pantheon Books, 1972), p. 125.

14 *Perspectives,* No. 2 (1972).

15 *Ireland, Some Problems of a Developing Economy,* Tait and Britstow ed. (Dublin: Gill and Macmillan, 1972), p. 159.

16 Address to Social Study Conference, Falcarragh, Donegal, in *Irish Times,* Aug. 11, 1972. My only reservation would be about

the description of Ireland (contemporary) as "a nation born in revolution." President Eamon de Valera has correctly noted that "ours was not a revolution in the ordinary sense—it was not an internal revolt; it was a revolt against external domination." Earl of Longford and Thomas P. O'Neill, *Eamon de Valera* (Boston: Houghton Mifflin Co., 1971), p. 465. The difference is critical; a transfer of power within a ruling class (U.S. Revolution, Irish Revolution); destruction of a ruling class to establish a new class in power (French Revolution).

17 The Republic's politicians have made much capital out of the increase in population of 3.3 percent, to 2,978,248, between 1966 and 1971, claiming that it shows that the tide of 125 years of emigration has been definitely halted. What they do not add is that job obsolescence through technology has meant the elimination of nearly as many jobs as those created by new industries, a process projected to accelerate in coming years. Jack Jones, general secretary of Amalgamated Transport and General Workers Union, put unemployment in both parts of Ireland at 9 percent, more than twice the rate in Britain (*Irish Times*, June 16, 1972). Basic reason for decline in emigration has been recession in Britain coupled with growing resistance to employing Irish there because of Northern Ireland conflict.

18 Investment figures in *The New York Times* Economic Survey of Europe and the Middle East, Jan. 14, 1973. Relation of investments and profits of the multinationals in *The Chilean Road to Socialism*, Dale L. Johnson, ed. (New York: Anchor Press/Doubleday, 1973), p. 18.

19 *Documentos finales de Medellín*, Ediciones Paulinas, Buenos Aires, 1969. An English translation of the documents of the Second General Conference of Latin American Bishops at Medellín, Colombia, August 1968, is obtainable from the Latin American Division of the U.S. Catholic Conference, Washington, D.C. 20005.

20 See for example Alain Woodrow, "France in Search of a Destination," *Commonweal*, March 16, 1973.

21 Conor Cruise O'Brien, *States of Ireland*.

22 *Ibid.*, p. 312.

Selected Annotated
Bibliography

Ayearst, Morley. *The Republic of Ireland.* New York University Press, 1970.
  Scholarly and well-documented treatise on Irish government and politics, with detailed explanation of mechanics of proportional representation in elections.
Barritt, Denis P. and Arthur Booth. *Orange and Green. A Quaker Study of Community Relations in Northern Ireland.* Brigflatts, Sedbergh, Yorkshire: Northern Friends Peace Board, 1969; revised, 1972.
  Brief, refreshingly objective account of issues underlying conflict, valuable statistics.
Bell, J. Bowyer. *The Secret Army.* London: Sphere Books, 1972.
  A definitive history of the Irish Republican Army (IRA) from 1915 to 1970. The study is supplemented by hundreds of interviews with former and current members. Scholarly, sensitive, coherent.
Boyd, Andrew. *Brian Faulkner and the Crisis of Ulster Unionism.* Tralee: Anvil Books, 1972.
  The author, an Ulster Protestant, sympathetic to both the nationalist and socialist causes, blames Stormont's last Prime Minister for escalating violence and division in Northern Ireland.
Boyd, Andrew. *Holy War in Belfast.* Tralee: Anvil Books, 1969; New York: Grove Press, 1972.
  Blow-by-blow account of sectarian violence and its relation to British policy since the nineteenth century.
Coogan, Timothy P. *The Irish Republican Army.* New York: Praeger, 1970.

Though overshadowed by Bowyer Bell's definitive study of the same subject, this book is both highly readable and valuable. It captures the Irishman's ambivalence toward one of his country's most enduring institutions.

Cronin, Sean. *Ireland since the Treaty.* Dublin: Irish Freedom Press, 1971.

Quick overview of Irish history and politics, north and south, since 1920. Written by a moderate socialist.

De Paor, Liam. *Divided Ulster.* Harmondsworth, Middlesex: Penguin Books, 1970.

Irish historian places current conflict in historical perspective.

Devlin, Bernadette. *The Price of My Soul.* New York: Knopf, 1969.

First-person account of the radicalization of one of the few striking personalities to emerge from Northern Ireland conflict. Of permanent value.

Edwards, Owen Dudley, ed. *Conor Cruise O'Brien Introduces Ireland.* New York: McGraw-Hill, 1969.

Enjoyable symposium, including outstanding chapter on Northern Ireland by Douglas Gageby.

Edwards, Owen Dudley. *The Sins of Our Fathers: Roots of Conflict in Northern Ireland.* Dublin: Gill and Macmillan, 1970.

Irish historian offers part history, part political science, stressing that many who formally oppose partition in fact benefit from it.

Gallagher, Frank. *The Indivisible Island.* London: Victor Gollancz, 1959.

Irish newsman's history of partition, with statistics and maps detailing development of discrimination in voting, housing, and jobs.

Greaves, C. Desmond. *The Irish Crisis.* London: Lawrence and Wishart, 1972.

English monopoly capitalism is blamed not only for creating, but for perpetuating partition and conflict in Ireland.

Harris, Rosemary. *Prejudice and Tolerance in Ulster.* Totowa, N.J.: Rowman and Littlefield, 1972.

London university professor studies the rural community whose members "share a common culture and know each other well," yet are separated by seeing each other "in terms of stereotypes."

Hastings, Max. *Ulster 1969: The Fight for Civil Rights in Northern Ireland.* London: Gollancz, 1970.

Popular English journalist went to his Ulster assignment armed only with "a strong dislike for the principles of the Catholic religion," was shocked by what he saw. He came to respect Northern Ireland's Catholics and have "contempt for Protestants in action."

Heslinga, M.W. *The Irish Border as a Cultural Divide.* Assen: Van Gorcum, 1971.

Dutch geographer presents penetrating analysis of Irish society, north and south, and concludes that the country consists of "two nations."

Kee, Robert. *The Green Flag.* London: Weidenfeld and Nicolson, 1972.

English newsman offers extensive (870 pp.), sympathetic, popular account of development of modern Ireland.

Kelly, Henry. *How Stormont Fell.* Dublin: Gill and Macmillan, 1972.

The Belfast editor of the *Irish Times* (Dublin) gives lively and competent account of events leading to suspension of Northern Ireland's Parliament and executive by London.

Longford, Earl of, and Thomas P. O'Neill. *Eamon de Valera.* Boston: Houghton Mifflin Co., 1971.

Authorized biography of Irish statesman, evaluating modern history of Ireland from "nationalist" viewpoint.

Lysaght, D.R. O'Connor. *The Republic of Ireland.* Cork: Mercier Press, 1970.

Evaluation of Irish history, with stress on period since 1800. Offers a socialist viewpoint, raising many usually neglected issues about church and society.

Moody, T.W. and F.X. Martin, eds. *The Course of Irish History.* Cork: Mercier Press, 1967.

Symposium in which twenty-one experts review the highlights of Ireland, past and present. Originally prepared as a series of radio talks.

O'Brien, Conor Cruise. *States of Ireland.* New York: Pantheon Books, 1972.

A historian and literary critic rejects romantic nationalism underlying and supporting IRA violence, calling on the Irish to confess their mistakes in a book he himself describes as "Cruisocentric" and "a work of passion."

O'Brien, Conor Cruise and Maire MacEntee O'Brien. *The Story of Ireland.* New York: Viking, 1972.

A popular and balanced survey of Irish history.

O'Farrell, Patrick. *Ireland's English Question.* New York: Schocken Books, 1971.

An Australian history professor's impressively documented thesis that England created "the Irish question" by attempting political solutions to culturally rooted problems.

O'Neill, Lord. *The Autobiography of Terence O'Neill.* London: Rupert Hart-Davis, 1972.

Northern Ireland's third Prime Minister (1963–1969) exposes

the bigotry of a regime which he struggled unsuccessfully to moderate.

Riddell, Patrick. *Fire Over Ulster.* London: Hamish Hamilton, 1970.
An evaluation from the viewpoint of the "moderate" Orangeman, and his reasons for disliking and distrusting Roman Catholics.

Rose, Richard. *Governing Without Consensus: An Irish Perspective.* London: Faber, 1971.
An American, a professor in a Scottish university, tells how Northern Irish view their society. Based on 1,291 detailed questionnaires. Important, excellent.

Sunday Times Insight Team. *Ulster.* Harmondsworth, Middlesex: Penguin Books, 1972.
Expanded version of two thoroughly researched reports in London's *Sunday Times.* Excellent introduction to current violence in Northern Ireland.

Wallace, Martin. *Drums and Guns: Revolution in Ulster.* London: Chapman, 1970.
Belfast-based newsman condemns not only Northern Ireland's power structures, but the concept of the state as well, sees an eventual solution in agreement between Belfast, Dublin, and London governments.

Woodham-Smith, Cecil. *The Great Hunger.* London: Hamish Hamilton, 1962.
Scholarly account of the Irish famines of 1845–1849, the most traumatic event in Irish history in terms of its continuing domination of the collective subconscious.

Encyclopaedia of Ireland. New York: McGraw-Hill, 1968.
One-volume survey of all aspects of Irish life, north and south, valuable for reference.

The Gill History of Ireland. Dublin: Gill and Macmillan, 1972, 1973. Eleven volumes by different authors under general editorship of James Lydon and Margaret MacCurtain.
A popularly written yet scholarly overview of Irish history from earliest times, with considerable stress on social, cultural, and religious aspects. Most pertinent to Northern Ireland conflict are Joseph Lee's *The Modernization of Irish Society 1848–1918,* and John A. Murphy's *Ireland in the Twentieth Century.*

The Mailed Fist, with foreword by Tony Smyth of National Council for Civil Liberties. London: Dungannon, Campaign for Social Justice in Northern Ireland, 1971.
Describes use of brutality and torture on prisoners in Northern Ireland, with attested statements of internees collected by the Association for Legal Justice.

The Plain Truth. Dungannon: Campaign for Social Justice in Northern Ireland, 1969.

A 40-page pamphlet, with detailed statistics and quotations, formulating issues on which the civil rights movement in Northern Ireland was based.

The Ulster Debate. London: Bodley Head, 1972.

This report by the Institute for the Study of Conflict (London) assesses issues and possible solutions mostly from viewpoint of British "Establishment."

Index